CHATEAUX
BORDEAUX

CHATEAUX BORDEAUX
Editor
Jean Dethier
Head of publishing of original edition
Claude Eveno
Scientific adviser
Michel Guillard
Art Director
Marc Walter, Arbook International, Paris
Graphic design and layout
Sophie Zagradsky and Thomas Gravemaker, Arbook International, Paris
Commissioned colour photographs
Michel Guillard (Agence Scope, Paris)
Commissioned black and white photographs
Fernand Percival (Paris)
Archive photographs
Michel Dubau (Bordeaux), Jean-Claude Planchet (Paris)
Commissioned architectural drawings
Société Académique d'Architecture (SAA), Toulouse
Barthélemy Dumons and Sylvie Assassin (Toulouse)
Jean-Philippe Garric and Valérie Nègre (Rome)
Joseph Altuna and Marie-Claude Petit (Poitiers)
Philippe Gisclard and Nathalie Prat (Paris)
Gilles Mantel and Claire Mantey (Cannes)
Picture research
Jean-Pierre Bériac, Philippe Maffre (Bordeaux);
Marie-Pierre Lejard, Milovan Stanic (Paris)
Editorial assistants
Sabine Huet, Marie-Claire Llopès

Original edition published in the French language:
© Editions du Centre Georges Pompidou, Paris 1988
Collection "Inventaire"

First published in the UK by Mitchell Beazley Publishers
Artists House, 14-15 Manette Street, London W1VB 5LB
English translation © Mitchell Beazley 1989
Translated by Rosetta Translations
Editor
Alison Melvin
Senior Art Editor
Tim Foster
Editorial Assistant
Cathy Rigby
Production
Ted Timberlake
Managing Editor
Chris Foulkes

A CIP catalogue record for this book is available
from the British Library.
ISBN 0 85533 751 6

Typeset in Garamond by Servis Filmsetting Ltd., Manchester, England
Printed and bound in Italy by L.E.G.O., Vicenza

CHATEAUX
BORDEAUX

MITCHELL BEAZLEY

CONTENTS

APPENDICES

ACKNOWLEDGEMENTS

The Centre National d'Art et de Culture Georges Pompidou expresses its gratitude to M. Jacques Chaban-Delmas, whose commitment, along with the authority he has through his various responsibilities in the Bordeaux region, has stimulated the execution of this project, which he has supported from the start. The Centre also extends its thanks to the regional bodies, and in particular to the Conseil Régional d'Aquitaine and the city of Bordeaux for their financial contributions.

The Centre de Création Industrielle (CCI), a department of the Centre Georges Pompidou, wishes to acknowledge the numerous people and companies who have participated in the Châteaux Bordeaux project by their support and sponsorship. Neither the exhibition nor the book would have been possible without their assistance.

BANKING
BFCE – Banque Française du Commerce Extérieur, Paris

WINE COMPANIES AND ORGANIZATIONS
Association Crus et Domaines de France, Bordeaux
B.S.N. Emballage, Villeurbanne
Conseil Interprofessionel du Vin de Bordeaux (C.I.V.B.), Bordeaux
Maison de Luze, Bordeaux
Tonnellerie Seguin-Moreau, Cognac

WINE CHATEAUX IN THE BORDEAUX REGION

Château Beychevelle	Château Laroque
Château Branaire-Ducru	Château Lascombes
Château Canon	Château Latour
Château Castéra	Château Lynch-Bages
Château Cos d'Estournel	Château Margaux
Château Ducru-Beaucaillou	Château Maucaillou
Château Figeac	Château Mouton Rothschild
Château Giscours	Château Phélan-Ségur
Château Gruaud-Larose	Château Pichon-Longueville
Château Haut-Brion	Château Pichon-Longueville
Château Lafite Rothschild	Comtesse de Lalande
Château La Louvière	Château de Plassan
Château Lanessan	Château d'Yquem

The Centre de Création Industrielle (CCI) would like, in particular, to thank its sponsors in the wine trade who, in addition to their financial support, have commissioned original works from painters and architectural models from master craftsmen.

Association Crus et Domaines de France, Banque Française du Commerce Extérieur, Château Castéra, Château Cos d'Estournel, Château Ducru-Beaucaillou, Château Lafite Rothschild, Château Lynch Bages, Château Margaux, Château Mouton Rothschild, Château Pichon-Longueville, Château Pichon-Longueville-Comtesse de Lalande, Maison de Luze

We also wish to thank the following who have supported the Châteaux Bordeaux project by assuming some of the costs of the drawings and models for the architectural presentations.
Château Brane-Cantenac and Lucien Lurton for the project by Florence Lipsky, Pascal Rollet and Vincent Defos du Rau.
Barton & Guestier for the project by Patrick Dillon and Jean de Gastines for the Blanquefort site.
Christine and Michel Guérard for the project by Patrick Dillon and Jean de Gastines for the Château de Bachen.
In addition, we wish to thank all the artists who have lent us works of art specially prepared for the exhibition:.
Dominique Appia (Geneva), Michel Bez (Paris), Juarez Machado (Paris), Philippe Mazières (Bordeaux), Gérard Puvis (Paris), Edward Schmidt (New York), Société Académique d'Architecture (Toulouse), Philippe Venin-Bernard (Paris)

THE CONTRIBUTORS

JEAN DETHIER Belgian architect and town planner living in France since 1971. He has been Architectural Adviser to the department of architecture and design at the Centre Georges Pompidou in Paris since 1975. He has conceived and directed a dozen major exhibitions on architectural themes which have had a significant cultural impact both in France and abroad. He is the author of numerous articles and books.

HUGH JOHNSON The world's best-selling writer on wine, with international sales of his books totalling some seven million copies. The publication of his most outstanding literary work to date, *The Story of Wine*, in 1989 coincided with the showing of a major 13-part television series. Hugh Johnson's other great love is gardening, especially the history of landscape.

RENE PIJASSOU Director of the Geographical Institute at the University of Bordeaux, he also teaches at the Oenological Institute at the university. Since the 1960s, he has devoted a considerable part of his work to researching the history and geography of vineyards in the Bordeaux region. He has published several standard reference works notably on the Médoc (1989) and on Château Palmer (1974). He lives in Bordeaux.

PHILIPPE ROUDIE Professor of geography at the University of Bordeaux. He specializes in agricultural studies and in particular the problems facing the vineyard. He has written about 40 articles and books on various aspects of the history and geography of wine. In particular, he is author of *Vignobles et vignerons du Bordelais: 1850–1980* published in France by the National Centre of Scientific Research in 1988. He lives in Bordeaux.

NICHOLAS FAITH A British historian and journalist specializing in the fields of wine and business. He has written several books notably *The Winemasters*, a classic account of the rise of the Bordeaux wine industry and *Château Margaux* (forthcoming from Mitchell Beazley). He contributes to *The Financial Times*, *The Economist* and *Business*.

PASCAL RIBEREAU-GAYON The son of Jean Ribéreau-Gayon who was the founder of modern oenology. He studied science at Bordeaux then at Cambridge and California Universities. He is now director of the Oenological Institute at the University of Bordeaux. Pascal Ribéreau-Gayon is author of numerous scientific works on the chemistry and microbiology of wine, which have helped towards the improvement of production methods. He lives in Bordeaux.

ROBERT COUSTET Professor of history of art and architecture at the University of Bordeaux since 1970. He specializes in the art history of south-west France and particularly of Aquitaine in the 19th and 20th centuries. He has paid particular attention to the work of the Bordelais painter Odilon Redon. Robert Coustet has also contributed to our understanding of the history of wine architecture and town planning in the Bordeaux region. He lives in Bordeaux.

GERARD BAUER Town planner and architect. Professor at the Ecole d'Architecture in Paris (Tolbiac). He is head of research at the leading French consultancy for urban and regional planning: C.O.D.R.A. He is particularly concerned with finding practical ways to control and direct urban development and is the author of several books on this subject. He lives in Paris.

JEAN-PIERRE BERIAC After studying at the Ecole des Beaux Arts in Paris, Jean-Pierre Bériac chose history as his profession. He is director of the Departmental Archives of the Gironde in Bordeaux and has contributed to various books on the history of regional architecture, such as *Neo-Classical Bordeaux* with Philippe Maffre. He is an expert on the history of the Bordeaux landscape and in particular the gardens and parks of the wine châteaux. He lives in Bordeaux.

JEAN-CLAUDE LASSERRE AND PHILIPPE MAFFRE These two art historians work for the French National Historic Monuments Commission in categorizing the country's cultural, artistic and architectural wealth. Jean-Claude Lasserre is the head of this important cultural institution based in Bordeaux. Both have written numerous articles and books on the regional heritage and are keen campaigners for its preservation. They both live in Bordeaux.

THE CHATEAUX BORDEAUX EXHIBITION

The Châteaux Bordeaux exhibition was produced in Paris, France at the
Centre National d'Art et de Culture Georges Pompidou
Jean Maheu, Président

It was designed and created in 1987 and 1988
by the Centre de Création Industrielle (CCI),
– the design and architectural department of the Centre Pompidou –
François Burkhardt, Director
Georges Rosevègue, Administrator
Sylvie Wallach-Barbey, Managerial Assistant

Author and designer of the exhibition:
Jean Dethier, Paris

Assistant architect:
Philippe Dangles

Assistants:
Sabine Vigoureux, Anna Zabawski

Artists commissioned to produce pictures:
Michel Bez, Francis Martinuzzi, Gérard Puvis
and *Philippe Venin-Bernard* (Paris)
Ben Johnson and *Carl Laubin* (London)
Dominique Appia (Geneva)
John Wellington and *Edward Schmidt* (New York)
Juarez Machado (Rio de Janeiro)

Like the Châteaux Bordeaux exhibition, the idea for this book was conceived in response to two observations. The first was the remarkable blossoming of architecture that accompanied the economic expansion of the Bordeaux vineyard from the 18th century up until the end of the 19th century, inventing the concept of the "château", which symbolized quality, legitimacy and durability throughout the vineyards it represented. The second observation was that, despite the continued success of the wines of Bordeaux, there has been – apart from a very few exceptions – an absence of outstanding new architecture since the beginning of the 20th century.

The Centre de Création Industrielle (CCI) of the Centre Georges Pompidou is an institution that is devoted to a cultural approach to architecture and to the development of architectural creativity. It has considered the economically fruitful alliance between architecture and the vine that is so characteristic of the Bordeaux region, to present the heritage which has resulted from this and to judge the chances – or indeed to create the conditions – for a renewal of creativity in the viticultural architecture of the region in the context of increased international competition. The CCI, under the enlightened leadership of François Burkhardt, was more than willing to rise to this challenge since, by doing so, an original and productive synergy came about between the Centre Georges Pompidou and an important region of France. Furthermore the envisaged project had the added appeal of attracting architects from France and abroad to design new wine châteaux.

However, such an enterprise could never have been realized without the enthusiasm of men and women who were conscious of the underlying economic and cultural stakes. The meeting between Jean Dethier – the creator of several well-received exhibitions at the Centre Georges Pompidou – who conceived the Châteaux Bordeaux exhibition as well as this book, and Michel Guillard, editor of L'Amateur de Bordeaux, was the starting point. The enthusiastic and considered support of many of the best-known vineyard owners and important wine producers and their assistance, particulary financial, allowed the project to attain its full dimension and significance.

For this reason, the Châteaux Bordeaux event shows – both in terms of the amount of individual financial contributions it has received and in the exemplary relations established between the sponsors – what can be achieved by open, demanding and worthwhile sponsorship.

Finally, I must emphasize how much the success of this enterprise owes to the kind and supportive attitude of Monsieur Jacques Chaban-Delmas, the Mayor of Bordeaux, who has encouraged the project from the start and has given it the full cooperation of his city.

May I be allowed, whilst extending my personal gratitude and that of the Centre Georges Pompidou to all those who have worked for the success of Châteaux Bordeaux, to express one wish: that the awareness revealed by this project may be the start of a long-lasting renewal of creativity in wine architecture which will be worthy of the great heritage that the art of wine has bestowed on the Bordeaux region.

JEAN MAHEU
Président of the Centre Georges Pompidou, Paris

Approaching a region from the point of view of its history might appear paradoxical for an institution that is devoted to the exploration of modern trends. All the more so since these tendencies arise from a context which is marked by the merging of cultures and the increased availability of goods and services throughout the world. A constant interest in regional problems has shown us that our age is one of dialogue between the various legacies of tradition and the contributions of a contemporary creativity that is becoming universal. The new destiny of architecture is such that this dialogue cannot be continued without innovation on the one hand and remembering our past heritage on the other.

We are in a period of experimentation in which examining our history is more necessary than ever, but on condition that what is learnt is used to re-examine the issues that face us today. This is especially true in architecture, which over the last 20 years has suffered the ravages of the so-called "regional style" – the paradoxical consequence of the laudable desire to conserve historic sites. Mass-produced Provençal farmhouses, fake Breton houses – everyone now knows that using a reduced architectural vocabulary leads not to the preservation of regional character, but to the spread of characterless buildings across the countryside.

For history to be alive and inspiring, it has to be brought up to date and interpreted with a modern attitude and not just repeated parrot-fashion. Even when approached in this way, history's lessons are not always obvious. This reassessment of history is not easily taught and requires prudence and reflection, and fresh mistakes are already apparent among those who first freed themselves from the past. Neo-classicism is certainly one such reference which should be discussed and then passed over: the opposition of an élite and a vernacular past would not prevent it becoming impersonal as soon as it was systematized.

This is why the efforts of the regions should take the form of experimentation, the results of which should be discussed until pertinent lessons are found. This is why the CCI at the Centre Pompidou, in keeping with its role as an active institution, has decided, along with its partners in Bordeaux – brought together by Michel Guillard, whom I must thank – to consult European architects, in the hope that this event will allow us to reflect on the quality of life and the image of a great region.

FRANCOIS BURKHARDT
Director of the CCI at the Centre Pompidou, Paris

BORDEAUX IN PERSPECTIVE

HUGH JOHNSON

Those who know Bordeaux well, and are at home in the city and landscape which is the largest source of good wine in the world, are perhaps least able to see it clearly. It took a Parisian architect, introduced and inspired by a wine-loving photographer, to realize that Bordeaux is, collectively, a unique phenomenon. The region, the city, and its wine-making culture knit together architecture, landscape, the conduct of commerce and civilization into an entity with no parallel.

The achievement of this book and its companion exhibition is to draw our attention to this social creation: the château culture of Bordeaux. To call it a culture, to see the term written, is a mild shock: the pattern seems so natural and immutable: a farm, a manufactury, an elegant (usually) and understated (mostly) house, a product that is easy to trade in world-wide and which carries immense prestige. The whole combining to form an image, a trademark, a coherent marketing system. And this whole created two centuries ago and adapting, seemingly effortlessly, to every age since.

Described by an informed outsider, Bordeaux is a remarkable creation. But, again in the view of an outsider, it is a pattern and a system under threat. The châteaux, the central units of this subtle system, are growing old. None has been built since the First World War. Decades of depression took their toll, as roofless buildings still testify. And when money has returned, it has been spent in ways which were not always happy.

It is fair to argue, as one commentator has done, that Bordeaux is "a place of amnesia", a culture unaware of its richness and thus unprepared for the future. For – this is the argument – a strong sense of identity permeates Bordeaux's past, a sense which has now been lost and thus fails to inform the decisions Bordeaux takes about its future. One can instance the many châteaux where, despite generations of physical and often family continuity, there are no archives, no plans, no traditions even, about the early days of the château. Leave aside the natural prejudice of historians in favour of plans and archives, set apart those few châteaux (Margaux, Mouton, Latour) where the past is treasured, and one must agree. And so when the money came back to the Médoc in the 1970s the châteaux had no idea – no intuition – how to spend it. So they built sheds. A traveller through the Médoc today is

View of the exterior colonnades of Château du Bouilh, at St-André-de-Cubzac, built at the end of the 18th century by the architect Victor Louis. This château was to be the largest in the Bordeaux region, but it was never finished.

painfully aware of the sheds (the owners call them *chais*), just as he cannot ignore the expanding Shell oil storage tanks at Pauillac or the brooding power station at the confluence of the Garonne and the Dordogne. Bordeaux is at a point where it can slip into being a countryside of untidy farms and ribbon suburbs like many others, or it can find and follow its own inheritance of style. The aim of *Châteaux Bordeaux* is to urge Bordeaux – its people, its companies, those of us who drink its wine – to realize the excellence before it's too late.

In 1986, Michel Guillard, *amateur* of Bordeaux and skilled photographer, took his friend the architect and museum director to Bordeaux. Jean Dethier was looking for the theme for his next major Centre Georges Pompidou exhibition. He found it in the architecture of the Bordeaux châteaux, overshadowed for generations by the wine they made but in themselves an outstanding collection of buildings. Exploring, Dethier discovered the social and economic structure of which the châteaux are the physical presence. The following years saw an energetic outsider take Bordeaux apart. Professional researchers were despatched to every archive in the Gironde, public and private, from *département* to commune, to every château of importance, to the offices of architects and professors and *courtiers*. Backed by the prestige of the Centre Georges Pompidou and aided by the most senior members of the Bordeaux University faculty, rare discoveries were made. Boxes of papers were opened which had been sealed for a century. The archival sleuths found so many unknown or forgotten maps, plans and prints that only a tithe are here in this book. Unpublished drawings of Château Margaux jostle for space with 1920s perspectives of the elaborate gardens planned for Beychevelle. Estate plans from the 18th, 16th, 15th centuries have been unearthed. A map of Lafite, 200 years old, is new even to the present-day Rothschild owners. Gems of architecture were discovered, buried deep in unfashionable corners of the Bordeaux vineyard such as Cubzac.

Our view of Bordeaux's past is immensely enriched by this detective work. But these discoveries were not enough for Dethier. "Imagine!" he exclaims "in all the prosperous history of these châteaux, not one painter of international repute has been invited there to paint these buildings or the landscape!" He remedies this lack in an imaginative way, by commissioning a remarkable group of a dozen artists who specialize in architecture: the Société Académique d'Architecture of Toulouse. The 50 paintings that result are each the product of two months' work by a single artist. The views of the châteaux are linked by a passion for architectural exactitude but depart widely into fantasy in one direction and austere logic in the other. The whole is a new work of art: a collection of images that capture the architectural qualities of their subjects, as they are meant to do, yet also charm, amuse, enrage and engage every viewer.

Not content with this epic commission, Dethier has turned to other artists such as the Englishman Ben Johnson, to view whose interiors of Margaux is like walking those chequered floors. Six model-makers have been conjured to make models of 24 châteaux. Helicopters have been chartered, and Michel Guillard has brought back aerial photographs which are, in Dethier's words "a new vision of familiar scenes." To complement these images we have learned and perceptive essays from Professor René Pijassou, one of Bordeaux's most distinguished historians, from Nicholas Faith and from Jean Dethier himself. We have trenchant and extremely well-informed commentaries from the leading French experts on urban planning. We have observations about what is happening elsewhere in wine-making cultures related to those of Bordeaux.

We gain through these great efforts new perspectives on Bordeaux's past and present. But that is not the real point: the future is what concerns Dethier. "When you are rich," he says, gaze firmly fixed upon the proprietors of today's châteaux, "you have cultural duties." Book and exhibition are a polemic, an attempt to stir the *Bordelais* into a renewed love affair with their unique creation, the wine château. "Ideas in Bordeaux develop as slowly as the wine", observes Dethier after three years of cajoling. But he is having success. The persuasion process has included the commissioning of ten top European architects to design châteaux in the Bordeaux tradition – but to develop that tradition and to make it work anew. Four sites were chosen, two in urban Bordeaux, the home still of the *maisons de négoces*, and two at or close to existing châteaux. One of these proposed schemes, a new extension for Château Pichon-Longueville, is to become real following Jean-Michel Cazes' choice of a winner from the three competing architects. In the city, the firm of Cruse is to redevelop enormous redundant warehouses as a new bottling complex, thus keeping the connection with the Quai des Chartrons and avoiding a move out to a suburban industrial site.

Such hard commercial decisions reinforce Dethier's central message: that the future of top-rank wine is a cultural future just as much as a technical one. The heritage of Bordeaux is a guarantee and a symbol, a reinforcement of quality in a world searching uncertainly for true worth among ever-growing choice.

Bordeaux invented the concept of the château: the source of and method of making fine wine and simultaneously its trademark. The world has copied this concept, as the California châteaux in *Châteaux Bordeaux* display. It is my hope that this book, and its accompanying exhibition, do nudge the *Bordelais* into a renewed realization of what a good idea it was.

THE BORDEAUX

WINE HERITAGE

THE SOURCES OF BORDEAUX'S WINE CIVILIZATION

ARCHITECTURE AS THE CULTURAL

STRATEGY OF A REGIONAL ECONOMY

JEAN DETHIER

W hy has the Centre Pompidou, an institution that is devoted to the art and culture of the 20th century, decided to explore – by means of the Châteaux Bordeaux book and exhibition – a French wine region, whose origins date back to the Roman Empire and which is endowed with a long historical tradition?

Why has this national institution given one of its four departments – the Centre de Création Industrielle (CCI),[1] whose name gives a clear indication of its purpose, which is to deal with the cultural issues of contemporary society – the task of examining a region as rural and as apparently non-industrial as the wine-producing area and the wine châteaux around Bordeaux?

Entrance door on the covered terrace of Château St-Georges, built in the 18th century near St-Emilion.

This paradox is only an apparent one. During the course of the centuries, the wine-producing society of this region has invented numerous concepts of surprising modernity. Whereas the term "post-modernism" has been much used in cultural circles since the 1970s, an analysis of the wine civilization of Bordeaux reveals various facets of a real (though unrecognized) pre-modernity, brought about (often intuitively) by successive generations.

THE CREATION OF AN ATMOSPHERE OF EUROPEAN COOPERATION

Over the last four centuries, Bordeaux's wine culture, its unique synthesis of people and place, have formed a sort of active prototype of the present-day European Economic Community. Bordeaux has always been able to exert a lasting fascination and attraction on a whole host of active men and women from abroad who between them have boosted the status and quality of the most renowned wines in the world. In the early days there were the English, then came the Germans and the Dutch, the Belgians and the Irish, soon after that the Spanish and Danish and most recently the Americans and Japanese. In ancient times, the Romans introduced the vine to the area around Bordeaux. In the Middle Ages, the English used the established base in Bordeaux to create an international trade in these wines, which they have continued to enjoy ever since under the name of "claret". The Germans brought their financial know-how and also, in the beginning, the oak wood from their Brandenburg forests to make the *barriques* that were indispensible for the transportation of the wine. The Flemish (Belgian and Dutch) drained immense areas of marshland (at the gates of Bordeaux and in the Médoc) and made them habitable and usable by creating a dense regional network of drainage canals inspired by their own polders. The Dutch perfected the use of sulphur (the Dutch match) which made it possible to preserve and age the wine in barrels, thereby improving its quality and enabling it to be sold throughout the world (before this wines had to be drunk within a year). Throughout the centuries, the Spanish and Portuguese have provided a vital source of manpower during the grape harvests. As for the inhabitants of Bordeaux, apart from providing a vast territory (varying between 100,000 and 150,000 hectares/385 and 580 square miles, depending on the period) that is exceptionally well-suited to wine production, they have also made a decisive contribution in the form of oenology – the modern science of wine making.[2]

THE INVENTION OF A WINE CIVILIZATION

The remarkable interaction that evolved in the wine world among the inhabitants of the Bordeaux region, among the French in general and further afield, has given rise to an authentic regional civilization that is both internationally inspired and of international interest.

Here, there is a reconciliation between the regional and the universal. In the media-dominated society of the "global village", it is essential to achieve the right balance in order to avoid the dangers which could lead to economic decline in a business based essentially on quality and cultural factors. The pitfalls are on the one hand, the depersonalization caused by the "International Style", or loss of the region's vital identity; and on the other, pseudo-regionalist parody, or the sterile and disastrous imitation of a bygone age.

Any civilization, whether it is rural or urban, expresses itself through its own specific culture. We have therefore tried to discover the creative medium used by this wine-producing society to express its own identity and to project its image beyond the reputation of its wines. We have also tried to understand how this artistic creativity has managed to establish and glorify the wines of Bordeaux throughout the world. For the key to this ingenuity – or, as we would say today, to this marketing or media strategy – lies in its invention of a direct and close intuitive link between the product – the wine – and the artistic creativity which is its off-shoot.

The artistic means used to portray the nature of the wines of Bordeaux is not painting (hardly any painters have thought to depict the Bordeaux vineyard[3] and they have never been commissioned to do so), nor is it sculpture (apart from a few charming statues in the parks and viticultural motifs carved on the fronts of houses); it is not dance, nor music (the attempt made with the opera *Bacchus triomphant* at Bordeaux in 1906 was never followed up), nor literature (despite the presence in the region of famous authors, such as Montaigne in the 16th century, Montesquieu in the 18th, and François Mauriac and others in the 20th century).

The main art form that the Bordeaux wine world has associated itself with, in a unique synthesis, is architecture. It comprises a whole range of different types of wine architecture, encompassing both "viticultural town planning" in the urban environment and "viticultural regional planning" in the rural environment.

It is immediately apparent that this society has managed to balance the benefits and conflicts of vine growing within a complex bipolar wine economy. It has been able to disperse its various rural activities (the vine) and urban activities (the wine trade) and achieve a skilful equilibrium between town and country. Better still, it has managed to invigorate the town with the benefits of its rich rural environment and, conversely, to lend a degree of sophistication to the countryside. This was a remarkable success story well before what we know today as "regional planning" or "town and country planning".

THE INVENTION OF REGIONAL SOPHISTICATION

Bordeaux is in any case essentially a town of balance. Victor Hugo himself described it by suggesting that it was necessary to consider the sumptuous beauty of Versailles and the liveliness of the port of Antwerp in order to understand the unique character of Bordeaux. This town has won the justified reputation of being one of the most beautiful cities in Europe, since the 18th century when it had the good fortune of being administered by town planners of genius: Claude Boucher, the Marquis de Tourney and Dupré de St-Maur, the great intendants of the king of France. The outstanding planning of these three men transformed a fairly obscure medieval provincial town into one of the European centres of the Age of Enlightenment. A rather muddled old-fashioned town, which had disregarded the river for centuries, was quickly transformed into a radiant capital, displaying a new architectural splendour – designed in accordance with the serene rules of the neo-classical style – along its river front, which was by then the scene for intense international trade.

In order to celebrate this golden age in a monumental fashion, the authorities then called upon the most brilliant architects of the day, who – despite local intrigue – were also outsiders. They asked Jacques Gabriel and his son Jacques-Ange to design the Place Royale (which today is more democratically called the Place de la Bourse) and in 1773 Victor Louis (who had returned from the Polish court) was commissioned to build the famous Grand Théâtre, that architectural Mecca so indicative of the Bordeaux spirit. Behind its delicate but somewhat sober façades, this building is designed according to a dual polarity, with its auditorium and grand foyer, the latter providing an immense space where the bourgeoisie can flaunt its wealth. This idea of architecture "dramatizing social activities" was later taken up and adapted in the designs of various buildings that were orientated towards wine.

THE INVENTION OF VITICULTURAL TOWN PLANNING

At a distance of just 500 metres (550 yards) from that striking symbol of Bordeaux architecture, the Grand Théâtre, is the start of the famous Chartrons district,[4] which runs for two kilometres (one and a quarter miles) along the quayside. From the 17th century onwards, the quarter spread northwards, forming a sort of self-sufficient enclave, and bringing about the invention of a new type of viticultural town planning, of which it was the first and largest known example. This district had an air of being set apart, a kind of "European principality of *négociants*" who bought, stored, sold and dispatched the wines of Bordeaux all over the world. However, this was not (as is so often the case in the 20th century) merely an industrial ghetto.

The Chartrons was conceived as a town within a town, a dense and varied zone in which, over an area of about 60 hectares (148 acres), the business of the wine world was carried on and where the *négociants* lived (often in very prestigious houses) alongside a large population (about 12,000 inhabitants in 1900) also involved in the wine trade. The community was well provided for with public buildings and numerous places of worship (Catholic, Reformist, Protestant, Jewish, etc.) which gives an indication of its ethnic diversity. The Chartrons remains a remarkable example of economic, social, cultural and urban integration and today's politicians and town planners have urgent decisions to make about its future. Urgent because, as we shall see later, the Chartrons are seriously threatened, being unable (until now) to adapt their unique heritage to the modern world and in particular to the new and pressing needs of the urban aspect of the wine-making economy.[5]

In their wisdom, the inhabitants of Bordeaux have avoided a confrontation between the urban wine centre and the wine-producing hinterland. They have brought about a gradual transition between these two aspects of the regional economy by creating a hierarchy of urban and rural centres. Thus Bordeaux is not the only town in the *département* of the Gironde to serve as a base for the wine trade. Other centres have become established in, for example, the town of Libourne (23,000 inhabitants in 1985), 35 kilometres (21 miles) to the northeast of Bordeaux in the Pricurat wine district – much smaller than the Chartrons – which stretches along the banks of the Dordogne.[6]

In this hierarchy of wine centres in the Bordeaux region, there is also a multitude of wine-producing villages and hamlets, often with names known world-wide. It was by reference to their *terroir* that the idea of an *appellation*, the limiting of the origin of a wine to the boundaries of a rural commune, came into being. Examples are Margaux, St-Estèphe, St-Julien, Listrac, Moulis en Médoc, Cérons and Barsac in the Graves, Loupiac and Sauternes further south, and many others. Between the numerous wine villages and the few urban centres where the *négociants* are based, is a network of small towns with an intermediate viticultural role: Pauillac and Blaye, on opposite sides of the Gironde, Langon and St-Emilion. The latter (3,500 inhabitants in 1985) presents a good example of traditional viticultural town planning: a historic town, nestled in a natural amphitheatre (the Bordeaux theatricality again) in the hollow of a peaceful little valley surrounded by its famous vineyards. The land value of these vineyards has so far miraculously saved this small town from suburban sprawl. This wine-producing oasis is the only one in the Bordeaux region to have retained the serene beauty of its pre-industrial town along with the beauty of the vineyard that voluptuously surrounds it – a harmonious balance between townscape and landscape. St-Emilion is the last remaining symbol of the peaceful coexistence of the two economic and cultural aspects of the wines of Bordeaux: the town and the vineyard. It is also evidence of the two important creations of a great humanist civilization: viticultural town planning[4] and viticultural country planning.[7]

THE INVENTION OF
A WINE LANDSCAPE

All types of agriculture, whether they are small-scale or industrial, result in specific landscapes, but the beauty of the countryside created by the Bordeaux vineyard is very distinctive. That is, when it has not been spoiled by unplanned urbanization, by the careless putting up of electricity lines and by the proliferation of large advertisement billboards.

With its meticulous organization, the vineyard offers a grandiose spectacle that is architectural, theatrical and pictorial all at once. It produces a similar effect to what is known as "op art" which is perceived most vividly when the observer is moving. Then the kinetic sight of the parallel *règes* of the vineyard suggests a meticulous choreography depicted by an artist such as Léger, Mondrian or Vasarely. In fact, the vineyard itself could have inspired Monet with its subtle seasonal variations in colour and luminosity. As for the vine, the plant that can live as long as man, it represents a high degree of masochism: the best grapes are harvested from vineyards that are so stony (the famous *graves* of the Bordeaux region) that they are unsuitable for most other crops. The vine stock's tortured appearance brings to mind paintings or sculptures by Dubuffet, Bacon or even Picasso.

This unique blend of objective, imaginary or phantasmagorical visions gives the vineyard a particularly poetic power of evocation. Its orderly rows present a subtle image which is both peaceful and powerful. The sea of vines is accentuated by the slightest slope or it is contrasted with the outline of a *jalle* or of the complex division of the land which has been developed over generations. But what makes this landscape unique in the world is that it is crossed by three magnificent waterways: the Garonne and the Dordogne which converge near Bordeaux in the Gironde, whose great size is both majestic (its width extends to eight kilometres/four and a half miles) and exotic (its yellow-ochre colour from the silt it carries). Over a distance of more than 200 kilometres (130 miles) on the land bordering the river and its two tributaries, the jigsaw of vineyards is unfolded. But since the vineyards can only thrive on particular types of soil, they tend to be set in a natural chequered pattern of woods (*garennes*), forests (often pine), pastures and *palus*. Until the end of the 19th century, this ecological balance also allowed the wine growers a degree of self-sufficiency, providing them with firewood and livestock. The extraordinary socio-agronomic structure and its effect on the landscape have made the Bordeaux region into a sort of national park whose beauty (now impaired and under threat) should be protected by the adoption of urgent measures.[7]

THE INVENTION OF
THE WINE CHATEAU

Within a radius of 60 kilometres (37 miles) around Bordeaux, there are more than 20,000 wine-growing concerns which together make up the largest fine wine area in the world.[8] The smaller properties are sometimes no bigger than one hectare (particularly in the Pomerol region) and the larger estates cover areas of up to 200 hectares (495 acres).

At the centre of several hundred of these estates, the *Bordelais* have gradually perfected one of the most ingenious aspects of their dual economic-cultural strategy: the wine château. The first château in the area which was deliberately built for the purpose of wine was erected in 1525 in the immediate surroundings of Bordeaux: this is the famous Château Haut-Brion at Pessac (whose vineyard is today surrounded by residential suburbs).

Over the generations, this new concept was refined and adapted by the various social classes who successively adopted it: the aristocracy, the upper bourgeoisie, the businessmen and financiers of the 19th century and then the middle classes. By adapting to this sociological evolution, the design of the wine château was developed with numerous geographical and stylistic variations. Some hundred châteaux were built in the 18th century in a very elegant neo-classical style which was popular in Bordeaux at that time. Still more were built in the 19th century, drawing on all types of styles in a neo-historical eclecticism.[9]

Despite their extraordinary diversity, all these wine châteaux obeyed a single principle which makes them original: for the first time, the ancient notion of the castle or château (the *castellum* which dates back to the early history of mankind) had been modernized and adapted to the economic and cultural needs of wine production. Of course, there had been previous examples of this in Europe. For example, the *villa rustica* of the Roman Empire, in the countryside as opposed to the *villa urbana* in the towns and, above all, the magnificent 16th-century villas of the agricultural region of Venezia, whose structural, spatial and aesthetic design was perfected and transposed into numerous variations by the most famous architect of the century, Andrea Palladio. But these villas were intended for the aristocracy who generally lived on their estates and ran mixed-farming enterprises, whereas in Bordeaux, the owners of the wine châteaux almost always lived in the town and only very rarely visited their country estates. However, the Bordeaux château complex does, typically, include a residence, which forms the main focal point of its structure.

The second focal point concentrates on all the functional buildings intended for the production, *élevage* and storage of wine. These are mainly the fermenting room (with its cylindrical *cuves*) and the *chai(s)* (of which there may be more than one and which contain barrels of wine called *barriques*). Various residential buildings are arranged around the utilities which are intended for the use of the *maître de chais*, the *régisseur*, the vignerons and the master-craftsmen (coopers, wrought-iron workers, etc.). In some cases, these buildings are arranged as a large architectural whole that sometimes attains the size of a small village around the *maison de maître* forming a kind of self-sufficient rural community. Between the château and its vineyard the attractive grounds and gardens[10] emphasize the urbane sophistication of these oases of civilization, by punctuating the countryside with rare trees, geometrical flowerbeds, allegorical sculptures and architectural follies. The whole effect is carefully designed so as to be both very functional and very prestigious: creating a brand image for the château's wine that is made memorable by its architecture.

THE INVENTION OF PUBLIC RELATIONS AND THEIR ARTISTIC PRESENTATION IN THE CHATEAU

Few of these châteaux are often inhabited by their city-dwelling owners, but increasingly proprietors are using them for entertaining guests: personalities from France and abroad, *négociants*, businessmen and wine enthusiasts who naturally appreciate the privilege of being in such surroundings. Thus they are becoming delightful rural embassies for a great wine where the refined civilization of "luxury, peace and delight" (to quote Baudelaire) may be savoured.

The viticultural economy of Bordeaux seems to have been among the first to put to use the very modern concept of public relations. This practice has encouraged competition among the châteaux owners to improve and develop their properties and to design their beautiful grounds with a theatrical use of landscaping and architecture to create the maximum impact. Château de Malle provides a first-rate example of the application of this principle, with its delightful rustic theatre nestling in the midst of a wonderful 17th-century garden.[10] Many other châteaux have adopted this same concept of theatricality to a lesser degree, by using architectural scenography to emphasize the function of the buildings: the areas of production and *élevage*, the *chais* and the *cuviers*.

This desire — sometimes intuitive, sometimes deliberate — to create spectacular buildings has continued until modern times. In 1926, Baron Philippe de Rothschild called in Charles Siclis, the Parisian architect who specialized in theatre design, to Château Mouton. In 1984, his cousin Eric invited the famous Spanish architect, Ricardo Bofill, to Château Lafite-Rothschild. Both châteaux required

the architects to dramatize and exalt the spirit of the most precious, most symbolic and most explicit of the public buildings: the *chais*.

The châteaux owners attempts to attract greater numbers of visitors have sometimes been supplemented by the addition of a wine museum. There are several in the wine châteaux of the region, but the most famous — because of the exceptional quality of its works of art which are all related to wine — is without a doubt that of Château Mouton Rothschild at Pauillac, which was opened to the public in 1962. Another museum, devoted to the viticultural architecture of the Bordeaux region, is presently under consideration at Château Pichon-Longueville, also at Pauillac.

All this reveals a mastery of architectural virtues (when it is used advisedly) for the creation of a magical feeling to the place and for the formation of a brand image that is capable of conveying the château's reputation of excellence throughout the world. Magic and image are very evocative words and the wine-producing culture of Bordeaux combined these two concepts very early on to invent a three-pronged strategy for the advertising, marketing and packaging of its products.

THE INVENTION OF THE BRAND IMAGE: MARKETING AND PACKAGING

The term "château", with all its implications of aristocracy and prestige, became commonly used throughout the region and was combined with the name of the vineyard owner (or the name of a locality) to define a particular wine. This ingenious system of identification was used in innumerable variants (there are more than 4,000 specific châteaux names in the Bordeaux region today) and the word "château" ensured that a sort of family likeness was retained in each region. At least, this was the case until the 20th century, when this key word was taken over by other wine-producing areas in France and elsewhere in Europe and has even been used (still in French) in non French-speaking countries that produce wine, such as the United States and Australia. The people of Bordeaux never thought — or only too late — of securing the copyright for this term. Nevertheless, they are responsible for the very simple idea of extending considerably the meaning of the word by combining it with the visual and poetic force of a graphic image — the image of the château and its architecture.

A GLOBAL CONCEPT OF COMMUNICATION

Thus, in the 20th century, the word "château" and its artistic image have been combined on the labels of millions and millions of bottles of Bordeaux wine. This profusion of images which are produced in limited editions every year (first of all by chromolithography) has recently given rise to the notion of *oenographilie* which itself leads to the practice of collecting wine labels. Their diversity presents a sort of encyclopedia of the various architectural styles of the châteaux and the multitude of graphic and sometimes very creative representations of them. The commercial and media success of this branding of a wine by the architectural image of the château where it was produced has led to this practice being extended beyond the mere bottle label. Realistic or schematized drawings of the façades of châteaux are also reproduced on the wooden cases that the wine is packed in (they used to be literally branded), on the lead or foil bottle capsules and even on the corks. This visual communication is focused on the architecture of the château and leads to the modern notion of a corporate identity – the identity of a company expressed not only by its graphic image but also by a coherent collection of different parts, whose central theme, in this case, is the image of the château. Its architectural quality becomes an ambassador for the quality of the wine produced.

A GLOBAL SYSTEM OF CULTURAL AND ECONOMIC INNOVATION

Thus the wine-producing society of Bordeaux has invented a whole string of concepts which have been put to use on a large scale and which fit together like a jigsaw puzzle. This combines within a coherent unit elements as small as the product labels and as vast as regional planning, with all the intermediate stages linked together: town planning, landscaping and country planning and, of course, architecture.

This global system of architectural innovation forms the symbolic reference point of the artistic culture that is peculiar to the civilization of the wines of Bordeaux. Here is an example of a society managing to create a unique interaction between two complementary and mutually enhancing factors: the quality of the wine and the quality of the associated wine architecture.

THE DANGERS OF A LOSS OF CULTURAL IDENTITY

This portrait of an authentic wine-producing culture may appear to be idyllic. However, it now seems to me that this unique wine heritage is faced with several serious dangers:
– a too frequent amnesia concerning its own cultural and artistic traditions;
– an occasional inability to protect this heritage from the onslaughts and corruption of industrial society, especially since the 1960s (largely due to ignorance about the uniqueness of this tradition);
– a frequent inability to preserve, adapt or renew this cultural heritage by skilfully reconciling traditional values with the needs of the future.

On the whole (because there are obviously exceptions), the participators in this regional economy – which has up until now been expanding – have failed to adopt a collective cultural strategy, which is the indispensable long-term counterpart to an oenological strategy. In this respect, they tend to seriously underestimate – or even sometimes to ignore – the wisdom of their ancestors who (at least in a pragmatic way) created commercial strength through a careful balance between economic success and their wine culture. The recent oenological revolution in Bordeaux has made possible an extraordinary revival of the regional economy, after several decades of depression. However, on a cultural and artistic level, the 20th century has so far been a period marked by little progress. Bordeaux's new golden age of wine production which began a few years ago should as a matter of urgency be profitably used to establish a new renaissance of the arts, which is ahead of its time.

There are other valid and creative paths that remain to be discovered besides the dead-ends of the "International Style" and pseudo-regionalist imitation. It was the search for these paths that the Centre National d'Art et de Culture Georges Pompidou and its architectural design department wanted to set in motion, with the help of various regional and national sponsors and by inviting architects and artists from Bordeaux, the rest of France, Europe and the Americas, to sketch the first outlines of a solution.

See the second section of this article on page 165.

1 The Centre de Création Industrielle (CCI) at the Centre Georges Pompidou provides an analysis, with criticism and prognosis, of the fields of architecture, urban environment, design, visual communication and social innovation.
2 Cf the text by Pascal Ribéreau-Gayon on oenology p.57.
3 With the exception of the various interesting frescoes painted in a neo-classical or art-deco style in some public buildings in Bordeaux (in particular the Bourse du Travail) during the 1930s, some of which are reproduced in this book.
4 Cf the text by Robert Coustet on the wine trade and the city of Bordeaux p.139.
5 Cf the project for the redevelopment of the Chartrons p.207.
6 Cf the text by Nicholas Faith on the economy of the wine châteaux p.49.
7 Cf the article by Gérard Bauer on the wine landscape of the Bordeaux region p.125.
8 Cf the article by René Pijassou on the history of the Bordeaux vineyard p.27.
9 Cf the article by Robert Coustet on the history of wine architecture p.63.
10 Cf the article by Jean-Pierre Bériac on the gardens and grounds of the wine châteaux p.113.

*Château Mouton Rothschild
with its vineyard at Pauillac
and one of the masterpieces in
its famous museum: an
ancient tapestry depicting
vines.*

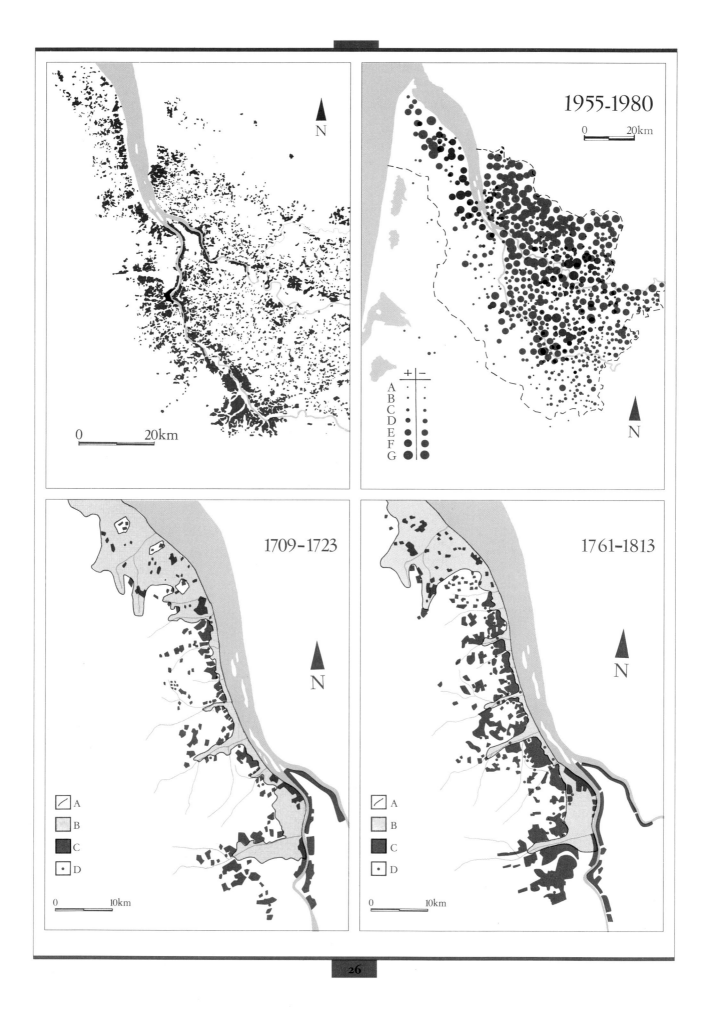

1955-1980

0 ____ 20km

A
B
C
D
E
F
G

+ −

1709−1723

A
B
C
D

0 ____ 10km

1761−1813

A
B
C
D

0 ____ 10km

THE HISTORY OF THE BORDEAUX VINEYARD

RENE PIJASSOU

The long tradition of wine production in the Bordeaux region is beyond dispute, but it is essential to dispel the myth that the *grands crus* date back to antiquity. More than 20 years' research, both in the field and through extensive public and private archive material, allows me to advance a more reliable view of the history of the Bordeaux vineyard. My conclusion is that the origins of the *grands crus* of Bordeaux are to be found at the beginning of the 18th century.

FROM ANTIQUITY TO CLARET

In the first century AD, the *negotiatores vinearum* of Burdigala (the Latin name for Bordeaux) grew tired of paying the high prices for wines from Campania or Narbonne, which were imported in amphorae by Roman traders. They therefore decided to plant their own vineyards. In addition to freeing themselves from the exploitation of Roman merchants, they also wanted to have a share in the profitable wine exports to new markets such as Britannia, which had recently been conquered by the legions of Emperor Claudius.

They had to choose a variety of vine that would be suited to the ecological conditions of the region and they acclimatized one, which they called *biturica*. No-one can tell what type of wine the early inhabitants of Bordeaux

produced. At the very most, we can hazard a guess that this wine, which was stored in amphorae or in barrels, was a good everyday wine, but not a *grand cru* by today's standards. In this early experimentation with vine types, it is important to remember two essential facts about the origins of the great wines of the Bordeaux region. First, the *biturica* was a specially-selected variety, intended to produce good *vin de pays*. Secondly, the selection of this variety was a step towards the creation of a commercial vineyard run by leading citizens of a port strategically placed on the Atlantic Ocean.

As to what happened to these first vineyards – which are in any case difficult to locate – after the Roman world collapsed under the onslaught of the Barbarians, nothing is known for more than six centuries. The vine no doubt retained its place around Bordeaux in the agricultural estates of the Archbishop and the ecclesiastical and secular nobility. The latter cultivated vines largely for their own consumption and to offer to guests. Whereas the ecclesiastical vineyards provided the wine necessary for the rites of the Catholic Church.

In the course of the 12th century, some glimmers of information start to appear. The conditions for wine trading had changed radically. The beginnings of decline in the Mediterranean world were offset by the rise of the northern countries. In addition, the Aquitaine became an English dukedom with the marriage between Eleanor of Aquitaine and Henry Plantagenet, who became Henry II of England. However, the rise of the Bordeaux vineyard did not really begin until the 13th century, after the King of France took La Rochelle in 1224. Bordeaux, which was a fairly modest town, became the leading port in exporting Gascon wines to England. The King-Duke (King of England and Duke of Aquitaine) granted generous tax and trade privileges to the Bordeaux merchants who controlled the shipping of wines to England. Thus Bordeaux was promoted to the rank of "England's cellar in the Middle Ages". In other words, it became the first region in the medieval world to export wine.

The Bordeaux middle classes then took up the cultivation of vines. Land was cleared for the planting of vines and the vineyards spread through the *graves* around the city, through the St-Emilion and Libourne regions, along both banks of the Garonne, upstream of Bordeaux, and across the Bourg and Blaye regions downstream. The low-lying land of the *palus* was also planted, but not to the same extent as today's vineyards. The Médoc, particulary the left bank of the Gironde estuary, was not used much for wine production during the Middle Ages.

The wine made in the Bordeaux region during the Middle Ages was not a *grand cru*, in the sense in which we understand it today. The people who bought the wine called it "claret", a term still used by the British today for the wines of Bordeaux. This was a "clear" wine, the *vinum clarum* of medieval texts; it was probably a rosé wine because the fermentation time allowed was short. Maceration had not been discovered and consequently the colour was weak. In addition, the claret was made from both red and white grapes which were pressed together and poured into the vat. Claret was a *vin nouveau* and was drunk as such. Indeed, during this period, people did not have the appropriate techniques at their disposal to age wines. Therefore, in the 14th and 15th centuries, "old" wine was

This fragment of the "Atlas de Trudaine" concerns the vineyard planted around the citadel of Blaye (on the banks of the Gironde) to the north of Bordeaux: the north is to the left. (National archives, Paris).

eight to ten months old and was worth half the price of the new wine from the previous autumn. Claret was a sort of "Bordeaux primeur" which started to become unpalatable in the May or June following the harvest.

The idea of a particular *terroir*, or a *cru*, was unknown in the Middle Ages. At the most specific, wine from the *graves* or from the *palus* was sometimes referred to in records dating from the 15th century. Perhaps an English wine lover might want to obtain wine from a particular lord, or from a particular property. But the *grands crus* did not exist. In the *Bataille des Vins*, a 13th century literary text, St-Emilion was considered to be a white wine!

THE WINE REVOLUTION

This situation changed very little in the 16th century and in the first half of the 17th century. *Bourdieux* started to appear, especially in the *palus* of the Gironde. These were specialized wine-producing holdings, planted in furrows or *règes*. One type of vine started to emerge with a distinct identity: the Verdot, which produced the so-called "cargo" red wines, for drinking by sailors at sea. The *bourdieux*, which were owned by the middle classes of Bordeaux, were administered through the intermediary of a *homme d'affaires* or *régisseur*. This was a new departure that had the advantage of freeing viticulture from the paralyzing feudal system.

At the start of the 17th century, the arrival of entrepreneurs and engineers from the Netherlands overturned the traditional methods of wine production in the Bordeaux region. The engineers drained the coastal marshes in Bas-Médoc, Aunis and Saintonge. At that time, the Flemish, those "wagoners of the seas", dominated world trade and the Flemish *négociants* who settled in Bordeaux in the first decades of the 17th century, transformed the city's commerce. Their great energy produced an economic revival which was first felt in the maritime ports, before spreading to the Aquitaine hinterland and to the Iberian peninsula. They set up their shops in Bordeaux, where they stocked and blended wines. They also offered other beverages to European customers:

"colonial infusions" (i.e. chocolate, tea, coffee) and strong beers and brandies.

The export crisis that hit the Bordeaux region was mainly the result of the production of new types of wines encouraged by the Dutch. The Flemish consumers appreciated sweet white wines and altered or adulterated wines. This Dutch way of improving weak wines encouraged the expansion of the peasant vineyards which produced large amounts of inferior red and white wines, that were only fit to be distilled. The diversification in wine producers supplying the international market may also be explained by the diplomatic and customs regulations that characterized the 17th century. Under the Dutch William of Orange, who became King of England in 1688, the British market erected trade barriers that were very prejudicial to French goods, in particular the Gascon clarets. The latter were subject to entrance duties that were more than twice those for wines from Iberia. This protectionist policy favoured the "black wines" of Spain and Portugal – which were in fact red wines as we know them today – and as a result these wines became very widely drunk in Britain.

How did the producers of the Bordeaux region react? Most of them continued to produce their traditional wines. However, others tried to produce different types of wine that would appeal to wealthy English wine drinkers, who still favoured the claret of the Bordeaux region. These claret lovers were recruited from the newest ranks of the British aristocracy who were eager for novelties and expensive high-quality products. The genius of the Pontacs, owners of Château Haut-Brion in Pessac at the start of the Bordeaux *graves*, was in recognizing the potential of the new British market. In addition to the estate of Haut-Brion, which it had owned since the 16th century, the Pontac family also had a vast amount of family land in Aquitaine and a substantial income. With their fortune established, the Pontacs easily made the transition from shopkeepers to nobility and entered the Bordeaux parliamentary aristocracy.

This fragment of the "Atlas de Trudaine" concerns the banks of the Garonne around Barsac and Ste-Croix-du-Mont southeast of Bordeaux; the north is to the bottom left. (National archives, Paris).

In 1666 the head of the family, Arnaud de Pontac, had the ingenious idea of sending his son François-Auguste to London, during the rebuilding of the City after the Great Fire, to set up a restaurant: a "New Eating House" with the name of Pontac. This was a type of 17th-century delicatessen, where the Pontacs offered meals for one guinea and sold the wine from their Haut-Brion estate (described as the "wine of M. de Pontac"). The Pontacs gained a select clientele of writers, including Saint-Evremond, Daniel Defoe, Swift, the philosopher John Locke, wealthy merchants and aristocrats. The illustrious public of the restaurant ensured that the reputation of these fine wines from Bordeaux quickly became established.

The famous English philosopher John Locke visited Haut-Brion on Friday 14 April 1677. In a remarkable description of the *terroir* of this future *grand cru*, he highlighted the exceptional quality of its wines, which were better than those produced in neighbouring vineyards. "The soil, which is composed of white sand mixed with gravel (*graves*), looks as though it could produce nothing; but such is the particular quality of the soil in Monsieur de Pontac's vineyard . . . that the merchants assure me that the wine from the neighbouring vineyards, whose soil is apparently the same, is clearly less good." This account is concrete proof of the concept of a wine-producing *terroir* or a particular *cru*. Moreover, it was perceived, especially at Haut-Brion, that this noble *terroir* was the source of high-quality wines.

These wines – the direct ancestors of the *grands crus* of Bordeaux – were produced with great care and attention. They were nurtured in barrels of new oak and were then decanted and perhaps also fined or clarified. When the wines were able to be exported to London (in times of international peace), these fine wines fetched prices five or six times higher than those of ordinary clarets. But in difficult times, such as during the 1690s, it was necessary to sell the surplus Haut-Brion, which was already a *grand cru*, by the glassful in the taverns of Bordeaux and even to sell it as "*vin de munition*" for the fleet of the Ponant based at Rochefort. Thus the bold and innovative approach of the *premier président* Arnaud de Pontac nearly foundered in the last decade of the 17th century.

Fortunately for the Bordeaux *grands crus*, disaster was averted. On the contrary, the innovations made at Château Haut-Brion served as an incentive to

the time. Gravelly *terroirs* and estates were thus planted with vines, as were the lowlands of the Ambès peninsular. A vast planting operation started in the southern Médoc, in the Blanquefort region, where the Pontac family had another wine château, and expanded towards the Margaux region, which it intensively cultivated, and gradually extended towards Pauillac and St-

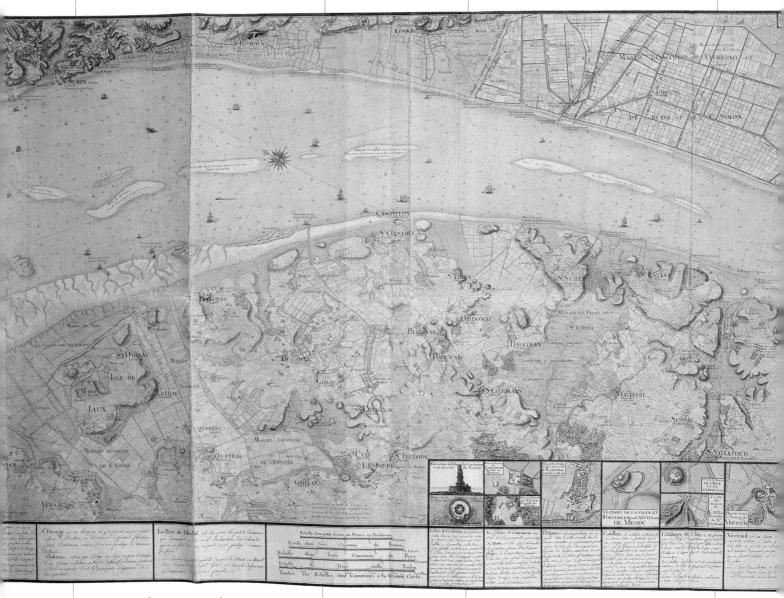

encourage investment from the parliamentarians of Bordeaux, often friends or relatives of the *premier président*, and also from the rich middle classes of the town. All these wealthy notables invested widely in wine growing and many acquired estates, particularly in the Médoc, which made little wine at

Estèphe to the north. In the second half of the 18th century, the vineyards reached the Bas-Médoc and the northern limits of the current *appellation* area.

The Intendant of Bordeaux between 1720 and 1730, Claude Boucher denounced the "planting mania" that had got hold of the middle classes and aristocratic parliamentarians of Bordeaux. This expansion took place, not only in the Médoc, but also in most other parts of the Bordeaux region: Graves, Sauternes, Bourg, Blaye, the *palus* on the banks of the Gironde and, to a lesser extent, in the vineyards of Fronsac, St-Emilion and Pomerol. Thus the present-day layout of the Bordeaux vineyard was in fact created

and Ludon. In the upper part, the important fort and port of Blaye and the town of Bourg can be seen. Among the 15 illustrations along the bottom of the map, we can see more detailed plans of two wine towns (Pauillac and Macau) and those of two wine châteaux (Margaux and Issan with their old grounds and gardens). (National archives, Paris).

Lestonnac, creator of the vineyard of Château Margaux and co-owner of Haut-Brion; the Ségur family, holder of the estates of Lafite and Latour, in Pauillac, and creators of the famous vineyards of the same name. The Marquis Nicolas-Alexandre de Ségur, the *premier président* of the Parliament of Bordeaux, was perhaps the most renowned of all. On his death in 1755, his

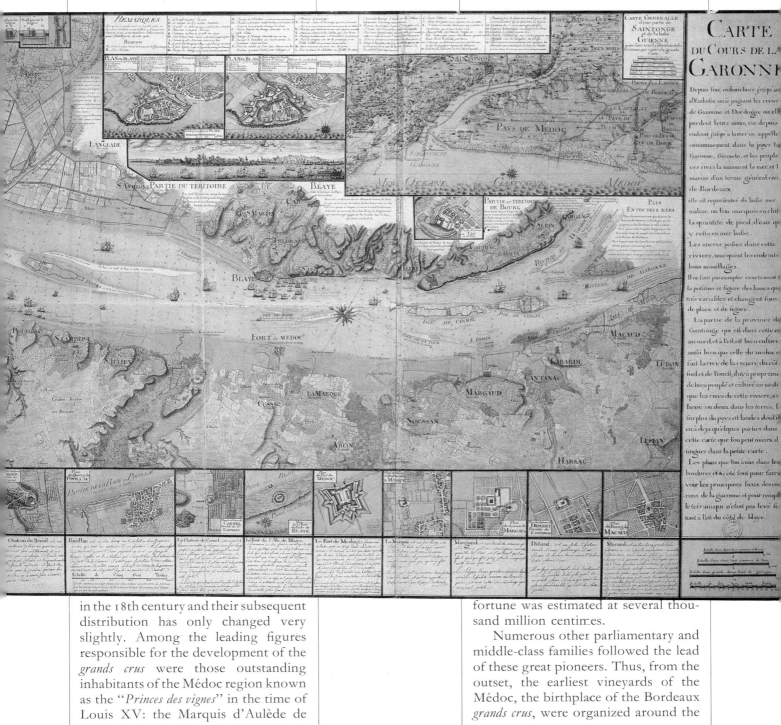

in the 18th century and their subsequent distribution has only changed very slightly. Among the leading figures responsible for the development of the *grands crus* were those outstanding inhabitants of the Médoc region known as the "*Princes des vignes*" in the time of Louis XV: the Marquis d'Aulède de

fortune was estimated at several thousand million centimes.

Numerous other parliamentary and middle-class families followed the lead of these great pioneers. Thus, from the outset, the earliest vineyards of the Médoc, the birthplace of the Bordeaux *grands crus*, were organized around the dominant properties of the wine châteaux. On the other hand, the transformation of the St-Emilion, Pomerol and Fronsac vineyards took place later and less completely. It took shape in 1760-80 and the innovations were the work of a few prominent Libourne citizens, including the Fontémoing, Boyer and de Carle families. There are several reasons for the slight delay between the viticultural development of these regions and that of the Médoc. Firstly, the structure of land ownership was different; the sharecropping system, which was unknown in the Médoc, continued for a long time around Libourne. Secondly, the prominent inhabitants were less wealthy and less adventurous than those of Bordeaux and they did not have the benefit of the support of the great Bordeaux *négociants*. Thirdly, trade in Libourne, although it was lively, proved to be less enterprising than in the Chartrons in Bordeaux. It won several markets on the Breton coasts, in the north of France, in Belgium and in Holland. However, it did not manage to get a foothold in the British market which was the only one to readily pay the high prices asked for the fine wines of the Bordeaux region.

During the 19th century, with the arrival of the railway and due to the impetus given by active owners, the great wines of St-Emilion, Pomerol and Fronsac made up for lost time and joined the first rank with their peers from the Médoc. The same was also true of the great sweet white wines of the Sauternes area, which appeared a little earlier than the red wines of St-Emilion. In 1785, M. de Lur-Saluces married the heiress to M. Sauvage d'Iquem and founded the present dynasty, thereby conferring a great reputation to the white wines from Château d'Yquem.

The fine red wines of Haut-Brion and of the Médoc first made their appearance on the London market at the beginning of the 18th century, under the name of the "New French Clarets". The most revealing evidence of this important event in the history of the *grands crus* is provided by old advertisements in the *London Gazette* between 1704 and 1712. One such issue of the magazine announced the public auction ("for sale by the candle") on 22 May 1707 of a lot of the "New French Clarets", recently arrived, "from the *crus* of Lafit, La Tour and Margouze". Haut-Brion was of course often mentioned in these advertisements, along with its peers from the Médoc. These new types of wine were already worth four to five times as much as ordinary clarets.

THE GREAT CHANGES

At the same time as the emergence of the great red wines of the Médoc and Haut-Brion, new methods of wine production were established. The great Médoc châteaux arranged their vines in vast *plantiers*, i.e. in large parcels arranged in *règes* and ploughed with a swing plough drawn by oxen. The maintenance of these vineyards was organized in a hierarchical way, led by a *régisseur* with the help of a *homme d'affaires*, the head of cultivation and a team of cattlehands and wine makers from the surrounding countryside. Thus, the large châteaux employed a staff of between 30 and 50 people on a permanent basis.

New methods of wine production improved the selection of the types of vine planted in the vineyards. In surviving documents from the last quarter of the 18th century, we may note the gradual appearance of the noble grape varieties of today, chosen from among the many local types of vine: Cabernet Sauvignon, Petit-Verdot, Malbec and, a little later on, Merlot and Cabernet Franc. About 8-10,000 of these vines were planted per hectare and trained to grow low. Care was always taken to use fertiliser sparingly and at long intervals. It was the aim of the best *régisseurs*, who carefully tended these precious vineyards like gardens, to obtain low yields: only 15-16 hectolitres per hectare. It was also common practice to keep a stock of old vines, the "mothers of the *grands crus*", as described by a *régisseur* at Château Latour at the end of the 18th century. Obviously this type of wine production required constant investment, and a long-term commitment which was only possible because of the large incomes and the secure positions of the founding families of the first *grands crus*.

The modernization of wine production was accompanied by the perfection of new techniques for the vinification and maturing of the great wines. New methods were slowly developed both in the *chais* of the great châteaux, by the *maître de chais* and his workers and in the *chais* of the Chartrons. Picking of the grapes was carefully carried out, early if possible, and the fermenting time was generally short. In addition there was a strict system of selection for the batches of wine from each harvest which improved the quality of the product. The *régisseurs* separated the *premiers vins*, i.e. the best wines, which alone carried the name of the château, and the *seconds vins*, which were of inferior quality, as were the *fonds de cuve*. This selection process entailed heavy financial sacrifice: the *seconds vins* were sold at a price that was three to six times lower than that of the *premiers vins* or *grands vins*.

The new wine was put into new barrels, made from oak from the north. Frequent ullaging, regular topping up of the barrels, was practised. Every three months, racking was carried out, a decanting operation to get rid of the solid impurities. Another technique used from the 1730s onwards was the addition after each racking of sulphur dioxide, a sterilizer, produced by the *allumette hollandaise* or *mèche soufrée*. Finally, after two years or more, the wines were fined in barrels. In the 18th century, the fine wines were kept for longer than today in the barrel, usually for four years or more. The wine was rarely bottled in the château, apart from the owner's personal reserve. Bottling was also fairly rare in the wine merchants' *chais*. The fine wines were first transported in barrels to the Bordeaux *négociant*, who exported the wine in casks to his foreign – usually English – customers. The wine was then bottled for the buyer by the importer.

We can see the fundamental part played by the city of Bordeaux in the creation of the great wines and the essential role of the Bordeaux *négociants* who shipped the *grands crus* throughout the world. The last decades of the 17th

This cabled column of baroque inspiration with a vine winding around it is a symbol of the complementary relationship between architecture and wine-production in the Bordeaux region. (Collection of Château Pichon-Longueville-Comtesse de Lalande, Pauillac).

century and, in particular the early years of the 18th century, were characterized, on the economic level, by the appearance of numerous merchants. It was at this time that the new district of the Chartreux, outside the old city of Bordeaux, took the name of Chartrons and became the symbol and home for the new commercial aristocracy of the Bordeaux wine trade. Most of the new merchants were of British origin, e.g. the Bartons who arrived in 1725 and the Johnstons who arrived in 1735. A little later, German, Danish and Dutch merchants started to establish themselves. Relations between the *négociants* and the great wine producers were cemented by a new generation of *courtiers des vins*, most of them from the British Isles. They also settled in the Chartrons. Thus Abraham Lawton, born into a family of wine merchants in Ireland, established his firm in Bordeaux at the end of 1739. He founded one of the most famous brokerage offices in Bordeaux and his descendants are still carrying on the same profession today.

The 18th century was the golden age of Bordeaux, the age of commercial prosperity and the appearance of a new wealthy and refined society. This is evident by the founding of the Chamber of Commerce in 1705 and the creation of the Académie Royale des Sciences, Belles Lettres et Arts de Bordeaux in 1712-13. The Académie was for a while directed by the young *président* of the parliament, Charles-Louis Secondat, Baron of La Brède, and the future Montesquieu, himself a wine producer. In addition, the building of beautiful, stately stone mansions in Bordeaux and the monumental neo-classical architecture of the trading district was a vivid illustration of the affluence of the town's élite and of a new style of living.

In fact, this new society, which was rich and elegant and loved beautiful things, had modelled itself on London rather than Paris. In London, the high society appreciated fine wines and frequented the coffee houses that had multiplied. It is also necessary to put the birth of the *grands crus* of Bordeaux into the wider context of the Enlightenment that was dominating Europe at the beginning of the 18th century. It was then that, quite naturally, the concepts of civility and refinement were linked with the tasting of fine wines from Bordeaux – hence the idea and expression of the "civilization of wine" which, from then on, was applied to the best products of the region.

The creation of the *grands crus* was accompanied by the gradual construction of a hierarchy of quality among the great wines. Thus, an analysis of the

wines: the first four classics – Haut-Brion, Lafite, Latour and Margaux; and a second and third class that were still largely incomplete.

Gradually the art of tasting and discussing Bordeaux wines came into being. In the past, people had been happy to drink draughts of wine straight from the barrel, without analyzing its particular qualities. The arrival of Venetian glassware encouraged

first brokerage books (1740-75) from the Tastet-Laurton firm highlights the existence of a classification of the great Médoc wines in the 1770s. In 1787, Thomas Jefferson, an American statesman, recorded in his travel diary the outline of the future classification of 1855 which the *négociants* had told him about. This list distinguished between three classes, notably among the red

enthusiasts to look at the wine when held up to the light. People started to appreciate the colour of the *grands crus*, but also to define the different qualities of taste: body, flavour and bouquet. By the end of the 18th century, the technique of maturing fine red wines, which had then finally become established, would make it easier to make comparisons among vintages on the one hand and among *crus* on the other. It was the *courtiers* and *négociants* of Bordeaux and the *régisseurs* of the great Médoc châteaux who invented the descriptive and rich vocabulary of wine tasting terms.

TOWARDS A FIRST OFFICIAL CLASSIFICATION

By 1815, the Bordeaux vineyards had more or less taken on their present appearance. Whereas the Médoc, Graves and Sauternes were very much to the fore, the vineyards of Libourne, St-Emilion, Pomerol and Fronsac were a little behind. The regions of Entre-Deux-Mers, Bourg and Blaye and the Premières Côtes de Bordeaux were quite a long way behind the leading vineyards in terms of quality.

During the 19th century, the hard times suffered by the wine-producing areas of the Bordeaux region were far longer-lasting than the periods of prosperity. From around 1825-50, the situation in the vineyards was very depressed. The protectionist policy pursued during the Restoration and the July Monarchy was of little help either to the exportation of the great wines or to the stability of prices. Owing to the lack of a solid and diversified banking system, the finances of the *grands crus* were on shaky ground.

The Bordeaux traders, who often acted as lenders and bankers to the châteaux, exploited the situation to increase their control over the *grands crus*. They adopted a policy of subscription – imposing long-term contracts of five or ten years at a fixed price – with many of the *grands crus*, including the most prestigious estates. Obviously, this practice proved to be very profitable for the merchants.

On 18 April 1855, the union of Bordeaux *courtiers* published the famous list of *crus classés* which, although it was not legally recognized, was nonetheless considered to be official. The occasion chosen for its publication was the Exposition Universelle held in Paris by the imperial government. The Bordeaux Chamber of Commerce had been given the task of staging an exhibition of the *crus* of the Bordeaux region and addressed itself to the *courtiers'* union. In

One of the preliminary sketches by the American painter John Wellington for his 1988 picture of Château Pichon-Longueville-Comtesse de Lalande. (Oil on wood, 100x150 cm, the artist's collection, New York).

response the latter presented a list of the 58 *crus* of the "red wines of the Gironde". It only contained the *grands crus classés* of the Médoc and Haut-Brion in the Graves. The union added 22 *crus classés* of sweet white wines from the Sauternes region. This list provoked much complaint and criticism both from wine producers in the Médoc who had been downgraded or classed other than they might have wished, and from properties in St-Emilion, which had been ignored. In fact, the development of the latter, although well underway, was far from being complete – hence the omission on the part of the Bordeaux *courtiers'* union.

The classification of 1855 took place at the same time that the Bordeaux vineyard was under its first serious attack from a fearsome enemy: oidium. For almost ten years, it left the Bordeaux region in the unfortunate position of facing a disastrous fall in production. In the Médoc, for seven consecutive years, from 1853-59, the harvest was one third its normal size. In the 1860s, the adoption of sulphuration, which had long been contested, made it possible to stamp out the fungus, but not to exterminate it completely.

THE BELLE EPOQUE AND HARD TIMES

Paradoxically, with the enemy being kept at bay, the serious oidium crisis led to an exceptional rise in the prices of the great Bordeaux wines and, consequently, to an exceptional level of prosperity. No doubt the sudden drop in supply of great wines encouraged the rise in prices. In addition, the widening prosperity in France as a result of the Second Empire extended the commercial euphoria of high prices and large profits into the 1880s.

Gold was plentiful in the Bordeaux châteaux. The 1863 vintage reached unrivalled heights. This was the time of the intensive reconstruction or erection of noble wine châteaux surrounded by sumptuous grounds in the area around Bordeaux. New and more efficient cellars were installed. The staff on the estates benefitted from a social policy that led to the building of houses, schools and clinics near the châteaux.

Selection of the types of vines planted was finally decided in favour of the noble grape varieties of today: Cabernet Sauvignon and Merlot in the Médoc; Cabernet Franc and Merlot in the St-Emilion area.

With the opening of the Bordeaux-Paris railway in 1853, the vineyards of St-Emilion, closely followed by those of Pomerol and, somewhat later, Fronsac, were overcome by the planting mania. Not only did the area planted with vines increase, but prices also rose and, though it did not catch up with the Médoc, St-Emilion took a large step down the road of quality improvement. This was also a golden age for the sweet wines of Sauternes. Throughout the wine-producing areas of the Bordeaux region, but especially in the Médoc, the spectacular rise in revenues attracted investment from Paris, in particular the Péreires to Palmer and Nathaniel de Rothschild to Mouton. James de Rothschild, head of the Parisian bank, acquired Lafite in 1868. Ten years later, Count Pillet-Will bought Château Margaux in the largest transaction of the *belle époque* period of the 19th-century vineyard.

The great prosperity of the 30 preceding years was brought to an end by a three-pronged attack from the phylloxera, mildew and the "great fraud". These hard times were catastrophic, because the crisis in the Bordeaux vineyard (and in France generally) dragged on – with only a few brief periods of respite – until the 1960s. The damage caused by the phylloxera happened more slowly and was less decisive than has sometimes been claimed. A common error was to assert that this pest entirely destroyed the Bordeaux vineyard. This was simply not true but such scaremongering inevitably tarnished the image of the great Bordeaux wines.

In fact, owners were able to prolong the life of their vines by treating them with insecticides. This was a costly solution, but it allowed the stock of old vines and thus the quality of the *grands crus* to be maintained. The expansion of the area under vine and the increase in the use of fertiliser explain the amazing rise in yields and, consequently, in

19th-century illustrations showing the new and more rational two-level cuviers then being built in the Médoc.

production, that characterized the end of the 19th century and the first decade of the 20th century. However, this regeneration of the Bordeaux vineyard was gradual and continued well into the 1920s. Mildew also took its toll on the vine. The Bordeaux wine producers were devastated by its effects: acidic wine, low in alcohol and lacking in balance. In the 1930s, wines "turned" when they were bottled. These problems contributed to the questioning of the premium position enjoyed by Bordeaux red wines, especially abroad. This loss of reputation, in particular in Great Britain, was worsened by the "great fraud" which was rampant in the Bordeaux region from 1895-1914. The shameless blending of Sicilian, Spanish and Languedoc wines with those of Bordeaux, cheating on the labelling, and deceptive *appellations* were some examples of the fraudulent practices that were rife on the Bordeaux wine market at that time.

Thus the great crisis in wine production revenues, with which phylloxera has wrongly been blamed, came into being. There were many unfortunate consequences for the wine producers of the Bordeaux region: insolvency, large loans and heavy debts; numerous sharp falls in prices and changes in the ownership of wine-producing estates; total domination by the merchants who imposed a system of subscription at a fixed price that was considerably lower than the prices during the *belle époque*. One good result, however, was the very strict legislation imposed by the State between 1905 and 1911 to end fraud.

The outbreak of the First World War prevented the revival of the wine business. In addition, due to a shortage of "Bordeaux mixture", (copper-based vine treatment), and of manpower, several harvests, including the 1915 harvest, were wiped out by mildew. Monetary difficulties and the devaluation of currency in the years 1920-24 did not allow the finances of the châteaux, which had already been seriously weakened, to be restored. The unfavourable world-wide economic and social situation hindered exports, in particular Prohibition in the United States. The recovery in 1924-29 was too brief to re-establish an equilibrium. Then came the great depression of 1929. Despite the slow re-opening of the American market, the management and revenue problems of the châteaux increased up until 1939. Vines started to be uprooted and numerous châteaux were put up for sale at derisory prices.

A new development during these very difficult times was the creation of wine-producing cooperatives. From 1932 onwards, the cooperative movement saved small and medium-sized independant producers who were faced with bankruptcy. The Second World War then broke out and the levies enforced by the occupying German authorities gave the illusion of a brief economic recovery.

THE NEW GOLDEN AGE

A slight recovery, particularly as far as the American market was concerned, was felt in 1950-51. But, paradoxically, the real economic revival of the vineyards was linked to a natural catastrophe: the winter of 1956 which severely hit production. This served as a starting point for a marked rise in prices, which was further aided by the general world-wide economic recovery.

Picture by the Argentinian painter Ricardo Wolfson, 1988. It shows the neo-classical organization of Château de Plassan built in about 1800 at Tabanac in the Premières Côtes de Bordeaux. (200x300 cm, the artist's collection, Florence).

Prices rose, although the crisis of the years 1973-74 temporarily held back the increase. There has been an exceptional series of great vintages since 1975. Behind these outstanding results, which have attracted foreign capital – British and Japanese – and investments by French insurance companies, there has been an extraordinary policy of modernization. This has involved the adoption of new technology; better selection of vines and increases in yield by the putting into practice of the new science of oenology. A scientific type of vinification – both for fermenting and for ageing – has been developed by the Institut d'Oenologie in Bordeaux and has spread throughout all areas of wine production. This technical progress explains the frequency of successful vintages and the absence of crop failures over the last 20 years.

On the whole, St-Emilion and Pomerol have caught up with the Médoc and Sauternes in terms of their reputation, and numerous other less prestigious *appellations* have made considerable advances in quality. But in France and throughout the world, Bordeaux still today forms the first bastion of quality wine production.

THE CONCEPT OF THE WINE CHATEAU

PHILIPPE ROUDIE

What could seem more natural than using the term "château" to denote a great Bordeaux wine? All the more so since no other wine-producing region in the world had made this correlation before the Bordeaux region developed it and made it one of the standard wine terms.

There are today nearly 4,000 properties in the *département* of the Gironde that habitually sell all or part of their wine production under a château name. In 1980, according to the most recent census carried out by the Ministry of Agriculture, there were nearly 19,000 wine-producing concerns, including 15,700 producers of *appellation* wines. In addition, according to the latest known harvest declarations (those of 1987) there were a little over 20,000 wine producers in the *département*. These are therefore the facts, which are indisputable: in the Gironde, one wine-producing concern in four (or five) produces a Bordeaux wine which

is identified by the name of the property from which it came.

THE GEOGRAPHY OF THE CHATEAUX

The distribution of the châteaux throughout the Bordeaux vineyard is extremely irregular and may be divided into three main geographical groups. This geography of the châteaux closely relates to the amount of wine produced as well as to its fame. The greatest density of châteaux corresponds exactly with the areas where there is the highest percentage of vines in agricultural land, in other words to the highest degree of monoculture around St-Emilion and Barsac (in the Sauternes region).

With a few minor variations, some areas that are important centres of wine production today still have relatively few châteaux, such as the Cubzac area and the north and centre of the Entre-Deux-Mers plateau, an area that has no *appellations communales*. On the other hand, there are areas where vines – in terms of space – only play a secondary role and where châteaux are present but not numerous. This is true of the northern Graves or the western Entre-Deux-Mers where the remnants of the former vineyards in the suburban areas are evidence of an ancient and glorious past. The vineyard area has often almost completely disappeared with the spread of urbanization but the *crus* that have survived – on account of their fame – are châteaux in the real sense.

Whatever the case and despite the exceptions, there is no doubt that the term "château" implies quality wine production. This is also confirmed by the fact that within certain *appellations* the best *terroirs* have the greatest number of châteaux, as is the case around Blaye and Bourg, where the châteaux are situated around the *côtes* rather than the hinterland.

THE LEGAL VOID

In a vineyard with a reputation as old as that of the Bordeaux region and in a country where the legislation governing wine production has taken up numerous complex documents, we might expect to find a precise, legal definition of the term "château" or, at the very least, a fairly precise regulation of its use. However, unlike the notion of *appellation*, there is no such legal precision governing the expression "château" which is paradoxically of a particular clarity due to the few documents that refer to it. It is in this respect that the decree of 17 April 1942 – made when there were already nearly 1,400 châteaux (according to the Gironde directory of 1945) – is the most precise when it states that a château is linked to the existence of "a particular *cru*, a specific vineyard that has been known for a very long time by the name in question, in accordance with its meaning and with local, faithful and reliable usage such as it results from the law of 6 May 1919 and subsequent laws." It very soon came about that "according to jurisprudence, the expression 'château' (became) applicable to wines coming from any particular wine-producing property of some size containing appropriate buildings."[1]

In the 19th century it became popular to depict the architecture of the wine châteaux on fine china. In Bordeaux, this practice was popularized mainly by J. Vieillard's workshop.

FROM TOP TO BOTTOM: *Châteaux Lafite, Pomys, d'Yquem, Haut-Brion and Margaux. (Collection of the Musée d'Aquitaine, Bordeaux).*

CHATEAUX WITHOUT CASTLES

The law is thus not very clear about the interpretation of the term "château", at least with regard to the architectural aspect. Among the thousands of wine-producing concerns that use the term for their wine, there are very few who could apply it to their buildings, since most of today's 4,000 or so châteaux are nothing grander than rather bourgeois rural residences and sometimes even simple peasant homes. There are also cases – and these are not just the odd exception – where, not only is there no château, but there is no building whatsoever! On the other hand, most of the outstanding châteaux in the Bordeaux region are not numbered among the best *crus* of the region – apart from a few exceptions that are as remarkable as they are prestigious (Margaux and Beychevelle in the Médoc, Filhot, d'Yquem and Malle in the Sauternes region, St-Georges in the St-Emilion region etc.). Besides, many of these buildings, although they are of great cultural interest, do not have any adjoining vineyards or agricultural land. Hence the aesthetic confusion of many visitors who know little about wine production and the vine and who embark on a tour of the *grands crus*; and likewise the confusion – gastronomic this time – of art and archaeology enthusiasts who visit these historical residences. The "châteaux du Bordelais" are wine-producing properties that most often have no château, just as, on the other hand, the châteaux of the Loire have no vines!

Since the Bordeaux château is not a historical residence, does it originate from the large aristocratic properties where vines were traditionally cultivated? A study of wine production and how it was organized will provide some answers. In 1980, the Gironde contained 900 properties with more than 20 hectares (49 acres) of vines, covering a total of one third of the vineyard area in the *département*. Their geographical distribution reveals the pre-eminence of the left bank of Garonne-Gironde axis, the Libourne area, the central Entre-Deux-Mers and even the Côtes de

Bordeaux or the Côtes de Blaye. This corresponds to the areas where the châteaux are situated with the exception of the Graves and the Sauternes area. However, it is not possible to correlate the presence of a château with a great vineyard because of the simple fact that there are at least four times more châteaux than there are estates of over 20 hectares (49 acres) of vines! In fact many of the best châteaux *crus* of the Bordeaux region are only small properties – particularly in St-Emilion and Pomerol.

THE CHATEAU AND CRU CLASSE

There is another correlation that we should mention, that of the "château-cru classé". This notion was thought up by the Bordeaux region and it is the only area to take advantage of it. This is obviously not the place to relate the story of the classifications of the Bordeaux wines but, to understand what follows, one must remember that there had long been a practice – established at least as far back as the 17th century – of drawing up lists of parishes and properties, usually referred to by the name of their owner ("le cru de Monsieur . . ."), in the decreasing order of the quality of their wines. These lists became more and more frequent and were drawn up by enthusiasts or wine professionals (*courtiers* or *négociants*). Eventually, they became used as actual market price lists for the different wines and publicized individual properties.

Among these classifications, the list of 1855, drawn up by the Bordeaux union of *courtiers* for the Exposition Universelle in Paris, was most successful, no doubt because it had Napoleon III's blessing. For once the classification had been requested by the Paris authorities and had not been left to the initiative of local individuals. Restricted to the regions of the Médoc for red wines and to the Sauternes area for whites (58 red *crus classés* and 21 white), this classification, which acquired an official status, was for a long time the only valid one in the Bordeaux region. A century later the Graves and Libourne areas followed its example by promoting about 15 and 80 *crus classés*

respectively. After some recent changes to these two classifications, there are now a little under 200 *crus classés* in the Gironde, about 30 in the Sauternes area, about 15 in the Graves, 60 or so in the Médoc and less than 80 in St-Emilion.

The notion of the château cannot be identified with that of a *cru classé*, since while there are 4,000 châteaux, only 200 of them are classified. Moreover, not all the *crus classés* claim to be châteaux, and there are four *clos* among the St-Emilion *crus classés*! In addition, there are some good areas where there is no existing classification, e.g. Pomerol's Château Pétrus, one of the most famous *crus* of the Bordeaux region, is not a *cru classé*! These are therefore two unconnected concepts: *crus classés*, whose number is presently fixed and for which any future change will literally be a matter for the State; and châteaux, whose number is continually increasing. We can see in passing that the situation today is the opposite of that in the middle of the 19th century. At the time of the 1855 classification, there were more than 80 *crus classés* and not even 50 *crus* calling themselves châteaux.

THE ORIGINS

If the Bordeaux château is not a large estate or a historical residence and cannot be identified with a *cru classé*, can it be characterized by its aristocratic origins? In order to provide a detailed answer, it would be necessary to study the historical records of all the châteaux in the Bordeaux region, which is not possible here. However, in the light of what is already known, we can put forward some suggestions.

The oldest estates (if not the most numerous) – apart from the peasant wine properties, whose traditions are lost in the mists of time – seem to be those created by the clergy of Bordeaux (archbishops, chapters of the principal churches etc.) and the main monastic orders, although the latter also improved the existing vineyards. But, generally speaking, the clergy lost most of its vineyards before the term "château" was first coined. In fact, the oldest estates which were the forerunners of today's châteaux were created by the merchant and parliamentarian middle classes of Bordeaux, and dated back to when the Bordeaux region first made its appearance as a great wine-producer and when wine became a substantial source of revenue. Thus, from medieval times the gradual formation of the wine-producing estate was a continuous development which has continued into the 20th century.

The fact remains, however, that the origins of many of today's important wine properties, even before they assumed the title of château, dates back to the noble estates of the *ancien régime*, where great vineyards were developed and even created. This is particularly evident in the Médoc where the parliamentarians of Bordeaux in the 17th and 18th centuries ennobled themselves by buying land and creating prestigious vineyards. Conversely, particularly in the Libourne area (St-Emilion and Pomerol), there were few estates and hardly any Bordeaux landowners. This region was marked by the unusual way properties were divided up into units intended for all types of agriculture (including vine growing) and was well-populated with rural craftsmen, small traders and peasants. Be that as it may, these small properties only came to be called "châteaux" as the quality of their wine improved and as foreign markets, particularly in Belgium, started to discover them.

In fact, it is one of the biggest paradoxes of the Bordeaux region that it has only very recently discovered or invented the château, at least as far as the designation of a particular *cru* is concerned. A useful statistical and chronological way of approaching this

Portrait of Thomas Barton, originally from Ireland, who established himself as a wine merchant in Bordeaux in 1725. (Collection of Château Léoville Barton).

phenomenon is to count the *crus* using the word "château" in their name and to calculate their percentage of all wine producers by referring to the numerous books on the Bordeaux vineyard. With regard to the latter, there are the works of Franck for the 19th century and later there are directories, listing producers, by giving the name, title, owner and production of the *crus*. These reference works, multiplied at the end of the 19th century and in the course of the 20th century, but the one by Charles Cocks[2] (first edition 1850) is perhaps the most reliable of all, largely due to its co-author and editor, Edouard Féret. Thirteen editions appeared between 1850 and 1982 and it is today a bible for all Bordeaux enthusiasts, widely used by professionals and has been translated into several languages. It is simply a matter of counting all the producers, commune by commune, in each of the editions, and then adding up those using the term "château".

Out of the 668 *crus* mentioned in 1850, there were only 48 châteaux, 40 of them situated in the Médoc and the others in the Graves and Sauternes area. The best-known *crus*, notably those that were classified five years later, were not all mentioned as châteaux, and there were no châteaux in the Libourne area around Blaye or Bourg, nor in the Côtes de Bordeaux.

Eighteen years later, with the renewed success of the wines of Bordeaux in northern Europe and the prosperity resulting from the free-trade policies of the Second Empire, the number of named *crus* had increased by threefold, but the number of châteaux had

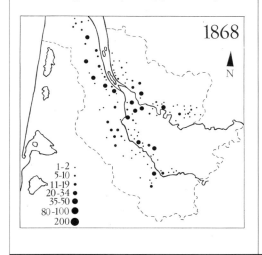

1868

N

1-2 ·
5-10 ·
11-19 •
20-34 •
35-50 ●
80-100 ●
200 ●

Maps drawn by Philippe Roudié showing the increase (between 1868 and 1969) in the number of wine-producing concerns in the Bordeaux region using the term "château" on their labels to market their wine. The numerical key is shown in the map on the left.

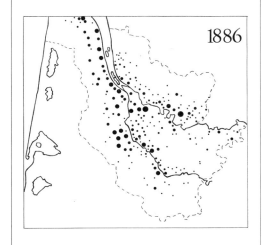

1886

increased seven times over. From then there was no let-up in the increasing use of the term "château": nearly 700 in 1874, nearly 800 in 1881, more than 1,000 in 1886, 1,300 in 1893, 1,800 in 1908, nearly 2,000 in 1922, 2,200 in 1929, 2,400 in 1949. Even though the number of particular *crus* was increasing at the same time, it is obvious that the proportion of châteaux among the total number of producers trading under the name of their *crus* steadily rose from 10 percent in 1850, to 24 percent in 1868 and 35 percent in 1893.

An analysis of these statistics shows that the linguistic phenomenon of the château dates from the Second Empire, which roughly corresponds to the time when prestigious residences were being built, particularly in the Médoc. But, whereas the building of châteaux ended with the vineyard crisis at the end of the 19th century (phylloxera, mildew, First World War and the economic crisis between the wars), the use of the term "château" spread throughout the Bordeaux region, not just the Médoc. It is obvious that this proliferation did not go hand in hand with the *terroir* being ennobled by a castle-like residence but it tended to affirm the pre-eminence of certain vineyards, providing individual *appellations* before the term had been coined. It is also evident that the custom of bottling the wine at the property itself (the term "au château" began to be used), which guaranteed the wine's authenticity, played an important part in establishing the importance of the concept of the château.

It therefore becomes essential — though very difficult — to try to under-

Portrait of one of the members of the Rothschild family who acquired Château Lafite in 1868. (Collection of the Château).

stand the great and continuous success of this château concept. From the outset, it should be stressed again how the lack of any legislation governing the use of the term resulted in its misuse. This is best illustrated by the comments of contemporaries of the period, in particular Charles de Lorbac (in fact, Cabrol, a Bordeaux author): "These days, in the *département* of the Gironde, the word 'château' is taken to mean a large wine-producing property which, in order to earn this ambitious title, need have no more than a good oenological reputation. What was the most renowned wine in former times? The wine from the château and the reason for this is quite simple: the nobles were the only big owners . . . , and kept the best land for themselves . . . Thus the wine from the château was the most sought after . . . . but the Revolution changed many things . . . , the old authority of the nobles disappeared forever. The châteaux also lost their strategic significance; but one thing survived: the good reputation of a wine to which the precious classification of château was applied. The word remained and it retains its commercial rank to this day."[3]

In former times the word "château" was the only term that could signify the long-established quality of the *cru*. The old term *terre noble* could not be used in the middle of the 19th century by Médoc owners who had entered viticulture from the bourgeoisie world of trade and banking. The word *domaine*, though it was often used, did not make any distinction between wine production and other types of agricultural land

1922

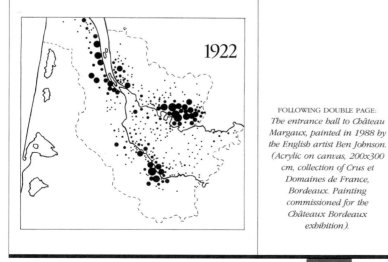

FOLLOWING DOUBLE PAGE:
The entrance hall to Château Margaux, painted in 1988 by the English artist Ben Johnson. (Acrylic on canvas, 200x300 cm, collection of Crus et Domaines de France, Bordeaux. Painting commissioned for the Châteaux Bordeaux exhibition).

1969

given over to forestry, cereals, pasture etc. As for the word *clos*, which is mainly Burgundian, though also used in the Bordeaux region, it did not seem to have a strong enough commercial impact. The word "château" remained: "since the products from the vineyard adjoining the château have come from a *terre noble*, the nobility of the land has made them noble wines."[4]

However, there was still one small problem: many of these châteaux were ordinary buildings rather than castles. Charles de Lorbac is quite clear in this respect: "More often than not, it must be said, the château is no more than a house of bourgeois appearance". However, with their new found wealth, the châteaux owners started to build new grand buildings in which the castle-like qualities were self-evident. In other words, for several hundred *crus* of varying prestige, the building of a new château justified a posteriori the older usage of the word.

THE NAMING OF THE CHATEAU

Once they had decided to use the term "château", the estate owners had to choose a name in line with this new classification. In most cases, this was quite straightforward – the name of the locality was used, since the *crus* were always linked to their respective *terroirs*. There was thus a number of châteaux that took the name of the commune, a common occurrence when the château surrounded a real castle-like building and inherited a rural estate. Then there were châteaux that took the name of traditional localities, derived from particular features of the soil ("*graves*", "*belles graves*" . . .), of the vegetation ("*orme*", "*chêne*", "*pin*" . . .), of the locality ("*la croix*", "*les moulins*" . . .) or of the house ("*borde*", "*mayne*"). But there was a problem as every château was entitled to use the name of the same locality, which in any case had very imprecise borders. Therefore, and this also had the advantage of publicizing the name of the property, the surname of the owner or founder of the property was often used, which explains the number of double-barrelled and family names, some of them renowned in the

Bordeaux region (like the Ségurs), others less well-known, including many foreign surnames, English ones in particular.

But with the huge increase in the number of châteaux, this use of personal names was no longer sufficient and people started to use all sorts of terms. Names such as "Bel Air", "Beau Séjour", "Bellevue", "Beau Site", "Beau Rivage", "Beau Soleil" etc. proliferated. As homonyms became more and more common, a period of usurpation proceedings started, to the delight of the local lawyers, who saw a whole new field of litigation opening up. It is evident that this practice of identifying a *cru* by giving it a name would have to be accompanied by documents authenticating it on behalf of the consumer, in other words a label. The first examples of wine labels date back to the middle of the 19th century, but in the Bordeaux region most of them came from the *négociants* who marketed the wine. Thus, beside the name of the *cru*, the name of the *négociant* firm also appeared and the whole was decorated with ornamental motifs which were increasingly based on illustrations of the architecture of the château or of its particular emblems. It gradually became commonplace to have a picture of the property or château, sometimes portrayed in a stylistic or flattering way and sometimes even replaced by the *chai* or fermenting room or a representation of the vineyard landscapes – the obvious admission of the absence of a real château.

The notion of the château became considerably more imprecise in the 20th century and was completely left to the initiative of the producers, even if they sometimes had to defend their right to use it in the courts, and today has tended to be used by all types of wines and not just those belonging to an *appellation*. There is nothing to prevent a wine grower linking a particular wine with a château name, which means that one owner, producing several types of wine that differ in colour or quality, can use several different châteaux names; the latter have almost become brands. Moreover, there is now the apparent paradox of a continuing increase in the number of châteaux but a decrease in the number of wine producers. If this trend continues, the point will soon be reached where each individual producer will be a château. In short, the term "château" has been devalued somewhat and now only means the wine from a particular property. People talk of "grands and petits châteaux" in order to re-establish a hierarchy of quality. In addition, unless a decision is taken to redefine the term "château" or some degree of awareness and self-control is established among producers, the misuse of this term will continue in Bordeaux and France as a whole and

THE THREE MAIN CHATEAUX AREAS IN THE BORDEAUX REGION

The Bordeaux vineyard is made up of three geographical units. The first includes the vines of the upper Gironde estuary, the southern Médoc and the Blaye region on either side of the inland sea; the second covers the middle stretch of the Garonne, Graves and the Sauternes region on the left bank and Côtes de Bordeaux on the right; and the third is linked with the Libourne region, or at least with the area stretching along the right bank of the Dordogne from Castillon to Libourne and even crossing the Isle around Fronsac.

These three areas are similar in that they are situated along the three great river axes of the Bordeaux region at their confluence (the Dordogne and the Garonne converge about 15 kilometres/9 miles north of Bordeaux and flow into the Gironde) and also in that they are situated opposite each other in groups of two, although not all the Gironde bank is a châteaux area.

These favoured sites also correspond to the most prestigious *appellations* (or groups of *appellations*); thus, in the Libourne area, the nucleus of St-Emilion and its satellites (Montagne, Lussac, Puisseguin, St-Georges), as well as Pomerol and Fronsac and even Castillon. In the Médoc, the greatest density of châteaux naturally corresponds to the string of *appellations communales* represented by Margaux, St-Julien-Beychevelle, Pauillac, St-Estèphe.... However, it is noticeable that the côtes vineyards are most often situated opposite these vineyards of communes of world-wide repute, e.g. Côtes de Bordeaux (and Côtes de St-Macaire) opposite the Graves and the Sauternes area, Côtes de Bourg and Côtes de Blaye opposite the Médoc ....

throughout the wine world from California to Australia.

1 P. Siré, "Les Noms des vins de Bordeaux", *Semaine juridique* 1480, 1959; cf also by the same author: "Les Châteaux de Bordeaux", *Semaine juridique 2472*, no. 18, 3 May 1972

2 C. Cocks and E. Féret, *Bordeaux et ses vins, classés par ordre de mérite*. Bordeaux: Féret et Fils, (2nd edition), 1868 (13 new editions up until 1982)

3 C. de Lorbac and C. Lallemand, *Les Richesses gastronomiques de la France. Les vins de Bordeaux*. First part: Les châteaux de la Gironde viticole, pp.32-33, Hetzel, no date (*circa* 1860-65)

4 P. Siré, "Les Châteaux de Bordeaux", *Semaine juridique*, op. cit.; cf also J. Déruppé, "Noms de châteaux et marques vinicoles" in *Région et Aménagement du Territoire, mélange offert au doyen Lajugie*, Bordeaux: Bière, 1985, pp.512-519

19th-century wine architecture in the Médoc: Château Pichon-Longueville-Comtesse de Lalande and Château Maucaillou.

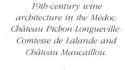

Château Gruaud-Larose and the chais of Château Beaumont. (Surveys and drawings: S-A, Toulouse).

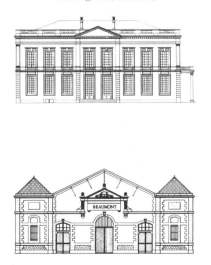

THE WINE ECONOMY OF THE BORDEAUX CHATEAUX

NICHOLAS FAITH

When the 17th-century diarist Samuel Pepys noted that he had tasted a marvellous wine called "Ho Bryan" at a London café called Pontac's the mention was casual enough. But the occasion was a historic one: the café was named after the owner, M. de Pontac, whose father had produced the wine. In commercial terms the diarist had been at the receiving end of the most integrated commercial operation ever conceived by the owner of a Bordeaux château. Although the British had been the major customers for "claret" for five centuries before the emergence of the café society of late 17th-century London, the wines had always been anonymous and drunk young. Since the 1660s they have been older and distinguished by the names of individual châteaux.

Yet since this isolated case in the 1660s Bordeaux's châteaux owners have not been in the habit of selling their wine direct to the final consumer outside France. Indeed it has taken three centuries for them even to achieve the same degree of economic control over their products, let alone their marketing, as M. de Pontac. This is not surprising. Only in Bordeaux is it possible even to discuss the economic life of a château, since only in the Gironde is a château conceived as an economic unit. In rural France as a whole the produce of a wine-making property is strictly anonymous, its identity deriving only from the region in which it is situated. The same applies in other French wine-growing areas where the basic unit is the "*cru*", the strictly deliniated patch of land which experience has shown can produce fine wine of a specific type.

So no individual owner dare pretend that he (or even she) is more important than the idea of quality enshrined in the name of the *appellation*. Even in Burgundy, the most individualistic of wine-growing areas, the label is dominated by the names of the *crus*: Montrachet, Chambertin and the like. By contrast, while Bordeaux has 37 *appellations*, their names are invariably relegated to the foot of the label whereas the name of the individual château, however insignificant, inevitably holds pride of place. Moreover the name of the château is that of a brand,

for it does not guarantee that the grapes are grown on a specific piece of land. The legal requirements are loose enough to allow ambitious proprietors to buy up vineyard plots from a relatively wide area within a given *appellation*. In the past 25 years this laxity has been of enormous assistance in promoting the independent economic life of châteaux, because ambitious owners can build up estates big enough to be worth promoting as brand names. The only effective control over such empire-building is the château owner's concern for the reputation of his brand name.

THE POWER OF THE CHARTRONS

Yet the very idea of the château as a distinct brand is so extraordinary that it can only be the result of a very unusual chain of social, cultural and economic circumstances. Moreover it has required repeated injections of external capital and thus of entrepreneurial attitudes to make this break with agricultural tradition the norm in the Gironde. Left to themselves, the local vineyard owners would not have transformed their properties into capital-intensive wineries though they have proved themselves apt pupils once outsiders have pointed the way.

In a sense even M. de Pontac, though the most important of the parliamentarians of his time, was an outsider. He was simply the first member of his class to invest his money, first in the Graves, the most promising gravel slopes near Bordeaux, and then, in the century and a quarter before the French Revolution, in a steady stream of property speculation in the Médoc. This was possible only because the soil of the Médoc is too poor to grow anything except vines and the most meagre crops of rye. So the land was cheap and the parliamentarians could build up enormous wine estates, often exceeding 50 hectares (124 acres).

But the parliamentarians had neither the capital nor the commercial capacity to follow M. de Pontac's example, and during the 18th century they steadily surrendered the economic initiative to the inhabitants of the Quai des

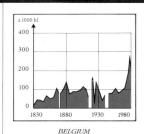

BELGIUM

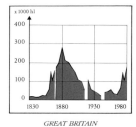

GREAT BRITAIN

Statistical analysis from 1830–1980 showing the exports of Bordeaux wines. The Y-axis shows the thousands of hectolitres dispatched.

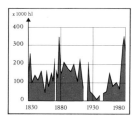

WEST GERMANY

UNITED STATES

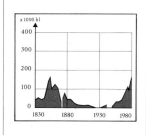

Chartrons. The vineyards could be exceedingly profitable, in a good year in the 1740s the owner of Château Margaux could sell her wine for four times the cost of producing it. Her wine, and that of an increasing number of other châteaux, was famous, but it was not their responsibility. (Nor was it entirely their produce. As late as the 1940s the Chartrons would reinforce even the finest clarets with at least 15 percent of stronger wines, usually from the Rhône.)

No sooner had the estates been assembled than most of them were confiscated at the time of the Revolution, which tipped the balance of power in favour of the Chartrons, ironically mostly citizens of an enemy power. It was not until the third quarter of the 19th century that the owners tried again. This time they were reinforced by outsiders, Parisian bankers with deeper pockets than the parliamentarians. The first sign of potential independence was the famous Classification of 1855, with its emphasis on the individual châteaux. In the following two decades came the first, sporadic attempt to bottle wines at the château, a development perceived then as now as the crucial step between the production of an agricultural raw material and that of a finished product ready to be sold to the consumer.

But this attempt was doomed to failure. The world slump of the 1870s depressed the wine market: the mildew of the early 1880s destroyed Bordeaux's reputation for quality; the phylloxera hampered the flow of wine. The Chartrons resumed control of a market already invaded by far more muscular and well-established brands of champagne and Scotch whisky. For virtually every château in the Gironde independence remained a dream for nearly a hundred more years. Virtually all the wines were destined to be sold *en primeur*, as soon as they were fermented, to the *négociants*, whose brand name was more powerful than the name of all but a handful of châteaux.

Outside the Médoc, the Graves and Sauternes the owners of the Gironde's vineyards were in an even worse plight. Their owners may have bought pages in

Bordeaux's "bible", Cocks and Féret, to emphasize the individuality of their wines, their world-wide fame, their unusual qualities. But these entries were dreams and aspirations, they rarely reflected reality. But the dream of independence never died: the very bulk of successive editions of Cocks and Féret between 1840 and 1949 emphasized the potential for economic independence.

FAMILY HISTORIES

It was Baron Philippe de Rothschild, the model for the modern château owner, who started the campaign to make the château, rather than the merchant's cellars, the economic centre of the universe, a campaign he started for reasons of pride rather than economic necessity. In 1924, backed by Philippe Moreau, a wine broker and head of a syndicate which had bought control of Château Margaux, he succeeded in imposing château-bottling on the first-growths, including Château d'Yquem. In his autobiography he has recorded the shrewd and far-seeing objections made by his "cousin" Baron Edouard, head of the other French branch of the family which owned Château Lafite (characteristically Baron Philippe dismissed them as merely one skirmish in his lengthy war with his "cousins").

Baron Edouard recognized that Baron Philippe's ideas implied more thoroughgoing a revolution than virtually anyone but a Rothschild could afford to contemplate in the 1920s – or indeed for 40 years to come. "Have you asked yourself" said Baron Edouard, "how many growers will be able to afford the necessary outlay? Have you worked out how much this wonderful idea of yours would cost . . . taking an average figure, say three harvests each of 400 casks, allowing three by four metres for each cask, that's going to mean quite a large area . . . plus space for storing approximately 100,000 bottles, add the cost of installing bottling equipment at each château . . . reckon on a million francs, at least. And what for? Simply to make a break with tradition and upset our old friends, the wine merchants".

For Baron Philippe château-bottling was a matter of pride, of ensuring that

Until the 1920s and 1930s, "étampes à feu" were commonly used to mark the wooden crates intended for transporting fine wines.

everyone appreciated the quality of the wine he was making. To Baron Edouard, and indeed to anyone concerned with economics, it implied a transformation in the role of a château: no longer merely a farm fermenting the grapes into wine, it became a "winery", in the Californian or Australian sense of the term. Since virtually all the New World wine makers buy in at least some of their grapes, the châteaux of the Gironde as they have emerged over the past quarter of a century are unique. They are integrated wineries, maturing and bottling only wines made from grapes grown on their own estates.

Nevertheless in the short-term Baron Edouard's figures proved conclusive. Confronted by the costs – and by the delays in payments inevitable if the wine remained at the château for the time (then nearly three years) it passed in cask before it was bottled – even the first-growths could not withstand the depression, and Margaux, for one, abandoned château-bottling, albeit not completely, for 20 years until some obviously fake bottles of the 1950 vintage surfaced in Belgium.

FROM CRISIS TO CRISIS

With château-bottling came the use of different names to market a château's second (or even third) wines. The idea was logical enough. The owner, taking responsibility for all the wine he produced, was inevitably going to find that some of it (in some years, like 1987, up to half of the total) was not worthy of the château. Hence the proliferation of second wines. This was not a novelty. Margaux had started to market its Pavillon Rouge in 1912, while Carruades de Lafite was produced throughout the 1920s. But the idea of second wines, like that of universal, compulsory, château-bottling, was swept away by the slump of the 1930s. Châteaux needed to sell every drop they could produce.

But in the depths of the slump Baron Philippe went further. He used his name, and that of the château, to sell wines not made from the estate's own grapes. He was following a precedent set by the great English wine merchants, the Gilbeys, who had bought

Château Loudenne in 1875, and had built a major winery there. They ruthlessly exploited the estate's name to promote their more ordinary wines, but it was Baron Philippe (with the help of his manager M. Marjarie) who dreamt up the idea of Mouton-Cadet, Bordeaux's first, and by far its most successful, brand name and the only one based on the name of an individual château. Here again he was challenging the power of the *négociants*, who had always relied on their names to sell lesser clarets. In the long run Mouton-Cadet helped run-of-the-mill châteaux by demonstrating that the Chartrons did not have the monopoly of selling claret for everyday drinking.

But recovery from the slump of the 1930s did not start until the 1960s. As Jean Miailhe, president of the Syndicat de Crus Bourgeois since 1962, told Jean-Louis Delpal: "although tens of hectares were pulled up after the First World War, 444 estates were recorded in 1932. Thirty years later, only 110 remained, several of which had been virtually abandoned."

The severity of the slump provided an opportunity for outsiders to buy into the Gironde. The first was the Russian-American Alexis Lichine. In the early 1950s he brought together a group of rich Americans to buy two châteaux, Lascombes and Prieuré (later renamed Prieuré-Lichine). He bought numerous additional parcels of land, many of which had not been traditionally associated with the two châteaux.

He was followed by French colonists returning from Algeria after its independence, the so-called *pieds noirs*. As Bernard Broustet wrote in *L'Amateur de Bordeaux*: "These repatriates arrived and found that the slump had made the prices of old estates accessible to them. Some of them had been able to save something of their Algerian inheritance; others arrived with little or nothing. Some knew how to make wine, others were ignorant. But all of them put their hearts into their work, and had the spirit of enterprise and a tremendous desire for revenge. Before doing up the beautiful, crumbling residences that they had settled in, they began tackling the vines. They

Plans of the town of Libourne where various wine merchants are established.
TOP:
Plan of the town at the beginning of the 18th century. (Archives of the département of the Gironde).
BELOW:
Detail from a 19th century plan showing various chais built on either side of the Dordogne. (Archives of the département of the Gironde).

started to pull up, to drain, to manure the soil, to replant. After the initial scepticism they had suffered from local people, who had been at times mocking, at other times hostile, they finally succeeded in becoming integrated at the same time as their wines made a name for themselves on the market." The most famous *rapatrié* was Nicholas Tari, who bought the virtually abandoned Château Giscours. But economically more important were the dozens of lesser-known buyers in the Entre-deux-Mers and the Premières Côtes de Bordeaux, indeed wherever properties were readily available.

Noticeably this did not include the region of Libourne. In Pomerol and in St-Emilion, the economic patterns were different from those prevailing in the Médoc. The properties were smaller, they were locally owned and revained in the hands of individual families for as long as comparable properties in rural France as a whole. The owners had achieved a relatively amicable working relationship with the *négociants* who sold their wine. Unlike the Chartrons, they were French, mostly from the Correze, up-river from Libourne. They were not selling to an unimaginably distant aristocratic clientele. They were hard-headed salesmen, peddling their samples door-to-door in Belgium and northern France. They were, and were perceived to be, partners of the growers, not imperialist exploiters. So when the owners started to bottle their wines they still continued to sell in the same way through the same outlets.

PROGRESS, A FACTOR OF INDEPENDENCE

This gentle evolution was inconceivable in the Médoc. It was only the crisis of the early 1970s which revealed that the Chartrons simply did not have enough capital to buy and mature the wines as they had for 200 years, it also discouraged the international groups who had bought into Bordeaux from taking over the role. The châteaux owners were ready for the challenge.

In the 25 years after 1945 the châteaux had equipped themselves with the two weapons required to achieve their independence: an improved understanding of the technical processes involved, and the capital required to apply their knowledge to their wines.

As Professeur Ribéreau-Gayon makes clear (see page 57) it was only after 1945 that the proprietors understood what they were doing. Knowledge, as so often, was a liberating force. In the words of André Cazes, Mayor of Pauillac, whose family own Château Lynch-Bages: "it was oenology, knowing what we were doing, which enabled us to transform our role, from merely providing the raw material to producing a finished product".

In this process the most important role was played by Professor Ribéreau-Gayon's colleague, Professor Emile Peynaud. He provided – and still provides for a handful of distinguished châteaux – an incomparable depth of scientific knowledge combined with a bluff practical manner which gives him an uncanny ability to work with *maîtres de chai* and *régisseurs* who would be suspicious of a more overtly "scientific" personage.

Thus armed, during the 1960s more and more of them bought bottling lines, and increased the capacity of their cellars. The new vines on the properties bought so cheaply in the 1950s and 1960s were bearing fruit. The owners included an increasing proportion of outsiders as well as a a new generation of well-educated locals who could not, by any stretch of the imagination, have been described as peasants. Even newcomers, like André Menztelopoulos, the Greek-born financier who bought Château Margaux at the end of 1976, and who assuredly had the money required to sell its wine directly, stayed with the old system.

The crisis had another important, relatively unnoticed side-effect. For the first time in history Bordeaux saw the sort of direct selling network between château and final French buyer which had long been an important feature of commercial life in Champagne and Burgundy and indeed in Pomerol. But this was a novelty in the Médoc, if only because the French themselves had bought so little of the wine. Yet it was the French market which absorbed, cheaply, rapidly – and direct from the

Wooden cases for shipping wines stamped with the image of their château of origin.

château – the unwanted vintages of the early 1970s, and shows every sign of doing the same for those other orphans of the international marketplace, 1980 and 1984.

NEW BALANCES OF POWER

Yet the owners recognised the frontiers of their economic power. Most of the wine continued to be marketed through the historic chain of intermediaries. It was offered by the owners through brokers who duly took their historic two percent commission. But they were not selling to merchants who would hold the stock but to firms which, in most cases were themselves little more than brokers. The stock was held either by the château or by the final, individual buyer. A few of the more sophisticated owners – like Jean-Michel Cazes of Lynch-Bages and Bruno Prats of Cos d'Estournel – financed their own *négociant* firms, but these were not designed primarily to sell their estates' wines, which continued to be sold through the Bordeaux market.

The shift in the balance of power, the necessity for owners to recognize the realities of the market-place, was clearly demonstrated in the 1980s. The owners saw how the superb 1982 and 1983 vintages they had sold relatively cheaply had subsequently vastly increased in price. So they actually raised the price of the mediocre 1984 vintage. They then had to bear directly the storm of opprobrium unleashed by angry Anglo-Saxon buyers. When the next mediocre vintage arrived in 1987 they had learnt their lesson, and prices dropped by at least a quarter. In a few short years they had learned that the market is just as demanding as the Chartrons had been But at least the responsibility was coined with an increasing profitability.

Indeed the ironic ending to the whole story is that the increased wealth brought by independence combined with rising production and rising prices has itself brought a major problem. Most of the estates, even the biggest and most famous, are still in family hands. Inevitably ownership becomes dispersed, increasingly distant relatives want income rather than the joy of

CHÂTEAU·LASCOMBES
À·MARGAUX

owning a share in a famous vineyard, and as the generations succeed each other taxes have to be paid. A few families – like the Moueix and the Thienponts – have been rich, and dedicated enough to be able to expand their holdings and to colonize neglected areas (the Moueix in Fronsac, the Thienponts in the Côte des Francs).

But others need to sell and they are lucky that French institutional buyers have begun to take an active interest in the Médoc, providing a solid foundation to the price of châteaux, even in times of relative depression like the late 1980s. In some cases the sellers had themselves bought estates cheaply only a generation earlier. Perhaps the most significant transaction of all involved the Forners. They are a Spanish family, driven out of Spain by General Franco, who had settled in Provence. At the end of the 1950s they found that their vineyards in the south of France were worth more than a comparable acreage in the Médoc. So they bought two châteaux, Camensac, a classed growth, and its neighbour Château Larose-Trintaudon, at 174 hectares (430 acres) the largest single property in the Médoc. Whereas previous generations of outside buyers had been bankers, anxious for prestige, the Forners were motivated by straight-forward economic motives: to buy cheap, to build up a property and then to sell it (though even they sold only Larose-Trintaudon). In other words they had set a pattern of pure capitalism: constructive, not speculative, to be sure, but, for the first time in the history of the Gironde they had demonstrated that a château is primarily an economic, not a social unit.

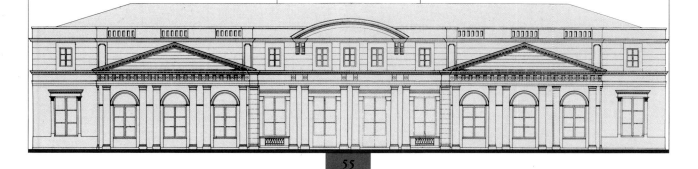

LE VIGNOBLE DE BORDEAUX

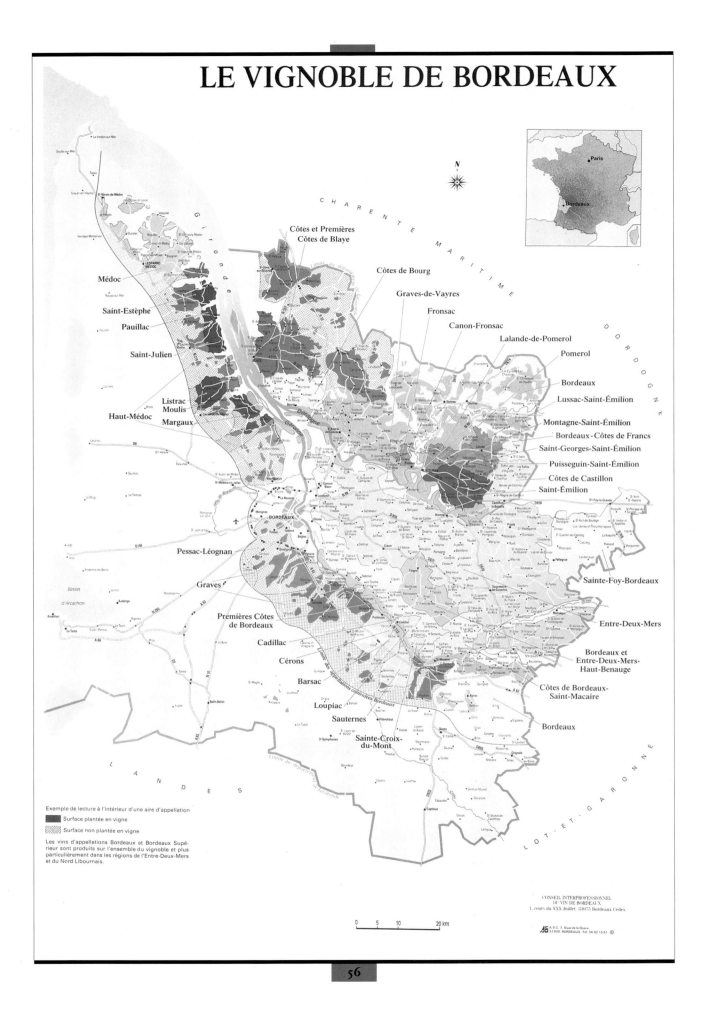

Côtes et Premières
Côtes de Blaye

Côtes de Bourg

Graves-de-Vayres

Fronsac

Canon-Fronsac

Lalande-de-Pomerol

Pomerol

Bordeaux

Lussac-Saint-Émilion

Montagne-Saint-Émilion

Bordeaux-Côtes de Francs

Saint-Georges-Saint-Émilion

Puisseguin-Saint-Émilion

Côtes de Castillon

Saint-Émilion

Médoc

Saint-Estèphe

Pauillac

Saint-Julien

Listrac
Moulis

Haut-Médoc

Margaux

Pessac-Léognan

Graves

Premières Côtes
de Bordeaux

Cadillac

Cérons

Barsac

Loupiac

Sauternes

Sainte-Croix-
du-Mont

Sainte-Foy-Bordeaux

Entre-Deux-Mers

Bordeaux et
Entre-Deux-Mers-
Haut-Benauge

Côtes de Bordeaux-
Saint-Macaire

Bordeaux

Exemple de lecture à l'intérieur d'une aire d'appellation

Surface plantée en vigne

Surface non plantée en vigne

Les vins d'appellations Bordeaux et Bordeaux Supé-
rieur sont produits sur l'ensemble du vignoble et plus
particulièrement dans les régions de l'Entre-Deux-Mers
et du Nord Libournais.

CONSEIL INTERPROFESSIONNEL
DU VIN DE BORDEAUX
1, cours du XXX Juillet 33075 Bordeaux Cedex

A.S.C. 7, Quai de la Grave
33000 BORDEAUX. Tél. 56 92 15 81

0   5   10   20 km

OENOLOGY:
A NEW SCIENCE AT THE CHATEAU

PASCAL RIBEREAU-GAYON

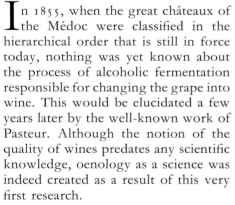

In 1855, when the great châteaux of the Médoc were classified in the hierarchical order that is still in force today, nothing was yet known about the process of alcoholic fermentation responsible for changing the grape into wine. This would be elucidated a few years later by the well-known work of Pasteur. Although the notion of the quality of wines predates any scientific knowledge, oenology as a science was indeed created as a result of this very first research.

History tells us that the Bordeaux vineyard is very old and that it has often been faced with economic difficulties which have demanded a continual refinement of the conditions of production. For a very long time, the dynamism of the leading figures in the wine trade of the Bordeaux region has shown their strong similarity with contemporary leaders of industry.

Ever since the 18th century, the improvement of wine-making methods has been one of the main necessities. This was justified by the desire to attain greater renown and was made possible by the lucrative prices asked for quality wines. A whole host of new ideas started to appear: the notion of the privileged *terroir*; the selection of varieties of vine; the principles of managing a vineyard; the limiting of yields; the notion of a *premier vin* and a *second vin* within the same concern; *élevage* in wooden barrels and improvement by ageing. Particularly remarkable was the widespread adoption of the use of the *allumette hollandaise*. The latter, when burned, gave off sulphur dioxide whose antiseptic properties prevented the bacterial adulteration of the wine, and yet, the very existence of bacteria was unknown in the 18th century. Similarly, the process of fining by using egg white was elucidated only fairly recently, whereas its effectiveness as a clarifying and stabilizing agent has long been recognized by wine makers.

There was much innovation during this period which was solely the result of experimentation, but was nevertheless very modern in its principles. It was due to these continuous efforts, rather than the alleged and rather confused tradition, that the wines of Bordeaux acquired their reputation. They have been able to retain this good reputation because technical precision has always been considered an essential element in maintaining the quality of the product, on a par with natural factors connected to the notion of the *terroir*.

DISEASES TO BE FOUGHT

The development of the biological and chemical sciences in the middle of the 19th century was well timed. The producers of quality wines were ready to take advantage of this new knowledge which also enabled the researchers and scientists at the University of Bordeaux to introduce a new scientific precision to technological progress.

In the same period, the appearance of some formidable diseases of the vine led to the first intervention by the University. First there was oidium, a powdery mildew, that destroyed a large part of the harvest in 1853, but an answer was quickly found by treating the vines with sulphur. The phylloxera crisis was much more serious as this insect attacks the roots of the vine. For the first time, the services of scientific experts were called upon; in its archives in Paris, the Académie des Sciences still has a record of the considerable research it undertook in order to find an answer to the problem. After treatment with carbon disulphide, the flooding of the vines in the winter did not prove effective; and required the vineyard to be transferred to low, damp areas which were less favourable for producing

good quality wine. The real solution, which is still used today, was found in grafting local vine varieties onto vinestocks of American origin which were resistant to the phylloxera.

The respite was short-lived because of the appearance of another parasite, mildew. The University of Bordeaux immediately got involved in the search for a treatment which was found in 1885 in a mixture of copper sulphate and lime, known as "Bordeaux mixture" and which is still sold for the treatment of various cultivated plants. The professor of botany, A. Millardet, was the mainspring of this operation in collaboration with his colleague U. Gayon, the professor of chemistry, and the *régisseur* of a Médoc *grand cru*, E. David. It was a good example of concerted action and successful collaboration between the research and business communities. The economic consequences of this discovery were considerable, as previously entire harvests had been destroyed by mildew.

FROM GOOD GRAPES TO FINE WINE

The vital role of oenology in ensuring the quality of wine is not immediately obvious. Wine making dates back to ancient times and is, on the face of it at least, a simple process. The crushing of the grapes starts the process of fermentation which converts the sugar into alcohol. But examined in detail, it is all much more complicated.

Obviously, no one denies that to make fine wine one must first have good grapes. It is indeed in the nature of favoured *terroirs* to regularly achieve a perfect ripening of the classic grape varieties. But the quality of the grape is only a potential quality; it will only be present in the bottle if the various stages of the conversion of grapes to wine are carried out under perfect conditions. The starting point is the grape juice, which comes from the living cells of the grape; it therefore has an extremely varied composition like that of all living organisms: glucids, protids, lipids, as well as vitamins, enzymes, minerals and trace elements. The grape juice is then converted by various micro-organisms such as yeasts and bacteria; these exist naturally on the grape and may be clearly seen when examined through an electron microscope. The juice is acted upon by these micro-organisms as soon as the grape is crushed. The number of possible biological and chemical changes is clearly very large; some are useful and should be encouraged, while others are harmful and are to be avoided. It should also be said that certain changes are only beneficial if they take place in well-defined circumstances.

The following example is particularly important. For a long time it was held that wine resulted entirely from the conversion of the sugar into alcohol by a process of alcoholic fermentation, caused by the yeast. Today, in the case of red wines at least, the role of a second fermentation is recognized. This is known as malolactic fermentation and consists in the conversion of the grape's malic acid into lactic acid by the action of certain bacteria, causing the wine to be softened and stabilized. But depending on the conditions in which they are active, these same bacteria may either cause the useful malolactic fermentation or the formation of acetic acid which is a serious problem. Therefore care must be taken to ensure that the bacteria are only active when they are beneficial to the wine.

This is where the role of the oenologist becomes apparent; he must know the composition of the grape and the wine, the nature and characteristics of the micro-organisms likely to develop, as well as the various chemical and biological changes which can take place in the grape and the wine. This skill is founded on a knowledge of the basic scientific disciplines; this used to be mainly chemistry but nowadays molecular biochemistry and genetic engineering are playing an increasingly important part. Oenology must continuously keep up with the progress achieved in these fields. It is important to understand the most favourable conditions for the production and preservation of the various kinds of wine and to put them into effect. In short the oenologist must guide and control natural phenomena so as to avoid damaging mistakes.

It is only under these circumstances that the undeniable importance of the individual characteristics of soils, vineyards and vintages will be highlighted and it is important that they should not be obscured by faults caused by accidents during the fermentation process.

COLLABORATION BETWEEN SCIENTISTS AND WINE PRODUCERS

The intervention of the University in the wine production of the Bordeaux region thus became prominent at the end of the 19th century. It was the result of a two-way process: on the one hand, wine producers were very attentive to the possibility of finding solutions for the numerous technical problems they continually faced; on the other hand, some well-known studies had shown that grapes, fermentation and wine making were a subject worthy of scientific research.

In 1880, Ulysse Gayon established oenology as a subject at the Bordeaux Faculty of Science. A former pupil of the Ecole Normale Supérieure, he had prepared for his doctorate thesis in Pasteur's laboratory. Appointed professor of chemistry at the Bordeaux Faculty, he quite naturally continued Pasteur's work in the field of wine and went on to found the Station Agronomique et Oenologique. He considerably refined the conditions for the vinification and preservation of wine as well as helping to perfect "Bordeaux mixture" to treat vine mildew.

After the Second World War, oenological research in Bordeaux entered a new boom era when Jean Ribéreau-Gayon became the head in 1949 of the Station Agronomique et Oenologique founded by his grandfather. He was the first professor in a French university to hold an oenological post. Together with his collaborator Emile Peynaud he is recognized as the pioneer of modern oenology and helped introduce into the study of wine numerous contemporary scientific concepts, such as pH, oxidation-reduction and colloids etc.

Since this time oenological research has developed spectacularly in Bordeaux. The improvement in the quality of the great red wines of the region, which was universally acknowledged after 1960, owes a great deal to this effort. In the first place, the microbiology of wine and the perfection of alcoholic fermentation made considerable progress. It was thus possible to avoid the main bacterial problems that were so damaging to the wine. In addition, the idea of malolactic fermentation – which is indispensible for the quality of red wines – was introduced, not only in Bordeaux, but also in vineyards throughout the wine world. Initially it was difficult to get this new concept accepted because it went against the old theory that regarded a slightly higher level of acidity as an indication of outstanding wine.

Finally, during this same period, oenological research made it possible to eliminate hybrid vine varieties from the large *appellations* and to replace them with traditional varieties that were indispensible for quality. These hybrid varieties of vine had been created between the wars, during the time of economic crisis, in the hope of reconciling excellence with resistance to disease. The result was a failure but the decline in quality was not appreciated at the time, because the wine produced was used for blending. This constituted serious fraud but it was not easy to prove. The virtue of oenological research was that it found that the red colouring in these hybrid wines had a specific molecular structure which could be identified by a scientific method of analysis using chromatography. The consequences for the quality of red wines as a result of this discovery were significant.

Such progress in wine-making techniques, based on scientific knowledge, have resulted in great changes, even in

the economic and commercial areas. Firstly, the oenological laboratory has become an indispensible part of all wine-producing concerns. Each year, the new vintage is vinified in tens of thousands of *cuves* which are regularly checked by chemical testing. Automatic testing, derived from medical analysis, has become important in order to carry out this considerable and totally indispensible work. Secondly, in view of the homogeneous quality, there is no longer any need to blend wines of different origins. Thirdly, bottling at the source of production, with the consequent guarantee of quality, has also become widespread. Finally commercial practices in the wine trade, in particular the role of the *négociant-éléveur*, have been modified.

While this dynamic oenological research was being undertaken in Bordeaux, the professional organizations and the large concerns remained very enthusiastic about the idea of technical progress, a factor which is clearly as indispensible for good quality as the notion of privileged *terroirs*. They both ensured that the results of the research were circulated and they even supported it by financing specialized projects. The Conseil Interprofessionel des Vins de Bordeaux (CIVB) is the main body for oenological research. The eight most prestigious châteaux names among the red wines (Châteaux Ausone, Cheval-Blanc, Haut-Brion, Lafite, Latour, Margaux, Mouton Rothschild and Pétrus) have joined forces with the University, to form a research convention for the study of conditions for the ageing of red wine in oak barrels.

In Bordeaux, the refinement of the techniques of vinification, especially for red wine, has been perfected to an extremely high level and is the envy of the world's other wine-producing regions. This is certainly one of the reasons for the vineyard's prosperity at the end of the 20th century. Today the region is recognized as an undisputed leader because of the quality of its red wines and recent progress in the last few years should allow the dry white wines to re-establish the fame they have to some extent lost. But it is not enough to advance the frontiers of science only in the laboratory, progress must also be put into practice in the *chais*. Oenologists have always been mindful of this transfer of technology and the application of research and its popularization form integral parts of their role. The research establishments are keen to take responsibility for putting new vinification techniques into practice. In the last few years, they have also played an essential role in the revival of the dry white wines of the Gironde. Research into the field of packaging has also been useful to producers.

Therefore, in Bordeaux, oenology constitutes a fully-fledged scientific and university discipline. Although it has been carried out since ancient times, the production of wine involves the interaction of very complex biological and chemical factors – on the one hand, their optimization is necessary for the quality of the product, and on the other, their study is of scientific interest. It is thus easy to see why a dialogue has been established between wine professionals and researchers. This collaboration is all the more important for the most prestigious Bordeaux wines because the optimum use of natural factors demands a high degree of technical precision.

19th-century engraved crystal glasses showing the emblematic buildings of the historical centre of Bordeaux: the Cours de Tourny and the Place de la Bourse with its Fontaine des Trois Grâces.

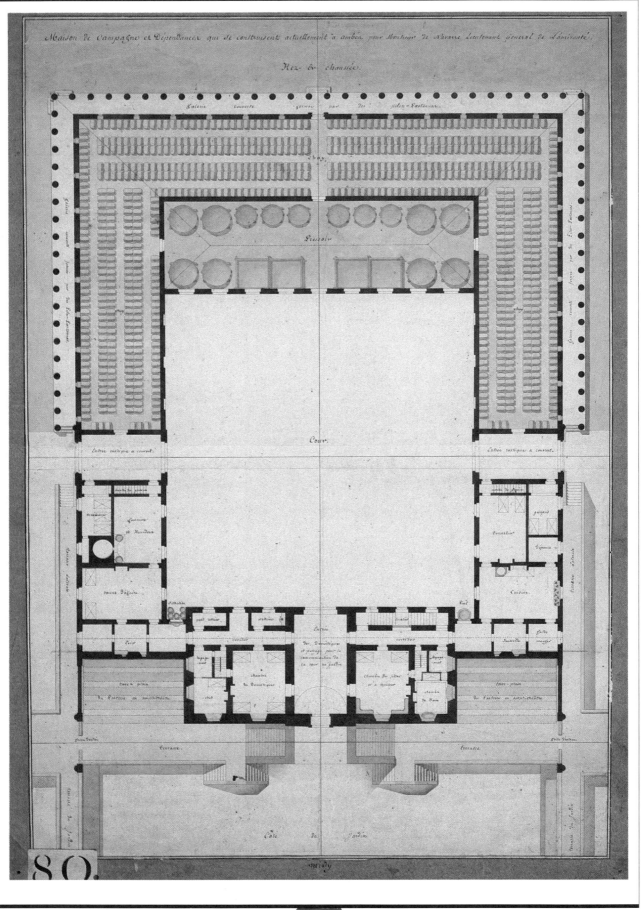

Maison de Campagne et Dépendances qui se construisent actuellement à Ambès pour Monseigneur de Navarre Lieutenant Général de l'Amirauté.

Rez-de-chaussée.

A HISTORY OF WINE ARCHITECTURE

ROBERT COUSTET

N o other region in France has as many châteaux as there are in the Gironde. There are thousands of them and their number is constantly increasing. However, the visitor will not find here the monumental constructions that have added to the reputation of the Paris region, or the Loire or even the neighbouring Périgord. The châteaux of Bordeaux are often so modest that it might almost be thought that the term has been misappropriated and in fact only exists on the bottle labels. The château phenomenon therefore requires some clarification.

CHATEAUX IN THEIR THOUSANDS

In the first place, it is common knowledge that the word "château" is used to describe a wine-growing estate and, in this specifically local sense, it does not necessarily have a precise architectural implication. The famous Château Pétrus presents a typical example. Architecturally speaking, it is nothing more than a charming country house, but, considering it from the point of view of the quality of its wine, no one would dream of disputing its right to use the title of "château".

In the second place, the people of the Bordeaux region have – either through their Gascon boastfulness or through natural generosity – increased the number of what could be called "courtesy titles". It is generally believed that only a person of noble birth with an outstanding social position and a large fortune can live in a château. This is how both the peasants and the *Bottin mondain* (French equivalent of *Who's Who*) described the residence of Madame Arman de Caillavet who owned an estate at Capian-Gironde, the inspiration of the famous writer, Anatole France.

History puts a new light on the development of the Bordeaux château. As with other regions of France, the Bordeaux area has a rich heritage of castle-like buildings: fortified châteaux from the Middle Ages, country residences, manors and country seats from the classical period. These buildings originally had no direct connection with wine growing, but with the development of viticulture, they now dominate the vineyards to which they bring added prestige. Olivier and La Brède in the Graves, Lamarque and Agassac in the Médoc, Camarsac and Cursan in the

Entre-Deux-Mers and Grand-Puch near Libourne have all long since given up their military role and become wine châteaux. The same thing has happened to the buildings of the classical period which, with their solemn style and architectural pomp, belong to the tradition of the nobility and served to reflect the social rise of the parliamentarians of Bordeaux and Libourne. The splendour of the 16th-century Vayres, the layout of its courtyards and its façade overlooking the Dordogne are above all designed to illustrate the power of the Gourgues family. The scale of Laroque went far beyond the needs of a late 17th-century agricultural concern, but satisfied the pride of the Lescure family. The plans of the architect Victor Louis for Château du Bouilh (1786) correspond to the lifestyle of the Comte de la Tour du Pin, a regular visitor to Versailles.

In short, a large number of Bordeaux châteaux are no different from those found in other parts of France. They only became *crus* very gradually, as the vine established itself as the main resource of the region.[1]

THE BIRTH OF THE WINE CHATEAU

The most characteristic feature of the

architecture of the châteaux of the Bordeaux region is the fact that the whole complex of buildings is connected to the vine both in origin and in function. These authentic wine-producing châteaux share particular characteristics which differentiate them from other types of châteaux.

We are fortunate to know the origin of this phenomenon. In the mid 16th century, Jean de Pontac, the head of a powerful family in the Bordeaux parliament, managed, by sheer perseverance, to create an estate in the *graves* of Haut-Brion, at the gates of the town. He planted it with vines, set about improving the taste of his wine and looked for trade outlets in England. The Bordeaux vineyard, in the modern sense of the term, had come into being. The new lord considered it essential to build a manorhouse as an outward sign of his ownership of the land. He assigned the master builder Jean Cheminade to the task of constructing a house from beautiful stone, without any carved ornaments, but with the characteristic features of the noble houses of the period: a high slate roof and corner turrets reminiscent of the military privileges of the feudal lords of long ago. In the 17th century, a second wing was added at right angles, retaining the

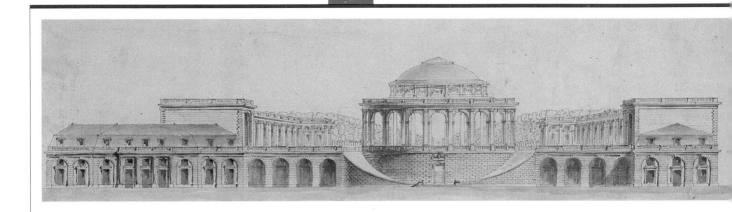

TOP:
Two variants developed in 1786 by Victor Louis for the overall design of Château du Bouilh, of which only the right wing of the right-hand drawing was built. (Municipal archives of Bordeaux).

MIDDLE:
"Bacchic celebration of the unlikely completion of Château du Bouilh", a triptych by the French painter Michel Bez.

commissioned in 1988
for the Châteaux Bordeaux
exhibition. (Charcoal and red
chalk mounted on canvas,
200x300 cm. Galerie Alain
Blondel, Paris).
BOTTOM:
Side façade of the service
buildings built by Victor Louis
before the French Revolution
and, in the middle of the
structure, the chapel that was
added later.

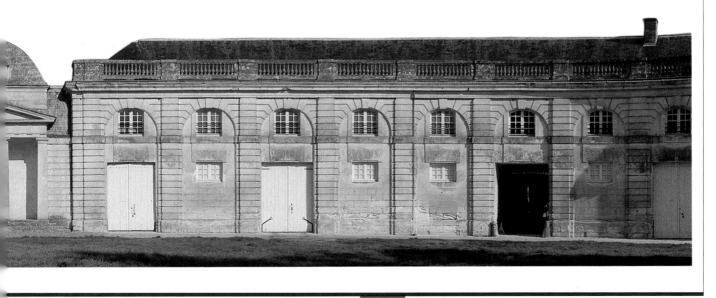

character of the original building.[2] We know nothing about the outbuildings and agricultural structures that must have adjoined this château. But Jean de Pontac had created the first *grand cru* of the Bordeaux region and the first recorded wine château. The urban landowner by building this residence had given great emphasis to the specific nature of a piece of land whose qualities were shown off to advantage. Jean de Pontac's achievement is so famous because it led to the outstanding success that is Haut-Brion. But it was not an isolated achievement. In 1545, Arnaud de Lestonnac, who also belonged to the parliamentary nobility, had a residence built on the d'Espagne or du Parc estate, which he had bought at Mérignac, near Bordeaux. This manor no longer exists, but we can form an idea of what it was like through the contract made with the master mason Jean Villetard d'Amboise. It provided for a large rectangular building on two levels connected by a staircase in a tower. It had a kitchen and a hall on the ground floor and two rooms upstairs. In upper and lower rooms, there was a fireplace of monumental design. But, most important of all, there was to be a *cave* with a capacity for five barrels of wine. Finally, next to this residential building, another one was situated. This was nearly 60 metres long and 13 metres wide (210 feet by 45 feet) and was intended to be used as a *chai* and cattle shed. This document confirms that the wine château appeared in the Bordeaux region[3] in the middle of the 16th century and it supplements the Haut-Brion example by allowing us to see its original characteristics. From its beginnings, the architectural complex that we call a "château" has performed a dual role: it is not only a symbol of ownership but it is also essential for the production of wine. Thus, it must be aristocratic in its residential role while remaining functional in its agricultural role.

A MODEST SIZE

The châteaux of Bordeaux have never needed to be enormous buildings. In any case, they were only partly inhabited. In the Médoc, the local owners

ABOVE:
Ornamental motif designed in about 1810.

(and later on, the Parisian or foreign owners) did not reside in their châteaux. They only stayed there once a year when their presence was needed during the harvest. At these times, the family would arrive with its servants – unless it was relying on the services of the estate's workers – and would stay for a few weeks. The châteaux near the town had an important leisure function and were used as second homes in the summer. Nowadays, luxury and comfort are no longer judged according to the number of living rooms and these châteaux are sufficiently large for those who have chosen to live in them permanently. In the general economy of a well-managed estate, the upkeep of the family mansion should not represent too great an expense.

The architects of the period were constrained by this economizing as schemes were only carried out if they remained within the bounds of what was considered reasonable. There are numerous examples of this prudence. In 1788, Louis Combes, a Bordeaux architect, was assigned the task of rebuilding Château Olivier in a neo-classical style. He produced some grandiose designs. The work was halted by the French Revolution, but there is no proof that his design would have been carried through to completion as were the plans for Margaux, which is very much the exception. In 1832, the Marquis de Lur Saluces asked Alexandre Poitevin, an architect to the legitimist nobility, to redesign Yquem. The latter thought of altering the old building by increasing the number of wings with high slate roofs to create a symmetrical effect. The result would have been impressive, but in the end it was not built. At the time of the July Monarchy, Gabriel Joseph Durand enjoyed the patronage of the upper middle classes of the Bordeaux region. They were very concerned about careful management and only had restoration, modernization and extension work done when it was absolutely essential. In general, Durand was only required to carry out minor improvements and his customers would always favour the cheapest estimate. They were anxious to keep spending down and not to incur expenses that could

*Château St-Georges built in
the 18th century near
St-Emilion.*
BELOW:
*Château La Louvière built in
the 18th century at Léognan,
Graves.*

OPPOSITE:
Top, *Château Laroque built in
the 18th century at St-
Christophe-des-Bardes.*
Bottom, *Château Figeac built
in the 18th century at
St-Emilion.*

compromise their wealth.[4] In 1859, the co-owners of Latour decided to replace the *pied-à-terre*, which "looked no more than a simple peasants' home to passers-by", with a building worthy of a *premier grand cru classé*. However, they rejected the grandiose scheme proposed to them by Duphot and instructed him to restrict himself to a small château that was both elegant and comfortable.[5] At Mouton, the Baron de Rothschild contented himself with a charming castle, but it is so small that it is now insufficient for modern requirements and former outbuildings have had to be converted for entertaining.

AN ARCHITECTURAL COMPLEX

In fact, the actual residence is only the nobler part of a much larger whole. From the 17th century until the 19th century, numerous texts give a definition of what was then more accurately (because the word did not allow for any confusion) called a "*bourdieu*". In 1810, a notarial deed described Ricaud's estate at Loupiac as "composed of a family mansion in the form of a small château, with a cellar, a stable, various buildings and a fishpond with a wide ditch beside".[6] This document makes a clear distinction between function and appearance. The expression "*maison de maître*" expresses the ownership of the land and is commonly found in contracts. *Petit château* merely gives an indication of the appearance of a building that is well adapted to its role and which is enhanced by its architectural quality and its additional decorative features (garden, ponds, etc.).

The outbuildings are equally important. They may be divided into two categories: those intended for use by humans and cattle and those that are directly connected with the vineyard. The first category is to be found throughout the rural world: cottages for the estate's employees and peasants, stables for the horses and oxen, barns and workshops for the equipment, sheds, outhouses, etc. The second group forms the complex called the *chais*, used either in the narrow sense of a place where barrels of wine are stored

or in the wider sense of all the buildings that are concerned with the manufacture of the wine, i.e. the presses, fermentation rooms, etc. All above ground, these make up the main body of the buildings.

In some cases, there may be no residence at all – as in *crus* that are of peasant origin and whose reputation is only fairly recent – but the agricultural buildings are indispensable. Without them, there would be no vineyard and no château. The best known example is Cos-d'Estournel, which so surprised Stendhal on route to St-Estèphe in 1838. The writer was enchanted by the strangeness of the imaginative architecture: "It is not Greek, nor Gothic, it is very amusing in what one could call the Chinese style".[7] But the strangest thing is that all this abundance of pinnacles, turrets, battlements and sculptures is only intended for cattle sheds and *chais*. Destournel neglected his own house, but considered that nothing would be too good for his oxen and his wine. More recently, Baron Edmond de Rothschild has done much the same thing, only in a more eccentric fashion: Château Clarke is no more than a luxurious country house, but the monumental appearance of the immense *chais* has been the focus of much attention.

A study of the architecture of wine production in the Bordeaux region should thus take into account all the buildings on an estate since they all have a specific function. The diversity of their roles and their complementary activities made necessary a variety of buildings which together form an indissoluble whole.

MAKING A LANDSCAPE

The expression "*maison de maître*" is the best way of describing the exact nature of a residence that must be kept within reasonable limits but which is nonetheless necessary – not so much for the proprietor's comfort but as a means of giving an identity to his property. However discreet it may be, the architecture of the château must clearly distinguish itself from the surrounding countryside by its "construction of a landscape" (A. Chastel).

This situation has been admirably

illustrated by Gustave de Galard, the most representative of the romantic painters of the Bordeaux region. In 1835, he published a collection of lithographs entitled *Album vignicole* with views of the châteaux that "produce the wine from the best *crus* of the Médoc and other parts of the *département* of the Gironde".[8] The collection might be found surprising as it does not concentrate on the more imposing buildings and only pays a relative degree of attention to the architectural character of the residences. But, on the other hand, he incorporates them in a rural setting which seems to be arranged in such a way as to enhance them like follies in a landscaped garden. The figures – bourgeois strollers or wine makers – confirm by their very presence that this is a *terroir* that has been constructed as an organic whole by the will and effort of men. The arrangement of the beautiful grounds, with their paths, ornamental lakes and clumps of trees help to introduce the presence of the château and to distinguish it from its rural environment.

Another frequently-used artifice reflects the same desire to stress the dominance of the *maison de maître* over its surroundings. It involves raising the house by placing it on a base, which is sometimes used as a *chai*, as at La Lignère and La Louvière. This method is particularly effective for châteaux that are situated on a flat terrain or in the *palus* on the banks of the Garonne. Plaisance, Droit and Alty (now in ruins) are thus protected from floods and enjoy the view of ships going by on the river. In addition, the steps leading up to the main level highlight the subtle theatricality of the house. The most common way of accentuating the monumental nature of a residence is to place it on a terrace. This arrangement may be found in many châteaux, for example at Crock. It is particularly frequent in the Médoc, where examples include Lafite, Beychevelle, Langoa, Ducru-Beaucaillou, Calon-Ségur, etc. The terrace separates the château from its surroundings and allows it to see and be seen more easily. It shapes the landscape by marking it out with balustrades and accentuating it with steps.

Fresco painted around 1938 at the Bourse du Travail in Bordeaux, symbolizing the relationship between viticulture and architecture.
OPPOSITE:
Two 19th-century châteaux in the Médoc. Top, Château Maucaillou at Moulis. Bottom, Château Gruaud-Larose at St-Julien.

Architecture and nature are thus combined in a structure that becomes less rigid the further you are from the château but which underlines its dignity and nobility and gives expression to its pre-eminent position.

A DOMINANT POSITION

A noble house reveals its nature in characteristic architectural details. Some are so explicit that they serve as outward signs to confer a château-like quality, by allusion and connivance, to buildings of a modest size.

The most effective of these pretences are those that lend a military air to the building: wide ditches, towers and turrets. Even in times of peace, this warlike device was retained for its symbolic value. In châteaux that have been designed along strictly classical lines, such as Lestrille and Malle, round turrets covered with freestone domes surround the central part of the building and this military-looking decoration is also to be found on the corners of the peaceful chartreuse de Peychaud in the *palus* of the Bec d'Ambès. During the Second Empire, architects dreamed of achieving a synthesis between the classical and medieval traditions and decorated opulent bourgeois houses with corner towers, bartizans and pointed pepperboxes. This is what Charles Burguet attempted at Châteaux Palmer and Pichon-Longueville, Duphot at Château Pichon-Longueville-Comtesse de Lalande and Bonnore at Sipian. Beaumont and Junayme also belong to the same style of architecture which exploits the symbolic and aesthetic function of the tower.[9]

The chapel is a traditional attribute of a château. It marks the nobleman's independence from the parish and the direct links, as it were, that he has with God. In the 19th century, it also acquired political undertones; in the new secular and republican society, it proclaimed the aristocracy's faith in the Catholic religion and the monarchy. Whereas the chapel at Haut-Brion only survives in written accounts, those at Lyde and Malle have been preserved along with their baroque décor dating from the early 18th century intact. In general the chapels were situated in a

tower or in a wing of the outbuildings. The unknown architect who built the chapel at Bouilh worked on a different scale and in a different style to that of Victor Louis. At Peyronnet, Alexandre Poitevin opted for the Gothic, and Filhot is in the Louis-XVI style. Very often, the oratory is separate from the main chapel in the grounds, where it forms an ornament, as at Chelivette, Morin, Beauséjour, etc.

The dovecot was a feudal privilege and a recognizable sign of nobility that was often used. The dovecot at Latour is so monumental in scale that it has become the image of the estate and has caused the actual *maison de maître* to be forgotten. The latter with its stone dome belongs to a type that is very common in the Bordeaux region.[10] Many other dovecots have conical roofs and tend to resemble – no doubt intentionally – defensive towers.

One of the original features of the Bordeaux region is the significance attached to portals. These were erected everywhere, even sometimes in the middle of the vines as at Issan. In the 18th century, they gave rise to sumptuous baroque constructions at Malle, Lafite, Beychevelle and La Lagune. The neo-classical period saw a preference for the simplicity of square piers and a plain entablature, but this did not prevent architects from producing some spectacular effects as at Châteaux Cosd'Estournel and Léoville-Las-Cases with their triumphal arches. Carefully designed by the best architects, the portals of the Bordeaux region are intended to give emphasis to the house and, by a process of metonymy, to confer upon it the dignity of a castle.[11]

THE CHARTREUSE

In the eyes of the people of Bordeaux, the *chartreuse* is the ideal residence. It fulfills the needs of the owner of a wine-producing estate in its small dimensions and by its architectural character, satisfies the taste of a society that is nostalgic for the 18th century. It is as difficult to pinpoint the time of its first appearance as it is to define its exact nature and today the word is very often used indiscriminately. Though this type of building has been used for a long time,

ABOVE:
Drawing of emblematic tower of Château Latour.
BELOW:
Drawings by Louis Combes made for Château Margaux in about 1810. (Bordeaux municipal library, Delpit collection).
OPPOSITE:
Top, *Château Latour surrounded by its vines.*
Bottom, *View of main façade of Château Margaux from the driveway.*

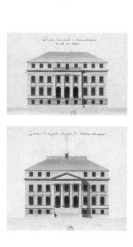

the first known record of it only dates from 1790.[12] Its popularity can be linked to the 18th-century fashion for small country houses. Like villas, or hermitages, the *chartreuse* is a place of refuge where the owner can in comfort live on his land. But the *chartreuse* of the Bordeaux region differs from other small French châteaux in its generally long and low design. This characteristic is the result of a regional tradition that dates back to the beginning of the 17th century. From the time of Sales (*circa* 1620) and Le Lyde (*circa* 1630) to Abzac (*circa* 1660) and Malle (*circa* 1710), numerous châteaux may be found whose accommodation consists of only a ground floor.[13]

In 1820, when G.-J. Durand was asked by the Comte d'Aux to carry out alterations on Château Talbot, he was careful to record the layout and elevation of the house, which at that time had the appearance of a classic *chartreuse*. The main body of the building was in the shape of an unequal quadrilateral with seven bays. Two wings with three bays slightly set back were at right angles and formed the outbuildings surrounding the courtyard. Divided down the middle by a corridor, the central body included a hall, a living room and a large room opening onto the grounds; on the courtyard side was another hall, a dining-room and some bedrooms. One of the wings contained the kitchen, another the bedrooms, the servants' quarters and the storerooms, while the third was taken up by the *chai*. Despite the small dimensions, such an arrangement was sufficient for a comfortable domestic life, elegant entertaining and also fulfilled its agricultural functions.

There are many variations on this basic pattern. Bel Air (1791), which is very small, does not have set-back wings but, to make up for this, the main body of the building is endowed with a pediment, pilasters and sculptures. Bacalan has nine continuous bays, the axis being simply marked off by partitions. Before the additions which have diluted its neo-classical rigour, Ducru-Beaucaillou had 17 bays with no break other than a slight central recess dominated by a pediment.

The *chartreuse*, a simple family mansion, is adorned with all the signs that could make it more like a château. In this respect, we have already mentioned the role played by the terrace. The terrace at Beauregard is equipped with dovecots and moats, the one at La Lagune has a majestic horseshoe-shaped perron and a magnificent enclosure. However, the usual way to enlarge a *chartreuse* is to extend it with a structure in the middle (Belin, Les Déhés before the later modifications in 1954) or by lateral structures (Peychaud, Beychevelle, Calvimont). Tauzia, with its dome-topped rotunda, is a rarer type that reveals a high degree of neo-classicism. These combinations have limits. Morin is a single-storey building, but its mansard roofs give the impression of its having another level. Mongenan consists of a main body with two low structures alongside. These are small châteaux rather than *chartreuses*, in that the usual balance is not perceptible. The *chartreuse* remains a single-storey residence in which, no matter what extensions have been added, the horizontal line should be dominant.

THE PALLADIAN STYLE

Since Palladianism has been in fashion, we tend to see examples of it everywhere. Nowadays, it is sometimes enough for a château to have two columns and a pediment for it to be described as "Palladian", which reveals a confusion between the use of decorative elements suitable for all types of classicism and the specific and much more complex vocabulary of the master of Vicenza. It is true that numerous designs prove that the architects of the Bordeaux region were aware of Palladio, but these plans were rarely executed.[14]

The Palladian château cannot therefore be defined simply as a residence that has been embellished with classical motifs. It is an agricultural estate which, like the rural villas of the Venice region, has been designed by the architect as a system in which "the parts have . . . a relation and correspondence with the whole" (A. Palladio). Such an architectural programme can only be carried out in a coherent fashion if it is rapidly

done. It therefore requires that considerable capital be immediately invested. This is no doubt the reason why this ideal system has only had a limited success, since owners prefer to build gradually according to their needs and their financial circumstances.

One of the oldest examples is La Lignère, built at Labrède. The architect is still unknown as is the date, which is probably in the last decade of the 18th century. The *maison de maître* and the adjoining buildings form a solidly welded whole. Facing a field bordered with clumps of trees, the main façade is raised on a plinth, to which a perron was later added. It is decorated with a graceful portico with arches. The outbuildings that make up the farm are in a more archaic style and are attached to the back of the house. The cool and dark basement is occupied by the *chai* and the wings contain the stables, the *cuvier*, an orangery and the peasant quarters. The vines stretch out beyond the gate and portal.

The architect of Plassan is also unknown and again its date is uncertain (late 18th – early 19th centuries). The U-shaped plan remains and the elevation continues the tradition of the *chartreuses* of the Bordeaux region, but the Palladian style is obvious and consists of much more than mere spectacular decorative features. A straight perron and porticos with triangular pediments conspicuously mark the middle of the façades overlooking the garden and the courtyard. The style is most clearly seen in the vigour of the long, juxtaposed geometric shapes, in the accentuation of the structure and in the desire to underline the hierarchy of complementary elements.

Château Margaux is the most perfect expression of Palladianism in the Bordeaux region.[15] The extremely wealthy Marquis de la Colonilla commissioned the architect Louis Combes to build it. This huge work was carried out quickly between 1810 and 1816, which explains the perfect consistency of the component buildings. The *maison de maître* is positioned in a dramatic way, with its powerful and precise shape rising up on a plinth at the end of a long avenue of plane trees. A wide and

CHATEAU LYNCH-BAGES   A PAUILLAC

· SOCIETE ACADEMIQUE D'ARCHITECTURE · MCMLXXXVIII · N· PRAT ·

straight perron leads to the portico which has four Ionic columns and a pediment with a bare tympanum. The solemn effect of proud solitude is accentuated by the position of the outbuildings, which are arranged in two courtyards on either side of the avenue; they are low buildings, having no communication with the château and, in a manner of speaking, under its watchful eye. The so-called "craftsmen's courtyard" is arranged like the square of a model village, with its Doric-columned hall, its fountain, the workers' cottages and the house of the *régisseur*. The other courtyard is reserved for vinification: press, *cuvier* and the wonderful *chai* with two bays separated by a line of 18 tall Doric columns.

Other examples of the Palladian influence can be found throughout the châteaux of Bordeaux, either in the actual architectural forms as at La Louvière, Phélan-Ségur or Chartran, or in the way the buildings are integrated into the natural sites. In fact, the phenomenon is part of the wider context of the region's neo-classicism, which is the preferred means of expression of the Bordeaux taste for discreet pomp and for order.[16]

LUXURY CHATEAUX

The balance of classicism, so suited to the moderation of the regional character, was upset in the second half of the 19th century. The neo-medieval style only met with moderate success in the Bordeaux area. Indeed, it was not very sensible to risk a fortune for the sake of installing staircases in towers, building disproportionate roofs and covering pointed gables with sculptures. Roquetaillade, lavishly restored by Viollet-le-Duc and Duthoit, is an exception and is not situated on a wine-producing *terroir*. However, there are picturesque examples of this neo-gothic architecture which has yet to be studied in the Gironde. The most attractive are the châteaux of the Marquis de la Grange (1856), Ricaud built in 1861 by Alphonse Blaquières and Breillan, which was further embellished until the end of the century. The relatively small dimensions of these châteaux destroy all the credibility of their pseudo-fortifica-

BELOW:
Façade of Château Bel-Air built from 1857 by the architect Lafargue (Bordeaux municipal library, Delpit collection).

OPPOSITE:
The residences of wine châteaux contain luxurious living rooms and reception areas for entertaining eminent guests. Out of consideration for the owners, we are not identifying the interiors of these châteaux.

tions and give them a theatrical air. In general, enthusiasts of gothic architecture contented themselves with restoring and making habitable ancient buildings. "Troubadour-style" adornments, intended to make them look more realistic in fact succeeded in transforming authentic medieval buildings into fake fortified châteaux. This is what happened at Châteaux Camarsac, Cursan, Thouars and Olivier; the latter is now in the process of being "de-restored".

The well-known Anglomania of the inhabitants of the Bordeaux region was shown in some buildings of a vaguely Elizabethan style. Duphot seems to have originated this trend which was particularly successful in the Médoc with Châteaux Cantenac-Brown built by Minvielle, Lanessan and Lachesnaye built by Garros and Mouton-Rothschild built by Maître. With their recesses emphasized by gables with stone and brick cusps, their twin chimneys and their oriel windows, these small castles added a touch of the English countryside to a few corners of the Médoc vineyard.

During the *belle époque*, buildings of an eclectic style started to appear. Their luxury was an indication of the wealth of their owners, who were often bankers from Bordeaux or Paris. However, the balance between the *maison de maître* and the estate was not compromised. The largest of these residences fully deserve the title of château, but at the same time they lost something of their unique Bordeaux character. This is true of Château de Parempuyre, built in the spirit of the Renaissance by Garros, and of Dulamon which was the work of Lafargue and has a neo-Louis XIV appearance. However, at Giscours, the relation between the *chais* and the château is so positively asserted that the word regains its regional meaning. In any case, it is usually by means of the wealth of their eclectic ornament rather than by their size that these buildings express their pretensions. The slate roofs decorated with mansards rise up proudly with their chimney stacks, their indented zinc ridges and their weather vanes. Such decorative extravagance is particularly inventive at Fonreaud or

MIDDLE:

Top, *the aristocratic elegance of a traditional residence: the neo-classical façade of Château Beauregard built at Pomerol in the 18th century.*

Bottom, *the functional arrangement of the chais and cuviers of Château Loudenne, built at the end of the 19th century at St-Yzans. The neo-industrial influence is obvious.*

IN THE MARGIN:
The residential or functional architecture of wine châteaux is often enhanced by carved motifs, with thousands of variations on the symbols of wine, the vine and viticulture.
Left, *bunch of grapes at Château d'Yquem.*
Right, *viticultural ornamentation on the façade of the chais at Cos d'Estournel.*

Tayac. Pastiches of varying degrees of plausibility may also be found. Thus, with its portico and its perron, Marbuzet could pass for a neo-Palladian villa, but the design does not create the necessary link between the château and the *chais*.

RUSTIC AND MODEL CHAIS

In the language of wine makers in the Bordeaux region, a *chai* (in the singular) is the building where the barrels are put and where the wine is matured. In the plural, the *chais* refer to all the utilities and outbuildings of the property. This usage shows in a symbolic way that all the activity of the estate is centred around the vineyard. Thus, in the Bordeaux region the *chais* include the buildings that are necessary for the running of the estate. Some châteaux have equipped themselves with purpose-built model farms. Those of Tours, of Giscours (called "ferme Suzanne") and of Lanessan have been built with the intention of combining rationalism with monumental proportions.

The big problem with *chais* as of wine storerooms has always been that of keeping them at a cool and constant temperature ($12-15°$ centigrade/$54-59°$ fahrenheit) and protecting them from humidity. Some châteaux near Ste-Croix-du-Mont, Libourne or St-Emilion use former subterranean quarries excavated from the rock especially for this purpose (Château Ausone). In the flat countryside of the *graves* or the *palus*, the cellar is placed in the basement under the *maison de maître* (La Louvière, Plaisance, Plassan). But the oldest and most common method is still to use long, low buildings with thick walls, pierced by a few small windows that can be closed by painted wooden shutters, and covered with a tiled roof. If the width of the building comprises several bays, they are separated by wooden posts (the line of columns at Margaux are exceptional). There in the darkness, on a well-swept and hard earth floor, the barrels are lined up and carefully wedged with wood or stone chocks.

Despite their rustic simplicity, these *chais* do not belong to vernacular architecture. We have seen how they form an

OPPOSITE:
The utilitarian buildings of many wine châteaux built in the 19th century are arranged around service courtyards next to the residence. Top, the service area for the chais and cuviers at Château Pontet-Canet at Pauillac (Médoc). Bottom, the lodgings of the régisseur and of the château staff dominating the entrance to the "Ferme Suzanne" at Château Giscours, Labarde (Médoc).

ABOVE:
The water tower at Château Cantenac-Brown built at Margaux (Médoc) in the 19th century in a neo-gothic style of English inspiration.

integral part of the château and that the Palladian system incorporates them in its monumental design. It is clearly shown in old texts, and in plans and designs (by Combes, Dufart and G.-J. Durand, among others) that these agricultural buildings represented an important part of the architectural scheme.

In the second half of the 19th century, there was a development – the most original invention of eclectic architecture – which led to the perfecting of a new *chais* system (in its wider sense, since it involved the cattle sheds, the fermenting rooms, etc. but not the wine cellar itself). The phenomenon is not well known. It is related to the advances made in vinification techniques and its origins should probably be looked for in the Médoc. Some estate owners and *régisseurs* were looking for efficient ways of processing the grape harvest and of storing the wine. The *chais* were then moved away from the *maison de maître* to form a unit, thereby underlining the increasingly important role of the cellarmaster and his authority in his specific field. At Châteaux Giscours and Pichon-Longueville, these new outbuildings were placed on either side of the château's façade and contribute to its general appearance. But they were increasingly being put to one side (Cantemerle) and often out of view of visitors (Palmer, Loudenne, Lanessan, etc.). Another characteristic is the use of industrial materials which had hitherto been unknown in the rural architecture of the Gironde: bricks, which could be perforated to ventilate the barns, cast-iron posts for the *chais* or the *cuviers* (Pontet-Canet).

But the most important changes concerned the *cuviers* which were now on two levels. The *cuves* were placed on the ground floor and reached up to the top floor, where access was through a hole in the floor. The presses, which were installed on the top floor, held the grapes which were brought in carts and winched up through a large opening. This system made the work easier and allowed for considerable savings in manpower.[17]

Architecturally speaking, the new *chais* were clearly distinguished from the residence. They were attractive to

the eye in various ways: in their multi-coloured appearance – pink brick (or rendering) was combined with the white (sometimes whitewashed) stone of the quoins and the surrounds of the various openings; in the rhythm and proportions of the openings which are clearly suited to their particular function – carriage entrances, skylights or oculi; in the play of the gables which break up the horizontal cornices and which are decorated with realistic sculptures – monograms interlaced with vine branches, barrels (Malartic-Lagravière), child grape-harvesters (Giscours) and other iconographic motifs related to wine production. Towards the end of the 19th century, these types of Médoc *chais* became widespread throughout the Bordeaux region. Since that time, they have been, with the *maison de maître*, an important part of wine architecture.

THE MYTH OF VICTOR LOUIS

Each *terroir* has its myth. It is often based on ignorance but nevertheless represents a cultural consensus. Thus, in the Bordeaux region, all the medieval fortresses are believed to have belonged to Edward of Woodstock, the famous Black Prince, son of Edward III of England, and all the beautiful classical residences are attributed to Victor Louis (1731-1800). The people of Bordeaux only know that he was the famous architect of the Grand Théâtre in Bordeaux. They have assumed from this that he was a genius and that his work is universally known and admired. They thus tend to credit him with many of the beautiful buildings of the town and, in the same generous spirit, all the 18th-century châteaux of the region. Neither the chronological facts nor stylistic evidence discourage them from making such attributions. If we are to believe Cocks and Féret (the official directory of the wines of Bordeaux) or the châteaux owners, then Louis must be taken as the designer of Morin, Le Tuquet, St-Georges, La Lignère, La Louvière, Bel-Air (Talence) and tens of others. In fact, the only château in the Gironde for which he produced designs is Le Bouilh, which was begun in 1786 and never completed.

However, the myth of Victor Louis is not without significance. It expresses the Bordeaux people's acceptance of a classical concept of aesthetics, consisting of harmony and moderation, and making good use of the beauty of the golden stone and readily dispensing with ornaments or else reducing them to a few sculpted motifs. It also accounts for the fact that the same architects worked in the town and in the countryside, thereby providing, in parallel with the economic interests, a close stylistic link between Bordeaux and its wine-producing *terroir*.

It is also true that the ideas of Victor Louis did in fact gain widespread acceptance. He imposed a style on a whole generation of collaborators and competitors. Recent research shows that Picque-Caillou and Chênevert should be attributed to Etienne Laclotte, La Louvière to François Lhôte, Nairac to Mollié and Vaquey to Roché, almost all of whom worked on the building sites of the Bordeaux area. The next generation turned away from the ideas of Victor Louis. The new leading architect, Combes, imposed neo-classicism and an ideal that was more overtly inspired by antiquity. He not only designed a scheme for Château Margaux, but also for Morin (still as he built it) and Fongravey, which was unfortunately greatly modified. Corcelles, the builder of the Chartrons Temple, also created Valrose and Labégorce. G.-J. Durand transformed Talbot at St-Julien and La Sauque at Labrède. For a minister of Charles X, Michel Bonfin built Peyronet, which Alexandre Poitevin completed in a neo-gothic style. The latter, though he was a fervent admirer of the Greeks and Romans, started the trend towards eclecticism, as is shown in his designs for Châteaux Filhot (neo-Louis XVI) and Yquem (neo-17th century).[18]

The people of the Bordeaux region affect a certain disdain for eclectic architects. However, the châteaux built by Burguet, Minvielle, Garros, Blaquières and many others, have character and fit in well with the wine-growing landscape. Above all, we should give these architects credit for being able to develop, with so many

variations in detail, the new *chais* of the Médoc type. There is no doubt that these rural buildings are original. They fulfill perfectly their functional and decorative roles. The châteaux of this period give the architectural heritage of the Bordeaux vineyard a diversity that is in keeping with the diversity of the wines themselves.

ECONOMIC CRISES IN THE 20TH CENTURY

The various economic crises and recessions of the 20th century have had obvious repercussions in the architectural field, which has the appearance of a period of stagnation or even regression. Changes in the vineyard have caused some destruction. The most scandalous are those which have disfigured the *palus* of the Bec d'Ambès. On this land, which is occupied by the autonomous port of Bordeaux, exceptional residences, such as Alty or Piétru, have been destroyed through sheer vandalism. Despite protestations, the Maison Carrée d'Arlac (property of the town) is in the final stages of collapse, while Château Dillon (property of the State) has been totally abandoned. A long list could be drawn up of such monuments that are now "between life and death".[19]

While the number of *appellations* is continually on the increase, no more châteaux are built *ex nihilo*. The rare exceptions are no more than rather unconvincing pastiches. Château Lafon-Rochet, built in the 1960s in the *chartreuse* style, is only interesting in that it perpetuates (though unfortunately in rather a clumsy manner) the atavistic taste of the people of the Bordeaux region for this type of residence. Bouscaut is still more recent, but this château is no more than a replica (rebuilt after a fire) that is not very successful on the architectural level.

The development of cooperatives since the 1920s could have provided an opportunity for a new type of wine architecture, similar to what had been achieved in the previous century with the *chais*. Not only was the opportunity missed, but the phenomenon gave rise to some real architectural disasters. The necessity of stocking large quantities of

FROM TOP TO BOTTOM: *The state of a disused wine château in the Côtes de Blaye in 1988; a former wine château in ruins near St-Estèphe; Château Piétru, demolished by a regional authority in 1988, just before being classified as a "historical monument"; a former wine château fallen victim to urbanization in the Graves; Château Dillon (18th century) left abandoned.*

OPPOSITE: Top, *the gutted and roofless residence of a fine neo-classical château among the vines at Baurech, beside the river, in the Premières Côtes de Bordeaux.* Bottom, *a disturbing image of the State's recent negligent ownership of Château Dillon in Blanquefort (Médoc).*

wine led to the building of warehouses and outdoor vats that are out of all proportion and spoil the most beautiful landscapes. The most upsetting example is that of the Union des Producteurs de St-Emilion, where the overbearing reinforced-concrete building disfigures a prestigious site. It is as if the cooperatives, by challenging the traditional structure of the château, are at the same time renouncing the image of quality that goes with it.

In the 1960s and 1970s, another opportunity for introducing a new, high-quality architecture connected with wine production was missed. It was during this period that several large *négociant* firms decided to leave the historic Chartrons district in Bordeaux and move into larger, more efficient and more accessible premises in the city's suburbs.

Recent prosperity has allowed many estates to modernize their equipment. The increased practice of bottling at the château has made the construction of new *chais* necessary and in the new *cuviers*, the chilly perfection of stainless steel has replaced the sensuality of wood. The example of Baron Philippe de Rothschild who was the first to put on show his *chais* at Mouton during the 1930s, was followed by many other owners. As far as modernization and expansion are concerned, the trail was blazed by Rigby A. Lee who endeavoured to restore both residences and *chais* while preserving their original character (Canon, Giscours, Langoa, Lynch-Bages). On the other hand, a strictly modern scheme was adopted for the immense *chais* at Clarke. For want of space, those at Haut-Brion were placed underground and the spectacular result started off a new fashion. In Bordeaux, the Mazières architectural firm, father and son, started to specialize in these massive reinforced-concrete cellars (Châteaux Margaux, Yquem, Pichon-Longueville-Comtesse de Lalande, etc). In this climate of competition, Château Lafite-Rothschild scored a point by calling on the Spanish architect Ricardo Bofill who has devised an underground hypostyle *chai* of circular design, which will once again be covered over with vines in 1989.

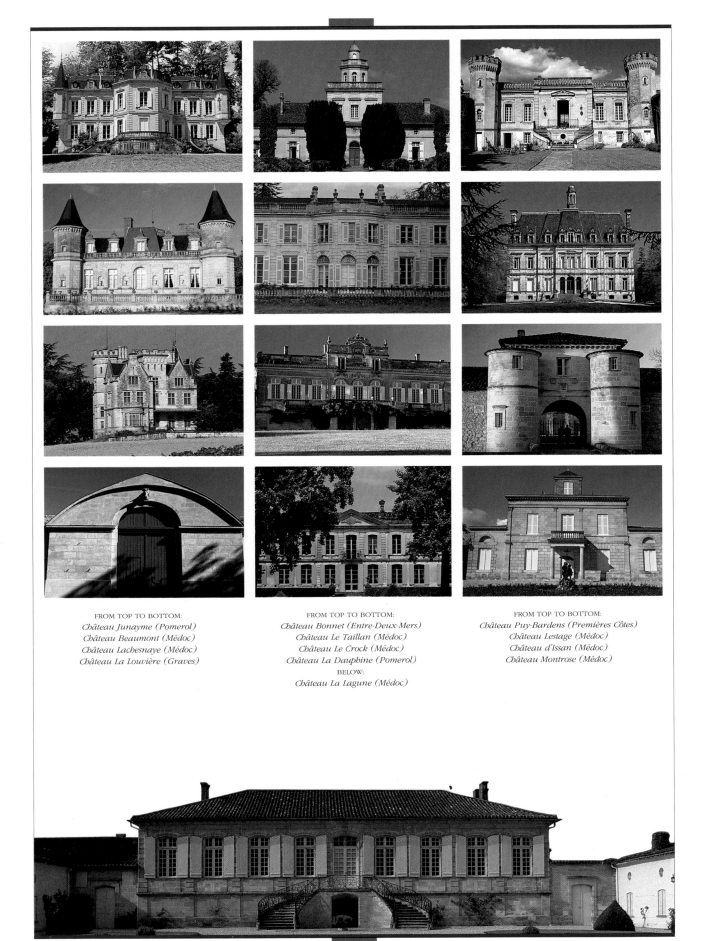

FROM TOP TO BOTTOM:
Château Junayme (Pomerol)
Château Beaumont (Médoc)
Château Lachesnaye (Médoc)
Château La Louvière (Graves)

FROM TOP TO BOTTOM:
Château Bonnet (Entre-Deux-Mers)
Château Le Taillan (Médoc)
Château Le Crock (Médoc)
Château La Dauphine (Pomerol)
BELOW:
Château La Lagune (Médoc)

FROM TOP TO BOTTOM:
Château Puy-Bardens (Premières Côtes)
Château Lestage (Médoc)
Château d'Issan (Médoc)
Château Montrose (Médoc)

FROM TOP TO BOTTOM:
Château Cantermerle (Médoc)
Château Chênevert (Graves)
Château Palmer (Médoc)
Château Larose (Premières Côtes)

FROM TOP TO BOTTOM:
Château Phélan-Ségur (Médoc)
Château Mille-Secousses (Bourg)
Château Beychevelle (Médoc)
Château Ducru-Beaucaillou (Médoc)
BELOW:
Château Laujac (Médoc)

FROM TOP TO BOTTOM:
Château de Sales (Pomerol)
Château Monbadon (Côtes de Castillon)
Château des Tours (St-Emilion)
Château de Plassan (Premières Côtes)

The present climate of economic and viticultural competition (which, in any case, is not limited to the Bordeaux region but is an international phenomenon) is thus favourable to the development of new forms of wine architecture. However, under the pretext of fulfilling the demands of a market that is becoming increasingly reliant on advertising, there is a great temptation to build expensive and ostentatious installations. It must be remembered that vinification is not a public spectacle. Although it is true that Bordeaux wine is not quite the same as other wines and that it serves as a model for a good number of its competitors, it must above all take care not to compromise its unique character.

The specific nature of Bordeaux wine results from the château method of production. The final elegance, finesse and subtlety of aroma should find a counterpart in the quality of the architecture associated with this product. Progress in wine architecture can only be made if vineyard owners remain true to the nature of their wine.

1 J. Gardelles, "Guyenne, Gascogne, Béarn, Pays basque", *Dictionnaire des châteaux de France*, ed. by Y. Christ: Berger-Levrault, Paris, 1981.
2 P. Roudié, "La construction du château Haut-Brion", *Vignobles et Vins d'Aquitaine*, Bordeaux: Fédération historique du Sud-Ouest, 1970.
3 P. Roudié, "L'ancien château du Parc ou d'Espagne à Mérignac", *Bulletin de la Société archéologique de Bordeaux*, vol. LXXVVII, 1986.
4 R. Coustet, "Expansion du néo-classicisme bordelais: travaux campagnards de Gabriel-Joseph Durand", *Bulletin de la Société archéologique de Bordeaux*, vol. LXXI, 1976-78.
5 Ch. Higounet (ed.), *La Seigneurie et la vignoble de*

ABOVE:
Wine label from the only château-residence built in the 20th century (around 1960) in a pseudo-neo-classical style: Château Lafon-Rochet at St-Estèphe (Médoc).
BELOW:
Two examples (with far too many others) of distressingly mediocre modern wine-producing buildings.
OPPOSITE:
The beautiful architecture of Château du Piat built at Tauriac (Côtes de Bourg) in the 18th century was threatened with decline until the 1980s. Fortunately, its owner, like many others in the region, is now gradually restoring it.

Château Latour, Bordeaux: Fédération historique du Sud-Oeust, 1970.
6 *Cadillac: aspects connus et inconnus d'un canton.* Commission Régionale d'Inventaire d'Aquitaine, no place or date.
7 Stendhal, *Journal de voyage de Bordeaux à Valence en 1838*, Paris, 1927.
8 G. de Galard, *Album vignicole*, Paris 1835.
9 *Le Château et la tour*, Actes du premier colloque de castellologie de Flaran (1985).
10 P. Coudroy de Lille, "Quelques pigeonniers en Langonnais et en Réolais", *Bulletin de la Société archéologique de Bordeaux*, vol. LXXI, 1976-78.
11 R. Coustet and F. Legrand, "Portails classiques et néo-classiques", *Revue historique de Bordeaux*, 1975.
12 Ph. Maffre, "Qu'est-ce qu'une chartreuse?", *Bulletin de la Société archéologique de Bordeaux*, vol. LXXXVI, 1985.
13 P. Roudié, "Manoirs et maisons de campagne du XVIIe siècle en Bordelais", *Actes du 104e Congrès national des Sociétés savantes*, Bordeaux: Fédération historique du Sud-Ouest, 1979.
14 J.-P.Mouilleseaux, "A la recherche de l'influence palladienne à Bordeaux et dans le Sud-Ouest", *Les Monuments historiques de la France*, no.2, 1975.
15 F.-G. Pariset, "Château Margaux et l'architecte Combes", *Vignobles et Vins d'Aquitaine*, Bordeaux: Fédération historique du Sud-Ouest, 1970.
16 Ph. Maffre and J.-P. Bériac, *Le Bordelais néo-classique*, Bordeaux, IACA, 1983.
17 E. Féret, *Dictionnaire-manuel du négociant en vins et spiritueux et du maître de chai*, Bordeaux: Féret et Fils, 1896.
18 A. Birot, "Une famille d'architectes oubliés: les Mollié", *Bulletin de la Société archéologique de Bordeaux*, vol. LXXIV, 1984; P. Roudié, "Documents concernant la construction de trois maisons de campagne", ibid., vol. LXVIII, 1976; B. Charneau, "La folie de Blanquefort: Fongravey", ibid., vol. LXXVI, 1985; R. Coustet, "Expansion du néo-classicisme bordelais . . . ", op.cit. and "Le château de Peyronnet; néo-classicisme et néo-gothique", *Actes du 104e Congrès national des Sociétés savantes*, Bordeaux, 1979.
19 P. Roudié, "Les avatars des maisons de campagne de la banlieue de Bordeaux", *Le Château près de la ville*, Actes du second colloque de castellologie de Flaran (1987).

CHATEAU BEYCHEVELLE

Château Beychevelle at St-Julien (Médoc). Surveyed and drawn by Valérie Nègre, 1988. (Wash, watercolour and airbrush).

NEW VISIONS OF THE WINE CHATEAUX

PORTFOLIO OF ORIGINAL DRAWINGS BY THE SOCIETE ACADEMIQUE D'ARCHITECTURE, TOULOUSE

It was in 1984 that the Société Académique d'Architecture was founded in Toulouse, France. This brought together a team of about ten young architects who share a common interest in the cultural strategies defined by Maurice Culot and Léon Krier. They appreciate their "rigour and their lack of respect for generally accepted ideas" (derived from orthodox modernism), their respect for the beauties of classicism and their taste for the erudite. The Société are ardent devotees of the architecture of the past and they search with tenacity and enthusiasm for the knowledge and the techniques that have unjustly fallen into disuse.

Their legitimate aim is thus to take part in the "Reconstruction of the European Town". To this end, they first concerned themselves with the heritage of their beautiful town of Toulouse and contributed to the development of ideas expressed in two emblematic books published by Maurice Culot at the Institut Français d'Architecture in Paris: *Toulouse: 1810-1860* and *Toulouse: les délices de l'imitation*. The group is developing an effective cultural and artistic strategy based both on theory and on architectural design as well as graphic or pictorial evocation of urban landscapes of traditional inspiration. In this way, it is contributing to a renaissance in the representation of urban architecture.

In order to allow this group to utilize fully its many talents and to enable the Châteaux Bordeaux exhibition and book to benefit from it, the Centre Georges Pompidou (CCI) has entrusted it with the task of creating a "corpus of the wine architecture of the Bordeaux Region". This undertaking is in keeping with a policy of commissioning creative people (architects, artists or craftsmen). In 1988, the work of the group led to the creation of about 50 large and original drawings, sketched and then enhanced with colour (80 x 120 cm/32 x 47 in) which show the artistic heritage of the Bordeaux vineyard in a new and important light. The portfolio includes paintings which compare particular themes which recur in various châteaux, and others which show individual châteaux. The following chapter includes 15 of the latter, covering a wide range of different styles of wine architecture in the Médoc, the Graves, the Sauternes and the St-Emilion regions.

JEAN DETHIER

.CHATEAU.

POMYS

A

B

JEAN-PHILIPPE GARRIC

Château Pomys, built in the 19th century at St-Estèphe. Surveyed and drawn by Jean-Philippe Garric, 1988. (Gouache).

*Château Figeac, built in the 18th century at St-Emilion. Surveyed
and drawn by Sylvie Assassin, 1988. (Wash and watercolour).*

TOP: *Château Cos d'Estournel, built in the 19th century at St-Estèphe. Surveyed and drawn by Valérie Nègre, 1988. (Watercolour).*
BOTTOM: *Château Phélan-Ségur, built in the 19th century at St-Estèphe. Surveyed and drawn by Joseph Altuna, 1988. (Watercolour).*

TOP: *Château de Malle, built in the 18th century at Preignac (Sauternes). Surveyed and drawn by Joseph Altuna, 1988. (Watercolour).*
BOTTOM: *Château de Sales built in the 17th century at Pomerol. Surveyed and drawn by Marie-Laure Petit. 1988. (Watercolour).*

*Château La Louvière, built in the 18th century at Léognan
(Graves). Surveyed and drawn by Barthélémy Dumons, 1988. (Watercolour).*

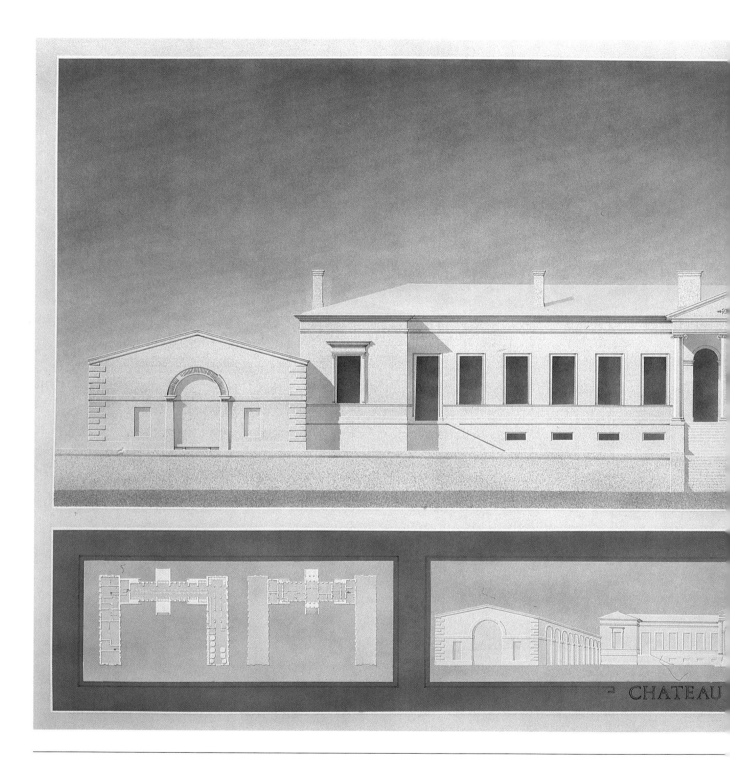

CHATEAU

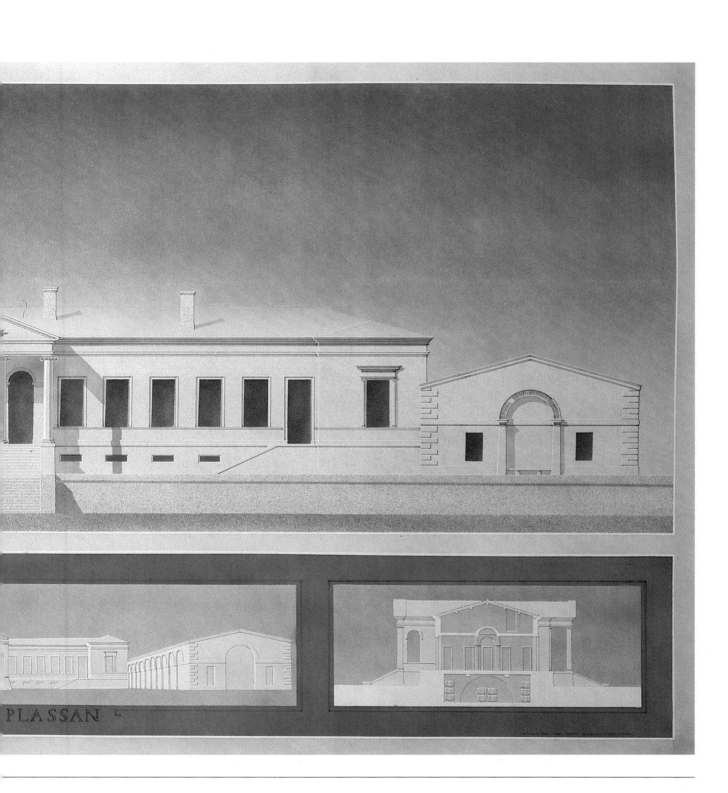

Château de Plassan, built in around 1800 at Tabanac (Premières Côtes de Bordeaux).
Surveyed and drawn by Nathalie Prat, 1988. (Airbrush).

TOP: *Imaginary view of Château Lanessan, built in the 19th century at Cussac-Fort-Médoc, Jean-Philippe Garric, 1988. (Oil on canvas).*
BOTTOM: *Imaginary view of Château Marbuzet at St-Estèphe. Jean-Philippe Garric, 1988. (Oil on canvas).*

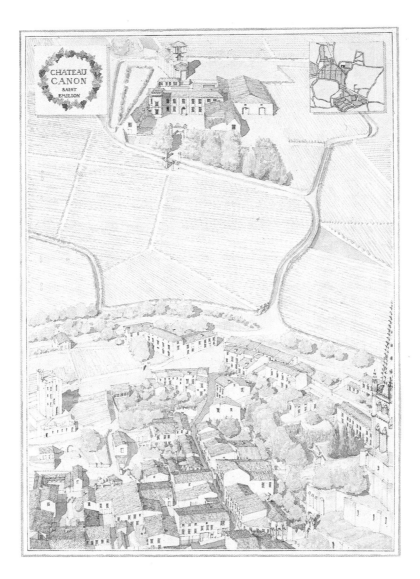

Bird's eye view of Château Canon and its vineyards surrounding the town of St-Emilion.
Surveyed and drawn by Joseph Altuna, 1988. (Watercolour).

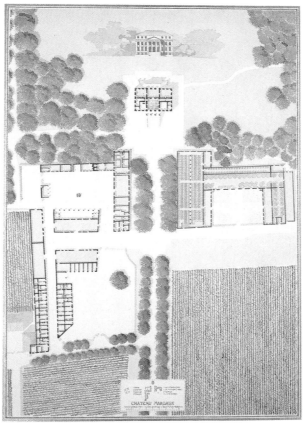

Château Margaux, built around 1810 by the architect Louis Combes. TOP: *The Cour des Artisans.*
BOTTOM: *Site plan of the château and its surroundings. Surveyed and drawn by Nathalie Prat and Valérie Nègre, 1988. (Watercolour).*

Château Margaux. TOP: *View of the residence in perspective.* BOTTOM: *The colonnade of the first-year chai.*
Surveyed and drawn by Philippe Gisclard and Jean-Philippe Garric, 1988. (Pastels).

PARKS, GARDENS AND LANDSCAPES

JEAN-PIERRE BERIAC

The wine region of Bordeaux is composed of a myriad of different elements, fashioned as much by the topographic variety of the countryside as by man.

In the Médoc, the vineyard stretches for 80 kilometres (50 miles) north to south along the banks of the Gironde, in a width that never exceeds five kilometres (three miles). The trained vine stocks cover the *croupes de graves* (gravel hillsides), interspersed with woods and meadows on the former marshes which are drained by *jalles*. As an extension to the Médoc, the old Graves vineyard – a large part of which has been destroyed by urbanization – also forms a band that follows the Garonne for almost 50 kilometres (31 miles), from the Blanquefort *jalle* to Langon. The Sauternes region is a continuation of this chequered pattern. Here the vines cover the gentle and extensive undulating hills and are occasionally broken by streams and small rivers. On the right bank of the Garonne and the Gironde in the districts of Bourg, Blaye, the Premières Côtes de Bordeaux and the sweet wine vineyards of Ste-Croix-du-Mont, the topography is more markedly hilly with the vines clinging to the steep hillsides. In late summer, the low-angled rays of the evening sun set the vineyard aglow. This same landscape reoccurs along the Dordogne, between Fronsac and Castillon. The hills rise from the Dordogne up to St-Emilion, then gently descend again towards the Isle, forming the Pomerol plateau.

A GARDEN LANDSCAPE

The land-holding pattern is complex, composed of a multitude of small properties and some large estates. In the Médoc, the average size of a property is less than 10 hectares (25 acres). Within the 5,000 hectares (12,500 acres) of the St-Emilion *appellation*, there are 1,000 châteaux.[1] The division of the types of land varies considerably from one property to another, as does the proportion of land planted with vines. Château d'Issan has 32 hectares (79 acres) of vines out of a total of 120 hectares (297 acres). At Margaux, only 85 hectares (210 acres) out of the 330 hectares (815 acres) are devoted to vines. On the other side of the Gironde, vines cover only 20 percent of the property of Château Grissac, but they take up 70 percent of the land at Grand-Jour.[2] If the areas devoted to wine production are compared to the size of the properties, it is clear that, even in the great *appellations*, the vine by no means takes up all the land, leaving room for other types of agriculture which necessarily leave their mark on the landscape.

Along with these facts concerning the structure and ownership of the land, we must also consider the various methods of growing vines: low-trained vines in the Médoc, taller with wider gaps between the *règes* in the Graves, vines that are trained at a height of more than 1.5 metres (5 feet) in the Entre-Deux-Mers. In general, the *règes* run at right angles to the line of the steepest slope, but in the vineyards around

St-Emilion they are arranged on short terraces and above Cadillac they follow the line of the slope.

In this strongly contrasting landscape, there are châteaux and *maisons de maître* with outbuildings and, often surrounded by parks and gardens. All the various architectural styles are to be found, from the neo-classicism of Nairac to the neo-gothic Lachesnaye, not to mention the ancient fortresses of Agassac and Vayres and the beautiful 17th-century homes of Malle and Abzac. Despite this great variety, the vine exerts a unifying force on the organization of the countryside and the quality of exploitation of the *terroir*. As early as 1787, the English agronomist Arthur Young summed up his vision of the landscape: "Flanders, a part of Artois, the rich plain of Alsace, the banks of the Garonne and a considerable part of the Quercy are cultivated more like gardens than farms".[3] There is the same fastidiousness in the growing of vines as there is in the beautiful grounds of the châteaux.

ARISTOCRATIC TRADITION AND THE FRENCH-STYLE GARDEN

The garden is of aristocratic origin. The gardens of Château de Vayres were created as early as the 1580s. Situated at the foot of a proud fortress, the various terraces were planted with orchards and vegetable gardens, with a parterre in the centre and stretching right along the banks of the Dordogne, in which the whole garden was reflected.[4] This was the proud showpiece created by the head of an important estate in imitation of the parks adorning princely residences. Other gardens in this period and until the end of the 17th century remained more modest in scale. They were characterized by the placing of small enclosures with parterres, allées and arbours around the house. The distinction between a garden created purely for enjoyment and one serving a practical purpose was not yet clearly defined. Sometimes these enclosures were backed by a wood, as at Cantemerle.[5] Even the garden plots at Margaux or Issan, created between 1640 and 1680, remained surrounded by

Château Figeac and its grounds among the vines. In the 19th century, the pseudo-landscaped garden spread into the enclosure of the former parterre.

walls. Mouchac is one of the few reminders of this bygone style.

The French style of garden was introduced fairly late in the Bordeaux region. Among the first important examples was Suduiraut[6] where, in the semi-circular forecourt, marked out by lines of deciduous trees, we can see the application of the principles defined by André Mollet in 1651,[7] as well as in the arrangement of the parterres and lawns on the rear façade. The same organization was used at Malle[8] in the 1720s. Here the succession of terraces rising towards the *garenne* and the small theatre decorated with characters from the *Commedia dell'Arte* created an Italian feel, characteristic of the cultural influences which had a permanent effect on the province. Such Italianisms could also be seen at Château de Cadillac-en-Fronsadais, which had a long slope with fountains, terraces and steps. This theme reoccurred at Vayres, where in 1695, Launay constructed a garden dominated by a large pavilion covered with an imperial dome. These devices blend the garden with the landscape.

Château de Sales at Pomerol, dating from the end of the 17th century marked a new departure.[9] The whole estate is organized around a north-south axis. The visitor first follows the shade of a long tree-lined avenue through the fields. Then a few steps away from the estate courtyard, symmetrical vistas created by other paths to the left and right reveal the dense wood and allow glimpses of the countryside beyond. Thus, the visitor has an overall view of the outbuildings and of the magnificent entrance to the main courtyard: a dovecot porch topped, here too, by an imperial dome. The terrace on the rear façade overlooks a parterre and a pond, with some orchards and a vegetable garden beyond. It is also the place where other visual openings in the foliage meet the main axis. This is a landscaped composition which encompasses the whole property. The notion of a garden gives way to the total structuring of the estate. We can go so far, in this case, as to talk of a "French landscape".

Sales is one of the most outstandingly successful gardens. One can see its

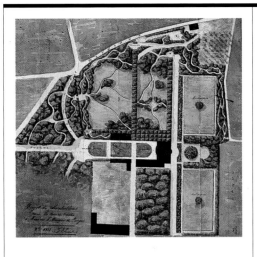

influence in hundreds of examples created in the course of the 18th century, but these were on a smaller scale and a less ambitious design. This trend transformed the garden into a social phenomenon. Although it was the exclusive property of the old nobility and the *noblesse de robe* up until the 1750s, it became more widespread until the French Revolution. The craze of owning a country property with *maison de maître*, *chai*, fermenting room, garden and some vines spread and became a visible sign of social success. The layout of these properties usually followed the same pattern. The entrance was made grandiose by a portal, behind which a drive, lined with elms or lime trees, ran up to the residence and its outbuildings. At the rear, an ornate parterre and lawns, flanked with rows of trees, stood in front of a wood interspersed with straight paths forming patterns or arbours. On one side were the orchard and vegetable garden. From the – often mediocre – centre of the estate, long paths led through the vineyard; these were often lined with free-standing fruit trees such as apple, peach or pear trees. The juxtaposition of these

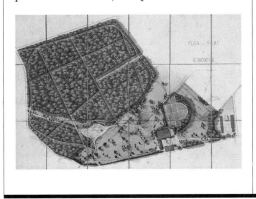

ABOVE:
Drawings of the grounds and gardens of Château du Taillan (Médoc) in 1812 (left) and of M. Thévenard's estate in 1823 (right). Both were designed by the architect Gabriel-Joseph Durand. (Archives of the département of the Gironde, Bordeaux).

Extract from the map of the Médoc drawn in 1759 showing the grounds and garden of Château d'Issan at Margaux. (National archives, Paris).
BELOW:
Original drawings of the 19th-century grounds. Left, Giscours at Labarde in the Médoc (Archives of the Château). Right, La Ligne in 1810 (Archives of the département of the Gironde, Bordeaux).

elements created the ordered landscape that had surprised Young.

The only differences between these properties, apart from variations in size and adaptation to the different terrains, was found in the richness of their decorative features. The wealthiest owners filled their properties with sculptures and built summerhouses, music rooms, factories, follies and ponds, with or without fountains. Some of these ornate decorations also fulfilled an identification role, such as the imposing portico on the side of the cliff at Château de La Roque at St-Germain-la-Rivière. The wealth displayed by these properties was justified both in terms of the pleasure they gave and in their role in asserting their owner's social position. To live in the fashion of nobility in the Bordeaux region at the end of the *ancien régime*, it was essential to have a wine-producing estate with beautifully-tended gardens. The modern notion of the wine château had taken shape.[10]

However, this did not mean that the château owner was not concerned with making economies. Although he might take pride in scientific curiosities,

he attached far more importance to the progress of agronomy. Thus, the introduction of the locust tree was intended to compensate for the shortage of *carrassons* (wooden stakes) and the Lombardy poplar allowed some damp areas to be exploited. Research into the different vine varieties, or the "*synonymie de la vigne*", was initiated in 1777 by François de Paule Latapie, with the blessing of the Intendant Dupré de St-Maur. This aroused much more interest than pure botany. These experiments were continued at the beginning of the 19th century under the authority of the new Société Linnéenne.[11] Amateur agronomists, like the Duc Decazes on his estate of La Grave, carried out their own tests. Among the garden designers at the beginning of the 19th century were professionals like Yves-Toussaint Catros at Margaux and brilliant innovators like the Baron d'Haussez, *préfet* and architect of the park at Cantemerle, as well as the Marquis de Brias at Le Taillan, and Yvoy at Geneste and Malleret.

ENGLISH GARDENS IN THE 19TH CENTURY

Although the wine château came into being at the same time as the French-style garden, it was not restricted to this type of landscaping and slowly a new style of "English" garden emerged. In 1789, there were only four or five examples including L'Hospital and the English garden did not really become widespread until the beginning of the 19th century. It was characterized by the transformation of the parterres into a simple patchwork, avoiding the great lines of deciduous trees of the classic garden. In the woods, the paths wound their way through the spaces between the rectilinear vistas, as at Paveil. At Margaux in 1810, Catros designed a composite garden. He replaced the old vegetable garden with a landscape garden and put an island in the northeast corner of the canal. He constructed a long, undulating path that followed the canal and returned towards the château after winding through the copses and put a serpentine path across the lawn, but was careful not to touch the *garenne* which was in the purest French style.[12]

Long before the 19th century when Barillet-Deschamps at Batailley,[13] and Eugène Bühler at Giscours,[14] treated the woods in the same way.

This timidity of design began to fade from the 1840s onwards, after which great landscapes started to be created. At Château Filhot, Louis-Bernard Fischer composed a panorama with vast lawns sloping down to a small lake and a plantation of exotic trees on the hill facing the main courtyard. He opened up a long vista towards the fortress of Budos and constructed a path linking Filhot to Yquem – the jewel among the vineyards belonging to the Lur-Saluces family – via the village where the same family occupied the *mairie*. At Giscours, Bülher constructed several lakes in the *jalle* that crossed the grounds and used clumps of trees to break up the expanse of the large meadows. In the distance at the edge of the wood, rhododendrons were reflected in the still waters. In 1881 at Le Taillan, B. Budd built a large balcony overlooking the vine-covered slopes and the marsh.[15] At the foot of the balcony, a few horses grazed in the shade of the stone pines. What had been achieved at Sales at the end of the 17th century, was looked at again in a different aesthetic style. The estate was not confined by walls, it was perceived by the eye and by the skill of landscape designers who knew how to direct the gaze. The long silhouettes of Atlantic cedars or Lebanon cedars, magnolias, Sierra redwoods, Carolina poplars, tulip trees and cypresses could now be seen in the Bordeaux region, alongside the oaks, chestnuts, planes, limes, holm oaks and stone pines.

THE LANDSCAPE IN THE 20TH CENTURY

The crisis at the end of the 19th century dampened this enthusiasm for landscaping. It was not until the period between the wars that there was any restoration of the gardens designed by the Bordeaux landscape designer Ferdinand Duprat, at Beychevelle and Margaux.[16] But, once again, the economic crisis and the years without harvests meant that abandonment was more common than novel design. From

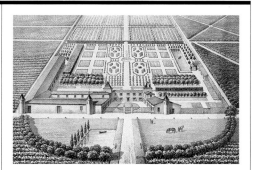

1945 onwards, these misfortunes were compounded by the substitution of the idea of "green spaces" for that of park or garden, which led to an impoverishment of the landscape's intellectual content. The aesthetics of château surroundings started to have more in common with motorway interchanges than with gardens. The uniform decoration for the main façade of a château became a lawn surrounded by a flowerbed filled with red sage, French marigolds and begonia, and at best planted with rosebushes.

Since the beginning of the 1980s, there has been a new stress on maintaining the beautiful grounds of châteaux and this has intensified in the last few years. New plants are reviving old gardens, such as the one at Langoa, where the owner has introduced shrubs in the style of Gertrude Jekyll in an 18th-century design. At Kirwan, the visitor immediately recognizes the small, typically Second Empire park, but above all is struck by the different pastel-coloured blossoms that appear throughout the summer. Creativity abounds. At Chênevert, inspiration is provided in the pictures of the house that date back to 1782[17] and a formal garden is being introduced into the old romantic framework of Lagrange which has been restored. At Château Castéra, the new owners are calling on the services of English landscape architects to restore and modernize the park and gardens. At Canon, in the shadow of the spire of an old church, André Gayraud has created a "secret garden" with a summer house and hornbeam arbour. From the small terrace, the eye is drawn, over the wall, to the serene vineyard landscape beyond.

This renewal has also led to changes in the type of staff required for the

garden's maintenance. For a long time, owners had made do with men "taken from the vine" but now they employ professionals or else train their own men. Technical innovations in the last 20 years have led to a considerable reduction in the numbers of permanent staff employed. At Château de Portets, there was a staff of about 15 men in the 1960s but only six are left today. The owners tend to rely on specialist contractors for the upkeep of their grounds and thus one of the links between the ornamentation and the working of the land is becoming more remote.

This brief survey of the history of gardens in the Bordeaux vineyard could apply to other non-wine-producing regions. However, a uniquely local character may be detected in the vistas looking onto the vineyard and, even more, in the fact that the paths – which start in the centre of the buildings and grounds – govern the dividing up of the vines through the whole estate and partly dictate its management. This logic, which was developed in the classical age, is still relevant today.

The château gardens are subject to the same influences as the estate, though slightly more remote. If the estate falls on hard times then the gardens can only be restored when the situation appears to have been resolved. There is therefore a delay between its recovery and the recovery of the vines, the modernization of equipment and even the restoration of the buildings, which is always carried out before the garden. The only exception to this is Château Clarke, where the residence burnt down at the beginning of the 20th century: the small park was restored before the château.

Despite the set-backs, the equilibrium of these two elements has proved to be remarkably permanent. The land that Olive de Lestonnac allocated for the grounds of Margaux in around 1640,[18] went through many successive upsets. The same was also true of the gardens at Château de Portets since at least 1673,[19] at Malle, Suduiraut and Olivier[20] since the beginning of the 18th century, and at Beychevelle since 1756,[21] etc. An examination of the landscape reveals clearly the type of land involved – often drained marshland, and practically always land of lesser economic value. The sacrifice for the economy of the estate is not very great. When the château and its outbuildings are situated in productive lands, the surrounding gardens are reduced to a bare minimum: 2,500 square metres (two-thirds of an acre) at La Mission Haut-Brion; at Cos-d'Estournel, ornamental vegetation is arranged along the buildings; and Château Latour makes do with a clump of trees.

Water was much sought after on the wine producing estate, where it met several indispensable requirements. Fish ponds maintained a supply of fresh fish. Water dips were useful for treating certain ailments in horses and could be used to wash the carts. There were also washing places and ponds for the barrels. Fountains and decorative ponds would never have existed at many châteaux without the strictly functional ponds. A simple process of diverting the general water system made this luxury possible. Gradually, other means of supply took over its functions but instead of being filled in, these ponds assumed an ornamental role thanks to the extension of the garden.

With these successive changes, the garden became the reminder of the estates former nobility. The moats which used to protect the fortified residences are still filled with water at La Brède, Agassac, Olivier and La Tour-Carnet but left dry at Laroque. Another sign of nobility, the dovecots are always placed near the house and the woods and *garennes* also play a lesser part in this nostalgia. Apart from providing timber for building and heating, they would give the owner the feeling of living in a noble style. The *garenne* at La

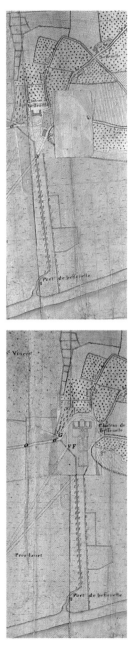

Lagune is still on the same parcel of land that it occupied in the 18th century.[22]

These symbols, which were formerly used because of the social prestige they brought to their owners, also fulfilled the consumer's desire to enjoy, not just a high-quality wine, but a sense of history. The wine from the château became the ambassador for an aristocratic tradition of refinement.

THE SPIRIT OF THE PLACE

Any disfiguration of the landscape results in a loss of revenue. The destruction of the elms was, and still is, keenly felt: 180 of them had to be cut down at Château de la Rivière, Grand-Jour lost the covering for its driveway and Bonnet the shade in its courtyard. However, modifications in the methods of cultivation have caused considerably more far-reaching changes to the landscape. In the Entre-Deux-Mers, a massive operation was carried out to regroup the land and to introduce tall vines. To facilitate the use of tractors, the *règes* were planted in the direction of the slopes of the hills. The destruction of fruit trees along main pathways in the properties was also the consequence of mechanization as they hindered the movement of the machines. Hills that were too steep, and which had been worked by hoe since the Middle Ages, were abandoned and their slopes covered with thickets. These few recent examples are just part of a long series of transformations. Crops were grown *en joualles* (in widely spaced rows) until the beginning of the 20th century. In the Médoc, the vines were attached to *carrassons* until the 18th century. The horizontal laths of wood were only introduced at the beginning of the following century and they were replaced by wire less than one century ago. As a result the long banks formed by the *règes* became more regular.

It is quite difficult to imagine what the bygone countryside was like. What did the Médoc look like before the *palus* were drained? A portrayal of Le Vigean (a locality near Eysines) in 1616[23] presents us with an ordered image of the vineyard landscape. With a few exceptions, what we see today is hardly ever older than 150 years. Therefore,

Le Parc
du Chateau Margaux
Médoc

F. Duprat, Arch.te Paysagiste
Paris 1927.

PARC
DE BEYCHEVELLE

Beychevelle
à Madame Achille Fould 1935

F.t Duprat, Arch.te Paysagiste.

the landscape is contemporary with the idea of combining a product, the wine of Bordeaux, with an image, the wine château. Its origin goes back to Gustave de Galard and his *Album vignicole* published in 1835.

In the Médoc, Graves and the Sauternes region, even when you cannot see the château, its presence is indicated by a mass of trees rising above the vineyard. A line of deciduous trees or conifers standing out on the horizon leads the eye to the main part of the estate. In other places, this game of discovery sometimes turns out to be more difficult. One has to pay attention to the colouring of the foliage and the presence of exotic plants. In general, the overall effect of the buildings and plants forms an image that is specific to each place. The construction which marks out the landscape gives it an identity. The perception we have of Lafite today has remained more or less unchanged since the start of the 18th century.[24] Is it possible to imagine Margaux without its avenue of plane trees? Malagar announces its presence by a line of alternating cypresses and stone pines halfway down the hill. Suduiraut can be identified by a small shielding wood and an entrance way marked by stone pines; Latour by a clump of trees in which a squat dovecot and some outbuildings can be made out. Sometimes a small structure that is both mineral (preferably a tower) and vegetable is the sole emblem of the property in the landscape. It is reproduced on labels and in advertisements and it gives its name to the *cru*. Nearly 100 château names contain the word *"tour"*, more than 60 the word *"croix"* and a similar number the word *"moulin"*. Vegetation also plays a role in these place names, with words such as *"bois"*, *"ormeaux"*, *"pins"*, *"pins francs"*, *"platanes"*, *"marronniers"*, *"charmilles"* and even *"cèdres"* and *"palmiers"*.[25]

Since it is a means of identifying the château, this image becomes established and hinders any change. Ricardo Bofill's work at Lafite is invisible from the road and Provost, by recreating the gardens of Lagrange, had to take into account the romantic setting inherited from the 19th century. Perhaps only

OPPOSITE:
Top, *gardens of Château de Malle at Preignac (Sauternes)*. Bottom, *fountain in the garden of Château d'Olivier at Léognan (Graves)*.

Philippe de Rothschild in his Château Mouton at Pauillac has been able, in a great feat of landscaping, to bring about a totally new creation, but one that is not without references to the past. The start of the straight 800 metre (875 yards) drive is marked with an obelisk which, with the ordered structure of the gardens, is a reference to the French-style garden. The three blind arches at the opposite end and the sculptures by Brancusi and Nevelson are of neo-classical inspiration.

In short, with a few exceptions, the parks and gardens in the Bordeaux vineyard date from the 19th century and determine the structure of the landscape. They are often open to the public and contribute to the prestigious brand image of the wine-producing châteaux.

1 Report of 25 August 1982 by H. Dumon's office at the CIVB.
2 Féret, *Bordeaux et ses vins*, Bordeaux, 1982 (13th edition), Féret et Fils.
3 Young (A.), *Voyages en France*, Paris.
4 Engraving of Chatillon, Archives of the Gironde, 4 L 563 and Drouyn (L), *La Guyenne militaire*, Bordeaux, 1865, vol.2, pp. 429–445.
5 Archives of the Gironde, 3 E 8706 f° 50.
6 Archives of Château Suduiraut.
7 Mollet (A.), *Le Jardin de plaisir*, Stockholm 1651.
8 Archives of Château de Malle.
9 Archives of Château de Sales.
10 Bériac (J.-P.), "Les jardins des Bordelais au XVIIIe siècle", *Actes des 9e journées internationales d'histoire de Flaran*.
11 A learned botanical society created in Bordeaux in 1818. Franck (W.), *Traité des vins de Médoc et autres vins rouges et blancs du département de la Gironde*, 7th edition, Bordeaux, 1871.
12 Archives of Château Margaux.
13 Archives of Château Batailley.
14 Archives of Château Giscours.
15 Archives of Château du Taillan.
16 Bériac (J.-P.), "Ferdinand Duprat architecte paysagiste et quelques autres", *Bordeaux-Aquitaine 1920-1940. Architecture, Urbanisme*. Bordeaux, 1988, pp.251-261.
17 Archives of Château Chênevert.
18 Information provided by M. Joël Perrin.
19 Archives of the Gironde, 4 J 2.
20 Archives of the Gironde, 2 Z 1297.
21 Archives of the Gironde, 2 Z 748 bis.
22 Archives of the Gironde, 2 Z 490.
23 Archives of the Gironde, 2 Z 1327.
24 Map by Claude Masse in 1708; National archives F 14 10059-9; Bordeaux municipal library, Delpit collection, box 49, board 2; Galard (G. de), *Album vignicole*, Bordeaux, 1835.
25 Féret, *Bordeaux et ses vins*, Bordeaux, 1982, op. cit., yellow pages, list of *crus*.

124

THE BORDEAUX LANDSCAPE UNDER THREAT

GERARD BAUER

Anyone who observes its landscape will realize at once that the Bordeaux vineyard cannot be described as homogeneous. The different *terroirs* of which it is composed are as varied as the wines they produce. This is where a good part of their interest lies – again as in the case of the wines. However, it would be too convenient if one type of landscape were to correspond to each great family of wines. In fact, the two elements rarely coincide. Since distinguishing between landscapes is largely a subjective exercise of trying to describe scenes in terms of their differences, the choice proposed here may not seem very thorough to anyone who knows the region well. It is merely the choice of an attentive walker; a local geographer would no doubt arrive at something different. In my opinion, six large categories of landscape typify the Bordeaux vineyard.

A RICH DIVERSITY

The first distinct landscape is that part of the vineyard which stretches in steep terraces along the northern slope of the Gironde. You can see a long way from these terraces, below is the river with its islands, behind that the plain of the left bank and beyond the immense forest of the Landes. The contrast between the small and carefully tended terraces and the majestic panorama they allow you to see is particularly striking at the start of the estuary between Bourg and Blaye.

My second type, which is completely different, is dominant in the

OPPOSITE:
Since the end of the 19th century, urbanization in the built-up area of Bordeaux has caused a certain amount of damage to the wine-producing landscapes of the Graves. This has now spread to the Médoc, the Bec d'Ambès and the Premières Côtes de Bordeaux. Top, Château Castéra at St-Germain d'Esteuil (Médoc). Survey and drawing by the SAA, Toulouse, 1989. (Watercolour). Bottom, deterioration of the suburban landscape which surrounds the prestigious vineyards of Château La Mission-Haut-Brion at Pessac (Graves).

Entre-Deux-Mers, for example. The roads wind along valleys, skirt around hills, occasionally scaling them and passing through a shimmering mosaic of vines, fields, meadows and woods, punctuated with small towns and large farms. This mixed farming landscape derives much of its charm from the fact that it is strongly evocative of rural life before the war, when there were many small, self-sufficient communities which are rare in France today.

Third comes the country of vast, almost flat clearings cut from the forest of the Landes and entirely planted with vines, from which emerge one or two châteaux placed on slight hills. There is a strong contrast between the pruned and luminous garden of the vineyard and the dark wall of trees that surrounds it. This landscape is best seen in the Graves.

My fourth type also occurs in the Graves and in some ways it resembles the preceding one. But here the forest has been superseded by the town. Plots of several tens of hectares of vineyard are completely surrounded by densely built-up areas that almost touch them. This landscape, which is probably unique in the world, can only be found in the immediate suburbs of Bordeaux (Pessac, Mérignac).

The fifth type is the exact opposite of the previous one. The town, whose boundaries are precisely defined, rises up out of a sea of undulating vines. This magnificent contrast, which is also very evocative of times gone by, can now unfortunately only be found in the area around St-Emilion.

I have kept to last a type of vineyard landscape in Bordeaux that, in my opinion, is even more exceptional and stranger than the others. Imagine an immense, continuous and largely flat garden, extremely well tended and covering hundreds of hectares. Nothing emerges from it except, here and there, strange pieces of architecture, stone lions, steeples, neo-gothic or Chinese châteaux with grounds full of rare plants. Sometimes the atmosphere is quite unreal. It is the kind of place the surrealists would have appreciated. "The most conventional of statues would wonderfully embellish the countryside. A few naked women in marble would be of better effect in a large, ploughed plain" (Max Ernst). Despite the great difference in scale, you might also be reminded of Zen gardens. This is in the Haut-Médoc.

I hope that, even with these brief descriptions, I have been able to encourage those who do not yet know the Bordeaux vineyard to visit it. But I am concerned that those who come in five or ten years time will not be able to enjoy this same rich heritage.

"VIOLENT CHANGE HARMS MAN AS WELL AS THE LANDSCAPE" LUDVIK VACULIK

I am not suggesting that the vineyard landscapes of the Bordeaux region should be regarded as sacrosanct, untouchable and beyond the reaches of time. All landscapes must necessarily change, since they are no more than the reflection of what happens within them. But I am convinced that this process of evolution could, without great effort, be more planned, thought-out and channelled and not so often left to chance. Our Swiss, British and Dutch neighbours have long since realized that their countryside is mostly very rare and that they must look after it to prevent people using it as they please. We French have not yet acquired this habit. We remain complacent in our belief that we have one of the lowest population densities in Europe, a surfeit of open spaces and a countryside

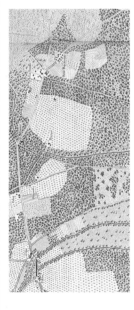

BELOW:
Map from the "Atlas de Trudaine" showing a vineyard nestled in a clearing in the pinewoods at Cajac along the old road from Bordeaux to Bayonne. (National archives, Paris).

OPPOSITE:
Top, *plan of Pauillac (Médoc) in 1759 and aerial photograph in 1988. In the 20th century, urbanization has been allowed to encroach upon the territory of these famous vineyards.* Centre and bottom, *St-Emilion in 1988. The photographs show the exceptional harmony that still exists between this old wine-producing town and the vineyard landscape that surrounds it.*

overflowing with so many beautiful landscapes that there will always be enough of them. The Bordeaux region is a typical example of an area where there is intense competition for the available space and in such cases it is important that it is left up to the community to decide upon the future of the countryside.

Wine production, like technical progress in general, has become very mechanized. Because of this, in the less prestigious parts of the Bordeaux region, a modern vineyard with tall and more widely spaced *règes* is being created. However, these changes have hardly spoiled the general character of the landscape. In any case, mechanization has adapted itself to the vineyard rather than vice versa and more progress has been made in the area of wine making than in that of growing vines. However, it is true that when wine-growing concerns are merged, the small vineyards, which are often planted in different directions, tend to be regrouped into larger parcels of land with all the *règes* planted in the same direction. Fortunately, this restructuring of the vineyard, which wipes out the chequered pattern of the land and thus destroys the individual character of the landscape, can only be done very slowly during replanting. It should also be remembered that the spread of bottling *au château* and of wine-producing cooperatives has given rise here and there (and may well continue to do so) to new *chais* whose architectural design is sometimes unfortunate. However, all things considered, the vineyard itself has generally retained its appearance and experts agree that there is no reason why it should need to change further. The transformation of the vineyard landscapes of the Bordeaux region seems to depend less on the modernization of wine production than on other external factors.

The evolution of general agriculture is one such factor. We may wonder whether the numerous mixed-farming enterprises such as those in the Entre-Deux-Mers will survive. In a market that is rapidly expanding and becoming more competitive, they risk being forced to specialize and to abandon the

BELOW:
*Two types of landscape. Top,
the vineyard of the Domaine
de Chevalier in a clearing at
Léognan. Bottom, the large,
efficient estates of the Médoc.
Here is the terroir of Château
Latour with its famous
symbolic tower and, in the
foreground, Château Pichon-
Longueville-Comtesse de
Lalande.*

OPPOSITE:
*Two other typical landscapes.
Top, the magnificent
surroundings of Château
Loudenne in the Médoc with
one of its three turrets.
Bottom, a more undulating
landscape in the Entre-Deux-
Mers where vineyards and
pastures alternate and where
polyculture is sometimes
practised.*

poorer land, thereby impoverishing the mosaic of textures that is characteristic of these beautiful old landscapes. The other threat facing the landscape in various parts of the Bordeaux vineyard is less insidious and much more conspicuous – urbanization, in particular, the urbanization around Bordeaux. The whole vineyard is, roughly speaking, shaped like a semi-circle with a radius of about 60 kilometres (37 miles) and with the metropolis (population in 1982 of 640,000 including suburbs, 840,000 with outer suburbs) at its centre. Bordeaux is suffering the same fate as other urban centres: as it grows, it becomes less dense and this increasingly diffuse expansion is accelerated by the facilities provided by cars, telecommunications, freezers, etc. Even though the neighbouring wine-producing vineyards are often some of the best, the city scatters its factories, power station, warehouses, offices, hoardings, shopping centres and, above all, its inhabitants, further and further afield. When roads are widened and a new infrastructure is created (motorways, high-speed railways, high-voltage cables), it is once again at the expense of the vineyard. In France, especially over the last 25 years, the boundary between the town and the countryside has been completely done away with.

At the same time, the new buildings in the outer suburbs are, almost without exception, stereotyped and identical. They have broken with urban planning and with the architecture of the old villages beside which they stand. In the case of Bordeaux, the general impression of disorder and mediocrity created by its recent expansion seems, by contrast, to be perhaps more marked than elsewhere. Firstly, because the rigour and elegance of the structure of the town centre and that of the vineyard – where it has not yet been suburbanized – both provide a particularly vivid expression of the deliberate planning of a landscape. Secondly, because the increasingly well-tended grounds and gardens of the châteaux highlights the banality and even the ugliness of many of the new buildings that are being erected on their doorstep.

This process, by which the city of

Bordeaux is being dispersed over several tens of kilometres through the surrounding countryside, is also taking place on a smaller scale in the other towns – and even in the villages – of the region. In the latter case, the problem is usually recent individual houses scattered here and there, alone or in small estates and sometimes in the middle of the vineyard. The succession of ministers in charge of urbanization have all raged about this urban dispersal, which is condemned by the name of "*mitage*" (literally "moth-eating"). But a blind eye has usually been turned, perhaps even more so in the Bordeaux region than in Burgundy or Alsace, just to mention the main wine regions. The public services have also played their part with water towers, overhead electric and telephone lines and unsightly road systems. In such an open and refined landscape, it takes very little to destroy the picture irrevocably.

The process by which urban expansion robs the vineyard landscape of its authenticity finds a parallel in the town itself: whereas the town, or rather its suburbs, are invading the vineyard, the wine trade is leaving the town in favour of the suburbs. For at least two centuries, the wine business had been centred at the heart of Libourne and especially in the large Chartrons district in Bordeaux. It played a large part in the quality of its architecture and in the activities on the quayside. Today, the Chartrons and the port of Libourne have been partly abandoned for *chais*, offices and loading areas that are more practical, but totally ordinary and scattered throughout the industrial estates around the city's outskirts. Bordeaux has not lost its role as the capital of the world wine trade – far from it – but its specific character has to some extent become less visible.

WHAT IS AT STAKE

A number of French town planning experts claim that the great upsurge in suburbanization which began about 20 years ago is now behind us. According to them, the town is becoming more populated again and there is a return to the centre. Disproving their prediction lies outside the scope of this chapter. I shall just say that it is an act of faith and that it contradicts urban evolution in general. In my opinion it would be dangerous to use this as an excuse not to worry about the potential risk of the gradual disappearance of the vineyard landscapes that are so characteristic of the Bordeaux region, all the more so since some of them — especially in the Graves and the Haut-Médoc — are already reduced in size. On the contrary, I think that no time should be lost in addressing the following question: does the public interest require that we continue to combine the exceptional quality of the wines of Bordeaux with that of its exceptional landscapes? This is not simply a matter of aesthetics. The debate is not an abstract one as high economic stakes are involved.

In the first place, this debate concerns the image that the wine-growing and wine-producing industry in the Bordeaux region wants to project to the outside world. Until now, considerable local efforts have been made to portray an image of refined activity aimed at combining the best technical innovations with the ancestral demands of distinction and even perfection. If this image is to be sustained, then it is essential to maintain the quality of the landscape and the places of production both of which are intimately related to it. The best proof of this is that, following Château Margaux's example, many owners — and not only the most prestigious — have worked and continue to work hard at upgrading their châteaux. A luxury product with a world-wide reputation, they rightly think runs the risk of losing its prestige if it comes from an unattractive and badly-designed building.

The conservation of the quality of the vineyard landscape also concerns the future of tourism, in which perhaps even more is at stake than in wine-production. All the well-known wine regions are enticing for many reasons: the visitor comes to admire the vines, to taste and select the wine, or to see for himself the *élevage* of a preferred *cru*. It is said (and this is confirmed in a recent study by the Bordeaux Chamber of Commerce) that, in comparison to its competitors, whether nearby (Cognac),

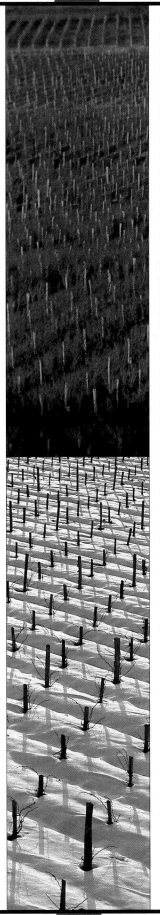

or further afield (Champagne, California, etc.), the Bordeaux vineyard is far from having achieved its full potential in terms of attracting tourists. In particular, it has not managed to attract long-stay visitors, since it does not offer sufficient varied and well-organized facilities for such tourists. It is well-known that tourism creates jobs and it would also lead to an increase, both directly by means of on-the-spot purchases and indirectly by renown, in the consumption of the wines of Bordeaux. No one doubts that, for many reasons, tourism that is centred on the wines of Bordeaux cannot develop around the presence of a few great châteaux alone and that it must be able to expand over as much of the vineyard as possible and include walks, visits to sites and other activities.

This line of reasoning leads, almost inevitably, it seems to me, to the necessity of considering the question of the future of the most typical vineyard landscapes. The best means of safeguarding and developing them should thus be listed in detail, debated and then taken up by the relevant authorities so that concrete decisions would ensue. But the development of tourism does have some disadvantages, it entails risks to the landscape (motels, camp sites, car parks, souvenir shops, etc.) and should therefore be carefully planned.

FORESIGHT AND SAFEGUARDS

The protection of the French landscape does not lack legal support. There are four levels at which action may be taken. The landowners form the first such level. I have already mentioned the importance that some people attach to the land in the Bordeaux region. Indeed nothing prevents the owners from going further and forming associations which, founded on the idea of the preservation of a common heritage, would group together all those sharing the same *terroir*. They would oblige the proprietors to respect a common register of responsibilities: rational choice of the most suitable sites for any new buildings; attempt to achieve the highest architectural quality; appropriate treatment of the landscape, etc. Town councils have direct legal power since

they have access to the plans of how the land is used, enabling them to lay down the areas that may not be built on and to fix precise rules for construction work, including the height and design of buildings, in other areas. The regional authorities can decide to nominate as "*parcs naturels*" those parts of its territory it considers essential to protect and to develop more carefully than the others. Once the charter of a *parc naturel* has been approved, it applies to everyone. Finally, despite decentralization, the State is still obliged to ensure the protection of sites, even if this sometimes means opposing the councils. The law states – and perhaps this is not realized by enough people – that the quality of urban and rural landscapes is of national interest. Moreover, the State can set up an area where the countryside is of outstanding beauty as a *parc national*, which will turn it, once and for all, into a sanctuary where changes can only be made with the strictest of guarantees.

The landscapes of the Bordeaux vineyard, which differ both in their quality and in the dangers they are faced with, require different strategies for their safeguard. For those landscapes closest to Bordeaux, the size and economic strength of the metropolis is such that the intervention of the State seems necessary. I have already said how beautiful I find the areas of the Haut-Médoc that have not yet been suburbanized and that their sort of beauty is unique in the world. This is why I would support the adoption of the most rigorous methods for its protection. Would it not be possible to create a national park of the Haut-Médoc? Like other parks, it would have to adapt its boundaries to the present situation and would probably be divided into several parts of varying sizes. In the first place, it would include the surroundings of Margaux and the vicinity of Pauillac, as far as Cussac to the south and the *terroir* of the famous threesome formed by Châteaux Mouton-Rothschild, Lafite and Cos-d'Estournel to the north. For the tourist, the journey from Bordeaux to this hypothetical national park would not be a very good introduction to the

charms that await him. Perhaps there is an opportunity here to develop a new means of access via the river.

Although its landscapes are perhaps not as exceptional as the Médoc, the vineyard of the Graves is in such potential danger that some areas could justify the same treatment. Of course, the greatest threats come from Bordeaux but they may also arise from a desire to clear some of the surrounding forest so as to extend the vineyard. Such forest clearance is certainly not to be condemned on principle, but, unless the appearance of the landscape is taken into account, it risks destroying the distinctive glades that characterize the whole region.

The few châteaux of the Graves which have been entirely surrounded by the suburbs of Bordeaux form a strong – and unintentional – landscape theme. But, owing to the fact that it was formed spontaneously and that the adjoining urbanization took place gradually and in an undirected way, the contrast between town and vineyard unfortunately does not produce its maximum impact. Needless to say, the vineyard in these places should be preserved as it is, whatever happens. On the other hand, a significant change in the peripheral urban structure could, if it was planned, reinforce further the interest of these areas. It is possible to imagine that the value of the land on the periphery of Châteaux Haut-Brion or Pape Clément should eventually make feasible the concerted construction of high-quality residential complexes, whose architecture would enhance the vineyard and vice versa. What a pleasure it would be to live a short distance from the remarkable historical centre of Bordeaux and to have a view of the vineyards that are beautiful all year round, perfectly maintained and for which someone else is responsible!

The Entre-Deux-Mers and the Fronsac areas, where the vine is only one element in a charming polycultural landscape, are fortunately not yet at risk from urbanization. However, the practice of dispersing building sites throughout the countryside is rampant. Moreover, as in other regions, agriculture will probably evolve increasingly

rapidly there. Perhaps there will be a need in the future for the region to mark off – with the aim of preserving a type of landscape that is characteristic of its historical heritage – some sites that are particularly typical and should be maintained in their present state. The money raised by a revived tourist industry could go towards the cost of ensuring the survival of an artificial type of polyculture. Since urbanization has now extended to a good part of the coastal road of the Côtes de Blaye and the Côtes de Bourg, which are of undeniable regional interest, it would also be useful to strengthen the controls governing development of the most attractive remaining areas.

St-Emilion presents a unique and paradoxical case, which is ideal from the point of view of protecting the landscape and the exact opposite of Bordeaux. It is almost a town planner's dream. The value of the town in terms of its architecture, structure and history is such that it is the town itself that protects the neighbouring vineyard from any encroachment. It achieves this by a rigorous policy of conserving the approaches to the town. Those interested in safe-guarding the landscape

Some typical examples of the destruction of the vineyard landscape in the Bordeaux region. Top left, *unplanned suburban housing surrounding the magnificent vineyard of Château Haut-Brion at Pessac.* Top right, *threatening urbanization near Château Chênevert at Mérignac (Graves).* Centre left, *a vineyard near Bordeaux invaded by new roads and suburban shopping centres.* Centre right, *a defunct vineyard in a recently urbanized part of the outskirts of Bordeaux.* Bottom left, *site of the former port of a superb wine château in the Médoc, recently disfigured by the erection of enormous wine storage vats.* Bottom right, *the Shell refinery (partially dismantled in 1988) and its immense storage installations for oil and gas at Pauillac in the immediate surroundings of the vineyard of a world-famous château.* Bottom centre, *in contrast the former Château Cordeillan-Bages at Pauillac, which was converted into a luxury hotel in 1988, is evidence of the emergence of wine tourism in the region.*

have nothing to worry about, except that this policy should remain effective.

Once again, the examples listed here in no way reflect the whole spectrum of the Bordeaux vineyard. They have been chosen because they seem to provide a particularly clear illustration of the variety of landscapes in the region, which is in itself an advantage to be maintained and developed, and the planning policies that could be put into practice. In any case, severe protective measures, requiring the intervention of the regional authorities or the State, must of necessity remain limited in scope. Fortunately, there is still plenty of important if less spectacular countryside in the Bordeaux vineyard. These wine landscapes should mainly be the responsibility of the local authorities, aided by the professional organizations. They will only retain their attractiveness if the owners and town councils are made aware of the considerable cultural and economic heritage that they are entrusted with. The less prestigious *crus* (representing the greater part of wine production) certainly have much more to gain, in terms of direct sales and enhanced reputation, than the well-known ones.

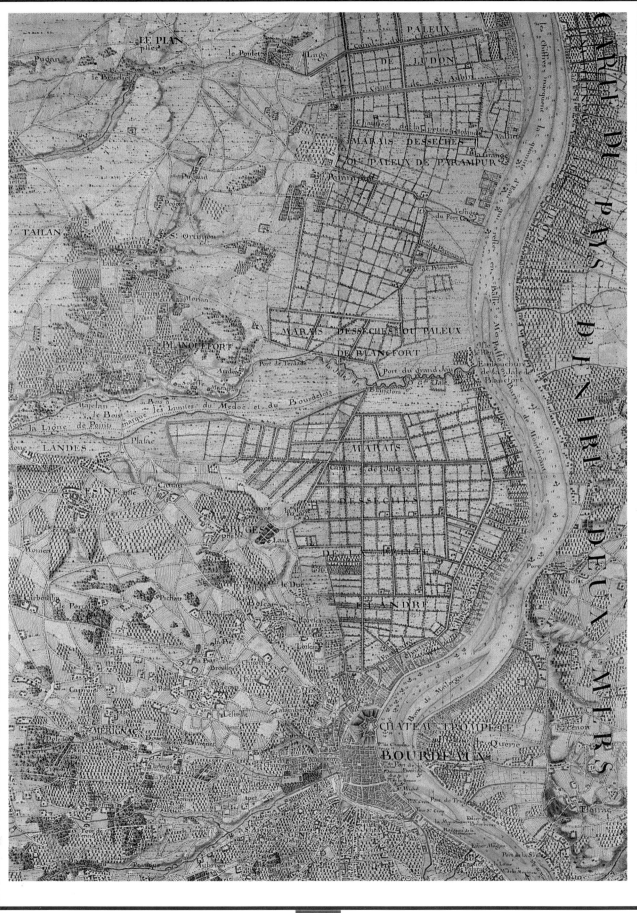

CARTE DU PAYS D'ENTRE DEUX MERS

LE PLAN

Pugan

le Poulet

Luga

PALEUX
DE LUDON

Pineuil

DE S.t Aubin

Chaussée

de la Petite Holande

Valliers

MARAIS DESSECHES

OU PALEUX DE PARAMPUR

la Grange

TAILAN

S.t Ortinon

Vestiges
du Fort Car

de Blancfort

BLANQUEFORT

Port de Terdade

MARAIS DESSECHES OU PALEUX

DE BLANCFORT

Embouchure
de la Jale de
Blancfort

Port du grand Jau

Jale

Bois des Limites du Medoc et du Bourdelois

LANDES

Plasac

MARAIS

ESINE

Canal

Canal de Jaleve

BRUGES

DESSECHES

DE LA

FLANDRE

MERIGNAC

CHATEAU TROMPETE

de Quérie

Cenon

BOURDEAUX

Floirac

THE WINE TRADE
AND THE CITY
OF BORDEAUX

ROBERT COUSTET

It is no accident that the town of Bordeaux has given its name to one of the most famous wines in the world. However far back we go in time, we can find evidence of the partiality of the people of Bordeaux for wine. In the 4th century, the poet Ausone (Decimus Magnus Ausonius), a prominent figure who was prefect of the Gauls, as well as a consul and a large landowner, devoted some of his verses to Burdigala (the Latin name for Bordeaux) in which he celebrated both the beauty of its monuments and the fame of its wines.

In the Middle Ages, the Archbishop, the monks and the Bordeaux bourgeoisie acquired land and planted vines. The vagaries of history caused the kings of England, as descendants of Eleanor of Aquitaine, to become the lords of Bordeaux for three centuries (1152–1453). Quite naturally, they favoured the wines from their Gascon estate. People did not yet speak of "Bordeaux wine", referring to it simply as "claret". Nevertheless, exports of the wine to England made the town prosperous. Twice each year, in the spring and the autumn, the English fleets sailed up the Garonne to "*aller aux vins*". This amount of trade obviously required specific facilities. Nothing now remains, but we can learn from texts that there were *chais* in which the grapes were pressed and vaulted *caves* in which the barrels were stored. The

basement of the Piliers de Tutelle, the most magnificent Roman monument in the city, was used as a cellar. We know that the inner harbours were lined with warehouses from which the barrels were loaded straight onto the ships. We have no indication as to the architecture of these functional buildings. It was probably not very grandiose because most of the profits from the wine trade were used for the building of churches, convents and the town walls.

When Bordeaux was returned to the French crown, the commercial link with England was destroyed. Deprived of their traditional customers, the Bordeaux wine producers looked for new trade outlets in northern Germany and the Netherlands. In order to make an impression on the international markets, they devoted themselves to improving the quality of their wines. Thus economic difficulties led to a quality wine being associated with the name of the town. However, the appearance of the city remained fundamentally unchanged throughout the Renaissance and the baroque period. Ships continued to anchor at the foot of its walls. Protected by its fortified towers, Bordeaux seemed to ignore the river that was responsible for its newfound prosperity and at the end of the golden age marked by Louis XIV's reign (1643–1715), it still retained its medieval appearance.

The 18th century was a period of unprecedented prosperity which allowed the town to be radically transformed. The king's intendants pursued a policy of modernization designed to show the benefits of centralized royal government. They demolished the town walls and lined the quays with identical houses that were arranged in a majestic façade along the Garonne. Sailors loaded ships with *barriques* in front of the palaces of the Place Royale, built in honour of Louis XV. Great Parisian architects – the Gabriels and then Victor Louis – introduced the most modern elements of the Louis-XV and Louis-XVI architectural styles. Their collaborators and their local competitors went on to develop their work further. Thus by the 18th century, Bordeaux had acquired its construction techniques, based on a mastery of the art of working with stone, and found its own style, combining moderation, balance and order. But most important the city became impregnated with a particular attitude based on the idea that the quality of life is associated with the quality of architecture.[1]

FROM A SUBURB TO A DISTRICT

After they had regained possession of Bordeaux, the kings of France built fortresses both to protect the town against possible reconquest by the English and to control a population that was quick to revolt. Thus the formidable Château Trompette was built beside the Garonne, downstream of the town. Under Louis XIV, Vauban was commissioned to modernize it. He gave it sizeable dimensions and, to protect its approaches, he surrounded it with huge glacis. Prevented from sailing up the river, the foreign merchants who came to buy wine got into the habit of anchoring downstream of Château Trompette. To facilitate these transactions, some of them settled there permanently and built warehouses and houses on the banks of the river. A small Carthusian monastry nearby lent its name to this suburb which became the Chartrons district.

After a period of slow growth from the 14th to the 17th century, the suburb

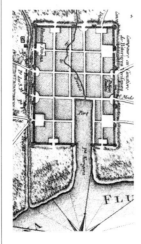

went through a time of rapid development due to the economic expansion of the 18th century. As the people of Bordeaux abandoned their traditional maritime activities, other European countries began to monopolize the wine trade. The Dutch came first, at the beginning of the 17th century, followed by the English and the Germans. They maintained their links with their own countries, remained faithful to the Protestant religion and formed a *noblesse du bouchon*, around which a community of craftsmen, sailors and servants gathered. The very cosmopolitan nature of the Chartrons was evidenced in the diversity of religions. A short distance from the former monastry (which had been replaced by the church of St-Louis), was a Calvinist church (Rue Notre-Dame), a Lutheran chapel (Rue Tourat) and the Anglican church of St-Nicolas (Cours Xavier-Arnozan).

The imposing presence of Château Trompette, separating Bordeaux from its illustrious suburb, was regarded as a hindrance. The intendants by-passed this obstacle by building promenades around the glacis, providing a link between the town and the wine quarter. At the end of the 18th century, the demolition of the fortress was envisaged, along with the construction in its place of a vast new district joining the Chartrons to the town centre. Victor Louis was the first architect to devise such an urbanization plan (1785), but the French Revolution put an end to his spectacular scenographic urban scheme. Nevertheless it was he who thought of arranging the new district around a monumental square opening onto the Garonne and the building work was started after the Napoleonic wars, when the citadel was finally demolished. Avenues lined with plane trees and a regular network of wide and narrow streets were placed on either side of the large Esplanade des Quinconces. The *négociants* quickly realized that this site was a godsend and they built new residences there, near to their *chais* and warehouses. The Chartrons were now no longer an isolated suburb and had become an important district of the town, while retaining its invisible but very real borders.[2]

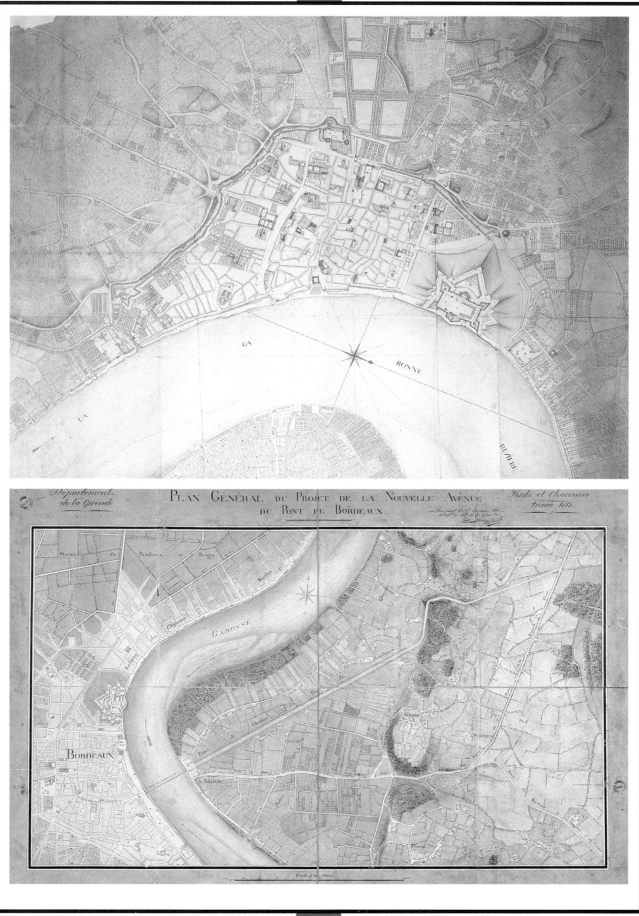

PLAN GÉNÉRAL DU PROJET DE LA NOUVELLE AVENUE DU PONT DE BORDEAUX

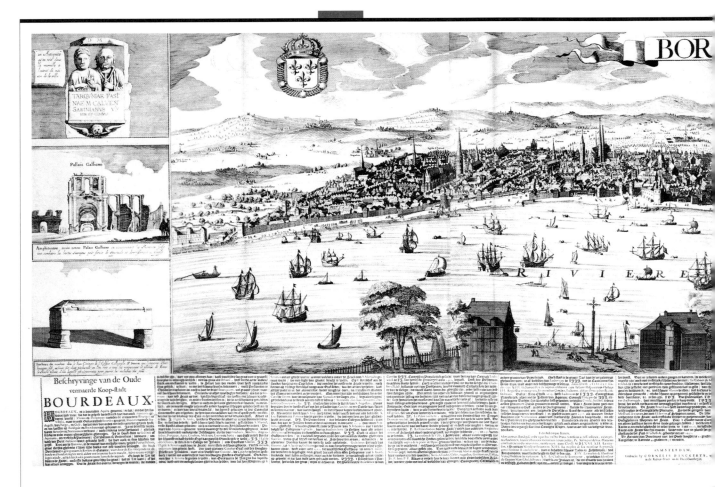

BOR

RIVIERE

Pallais Gallieno

Amphiteatre...

Beschryvinge van de Oude
vermaerde Koop-ftadt

BOURDEAUX·

ABOVE: *Bilingual engraving published in Amsterdam (Dutch, French) in the 17th century. (National archives, Paris).*

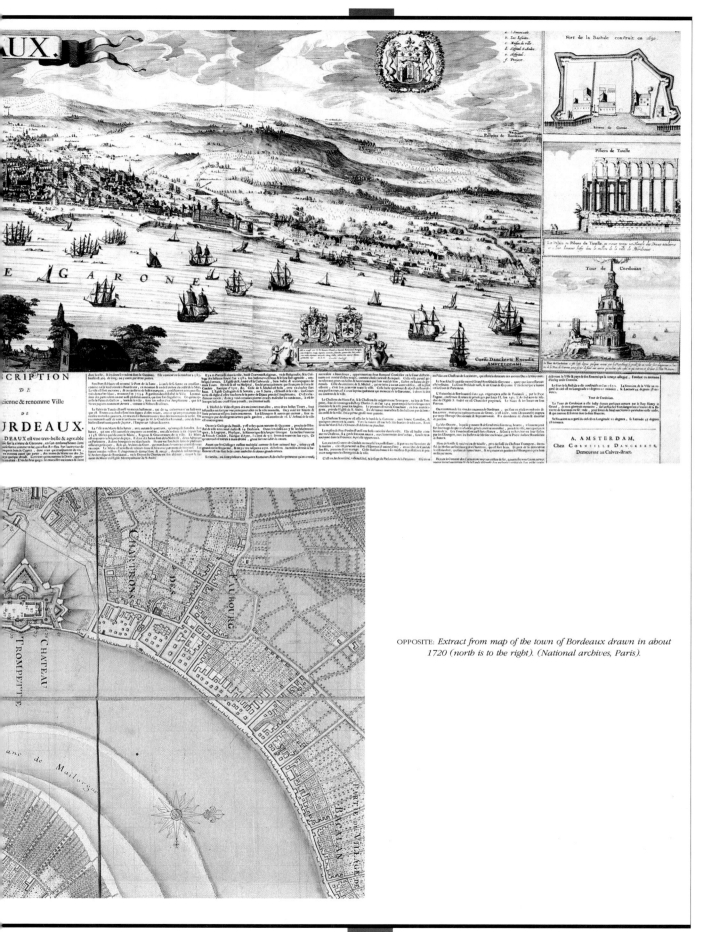

OPPOSITE: *Extract from map of the town of Bordeaux drawn in about 1720 (north is to the right). (National archives, Paris).*

PLAN
DE LA VILLE DE
BORDEAUX

A BORDEAUX,
chez
FILLASTRE FRÈRES,
Cours du Chapeau-Rouge,
Nº 4.

DIVISION OF THE LAND INTO STRIPS

The Garonne, which made the fortune of the Bordeaux vineyard, dictated the development of the Chartrons and also determined its topographic and architectural features. Access to the river was the most important requirement for the *négociants*. Thus the first line of buildings were built along the quayside and continued without break downstream. These buildings were tightly packed together and formed a continuous façade broken by only a few narrow streets that went off at right angles. In order to gain more space, archways were even put over the entrance to some streets (Ramonet, Barreyre, Poyenne, Denise) and were built on. The quarter gradually became more densely populated.

The Rue Notre-Dame was situated parallel to the quay and set back beyond it were the Chemin du Roi and the Chemin de Labarde (which became the Cours Portal and the Cours Balguerie-Stuttenberg in the 19th century). Thus, large blocks of varying dimensions were created. Within these blocks were gardens divided up into strips the width of the houses. Various sources give us the dimensions of the 16th-century buildings that determined the size of these garden plots: nine to ten metres wide (30–33 feet). The gardens extended back for about 100 metres (109 yards) to nearly 300 metres (328 yards) in some cases. Thus the division of the land into strips came about and this was to govern the architectural and urban character of the district.

A DUAL FUNCTION

The buildings most closely connected to wine in the Chartrons were for the *négociants-éleveurs* whose name reflects the twin activities carried out in the quarter. The trading function takes first place, dominating the entire economic system of the wine trade. The function of *éleveur* is more closely linked to rural life and is an extension of it in an urban medium. This enables us to understand the duality of the architecture of these buildings which combines commerce and vine growing, town and country.

The *négociant* needed a residence both for his commercial activities and his domestic life. The ideal position was on the quayside where the activity of the port was concentrated. The Pavé des Chartrons was less convenient but more elegant. If nothing better was available, his premises could be situated on the inner streets (Rue Notre-Dame, Rue Latour, Rue Raze, Rue du Couvent, etc.). These houses had to be monumental in appearance in order to satisfy a legitimate taste for comfort and as a reflection of the *négociant's* prosperity. On the other hand, these residences could not be compared in terms of grandeur with the residences of the nobility. Palaces (belonging to the Governor and Intendant – since demolished – and to the Archbishop) and mansions (belonging to the parliamentary aristocracy) were built in the old centre of the city. Wine was a trade and consequently it had to content itself with bourgeois architecture of a respectable degree of luxury but which was neither too ostentatious nor falsely modest.

The *élevage* of the wine, though it is indissociable from commerce, appears to be a subsidiary requirement. It demands a large team of craftsmen, warehousemen and plenty of space to nurture the precious wine and to store it until it is sold. The buildings in which this activity is concentrated are referred to by the generic name of "*chais*". Since they are hidden by the façades of the houses they have not received any special architectural treatment. The problems they posed were concerned with practical rather than design considerations: security, ventilation, workshops, stockrooms and passageways. The narrow confines of the division of the plots of land in strips could not be escaped. The builders of the old *chais* in the Chartrons had to come to terms with the limitation of space and were not overly concerned with architectural appearances.

A MODEST LUXURY

Until the 17th century, the residence was scarcely differentiated from the warehouse with the *négociant* keeping a few rooms above the cellar for his personal use. Drawings from the 17th century, in particular those of the Dutchman Van der Hem (active in Bordeaux from 1638–49), reconstruct for us the appearance of the buildings that ran along the river. They were heavy-looking, with thick walls, one or two storeys high and with a pointed roof covered with gutter tiles. Two examples still exist on the Quai des Chartrons. Their gables are decorated with baroque consoles and menacing faces of lions similar to those that were carved on the bows of ships.

The prosperity of the 18th century made it possible to build new houses that were more in keeping with the merchant's bourgeois lifestyle. Owing to the division of the land into strips, these houses remained narrow (two or three bays, very rarely four or five). But, they were usually two or three storeys high, reaching up to the cornice or balustrade hiding the roof. With the help of excellent stonemasons, the architects varied the design of the façades, whose decoration developed over the generations. The Rocaille style has left several examples that are decorated with picturesque masks. But up until the middle of the century, the fashion was more for austerity: the nobility of the façades was underlined by plain mouldings, pilasters with bosses and elegance was added by the wrought iron of the imposts and the railings. The Louis-XVI style gave way to all kinds of ornamental whims. Garlands and roses, medallions and ribbons, foliage and frets were used to decorate the bays. Neo-classicism saw a return to severity but it was ennobled by rigorous arcatures and impressive cornices.

It was in 1769 that the architect Etienne Laclotte, the greatest builder of his generation, produced the design for the line of similar houses that run alongside the Pavé des Chartrons. For this development, he designed an original type of façade which combined the rigid lines and garland decoration of the Louis-XVI style with the flexibility of a balcony on a squinch in a charming Rocaille style.[3]

Visitors who have been invited to the homes of *négociants* have always been struck by the elegant interiors of their

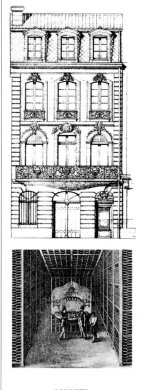

residences. On the *piano nobile*, one or two living rooms have French windows opening onto the balcony; the dining room is situated at the rear and lit by an inner courtyard. The walls are covered with painted panelling, delicately carved with Louis-XVI or Empire motifs; the fireplaces are of marble; the parquet floors are made of oak and mahogany.

The social rise of the *noblesse du bouchon* and the increasingly important role it played in municipal affairs led it, not to distance itself from commerce, but rather to separate its private life from its business interests. When the Rue d'Aviau was opened alongside the park in 1851, the leading families of the Chartrons acquired almost all the plots. Every residence was designed differently on the street side; but on the side of the park, the municipal architect, Charles Burguet, imposed a single plan of façades in the spirit of the 18th century. These residences became the official model of Bordeaux elegance, which continued to be influenced by nostalgia for its golden age.

A MOVE TOWARDS GREATER EFFICIENCY

In the Bordeaux vocabulary, the word "*chai*" has a very broad meaning. The *chais* of Bordeaux are the places where all the activities necessary for the *élevage* and sale of the wine are undertaken. They include the *caves* and warehouses, the *caveaux*, workshops for cooperage, bottling and packing for transportation, storerooms for crates, bottles and labels, as well as offices for administration purposes etc.[4]

The first *négociants* were no more than shipping agents whose job it was to export wines that had been made in the same year. The solid 17th-century houses were quite sufficient for their needs up until the 18th century when they were forced to enlarge their premises. Since the fronts of the new houses were reserved for living quarters, there was no alternative but to construct another building at the back on the far side of the courtyard and then, beyond a second courtyard, to fill in the garden with warehouses. As dictated by the division of the plots of land into strips,

LA MAISON DE NEGOCE CRUSE AU QUARTIER DES CHARTRONS A BORDEAUX

HERMAN CRUSE

ribbons of *chais* ended up covering the entire blocks. This arrangement had one advantage in terms of storage conditions: since the *chais* were stretched out beside one another and did not allow in any natural light, the temperature inside remained constant. On the other hand, solutions had to be found to the problems of moving around the *chais*, since this long chain of buildings had in general only one door at the front of the living quarters (or a second exit into a dead-end, in the case of the Pavé des Chartrons). The stairways, the corridors (confined to the ground floor of the living quarters) and the passageways gave rise to numerous different arrangements. Thus the architecture of the Chartrons quarter was achieved slowly and developed empirically without any overall planning.[5]

These structures had no architectural pretensions and the interior buildings had no decoration. However, the stairways were embellished with beautiful wrought-iron banisters, and the long bays of the warehouses, which were either vaulted with groins or emphasized with lines of perfectly dressed arches, produced an effect of mysterious grandeur.

The commercial monopoly of the old Chartrons continued until the last quarter of the 19th century. At that point, the district was expanded by the opening up of new streets (Cours de la Martinique, Cours du Médoc, Cours St-Louis) which led to large new building sites. In addition, further upstream, where the Gare St-Jean had been established, a bridge was built (the famous Eiffel bridge of 1860) which allowed the railway to cross the river and give this formerly disadvantaged area a commercial role. A large number of new firms set up premises around the Quai de Queyries and, for the first time in the history of Bordeaux, some activities of the wine trade were conducted away from the Chartrons.

Being finally freed of restrictions of space and with large areas at their disposal, the architects were able to rationalize the design of the *chais*.[6] They improved access and movement within the buildings. Modern construction techniques were used: cast-iron col-

umns, metallic lattice-work girders, electric lighting, etc. Alphonse Blaquières made the Calvet *chais* (Cours du Médoc, 1871) into a model of functionalism. However, the façades were sumptuous structures, in which use was made of ornamental features of the Beaux-Arts style. This triumphalism reached its climax when Alphonse Ricard erected a *maison de négoce* (1890), called "Château Descas", near the station. He bestowed on the façade an opulence, which with the high roofs and the luxuriant carved decorations, carried the architectural celebration of the glory of wine and its trade to their highest point.

THE FUTURE OF THE CHARTRONS

The *belle époque* was the heyday of the alliance between the wine of Bordeaux and its architecture. The 20th century has lived off this heritage without adding to it and there has been a gradual weakening of the close link between the wine and the town that gave it its name. Various inevitable developments have diluted the character of the Chartrons. Since 1924, massive projects carried out by the autonomous port authority have dramatically altered the monumental character of the quays. A line of reinforced concrete warehouses were built on the widened roadway and access to the river was blocked by iron railings. To the despair of the *négociants*, the wonderful façade of the Chartrons was cut off from the Garonne which had caused it to come into being. In the last few years, the port has moved downstream, the ships have deserted the town and the original warehouses have been left empty.

The Chartrons have suffered from the general movement away from urban centres that took place in European cities in the 1950s and 1960s. Road transport has supplanted the river and the quarter has become blocked with traffic. Lorries find it difficult to park and create obstructions that are difficult to overcome. Many *négociants* are leaving their beautiful old houses, which have become affected by noise and other forms of pollution, and moving to the peace of the residential suburbs.

Some firms have found it more convenient to establish themselves on the huge industrial sites near the motorways (Barton & Guestier at Blanquefort). These new *chais* have been designed according to the criteria of basic functionalism and are no different from the most commonplace of modern factories. The Chartrons have been deprived of their substance and the abandoned storerooms opposite the deserted quays are easy prey for property speculators.

However, some long-established and prestigious companies (de Luze, Schyler & Schröder, and, above all, Cruse), who are conscious of the commercial asset that tradition represents and of the image of quality that is associated with a historical architectural setting, attempt to convert premises in the district. Redevelopment projects for the quays and disused warehouses of the Chartrons (notably the one studied in 1988 on the initiative of the Centre Georges Pompidou, within the framework of the Châteaux Bordeaux project) have encouraged this stake in

ABOVE:
The Allées de Tourny; on the right, the Gobineau building (now the offices of the C.I.V.B.).
OPPOSITE:
The part of the Chartrons district built along the river; over a distance of nearly two kilometres, the lines of houses were initially designed to contain the offices and residences of the négociants. Behind them are the long and thin parcels of land containing the chais and warehouses.
BELOW:
Label showing the façade of the chais of a négociant.
Bottom, *inside the cellars of another company.*

the future. The construction in one of the blocks of a "Cité Internationale du Vin" could also contribute to the renaissance of the Chartrons, so long as it does not compromise its character. The architecture of the Chartrons expresses the enduring and unique nature of the wine of Bordeaux. Any modernist attempt that failed to take this into account would be a nonsense and would produce characterless buildings which would result in Bordeaux and its wine losing their identity.

1 R. Coustet, "Bordeaux ou l'originalité d'une tradition", *Archives de l'Architecture Moderne*, 1984.
2 P. Chauvreau, "La formation topographique du quartier des Chartrons", *Revue Historique de Bordeaux*, vol.XXI, 1928; vol.XXII, 1929; vol.XXIII, 1930.
3 E. Coutureau, "Le pavé des Chartrons, oeuvre d'Etienne Laclotte", *Revue Historique de Bordeaux*, 1981.
4 E. Féret, *Dictionnaire manuel du négociant en vins et spiritueux et du maître de chai*, Bordeaux, 1896.
5 A. Liquard-Gorgiard, *Les chais des Chartrons à Bordeaux*, unpublished paper, Ecole d'Architecture de Versailles, 1987.
6 N. de Maren, *Les chais bordelais du XIXe siècle*, master's degree paper, Université de Bordeaux III.

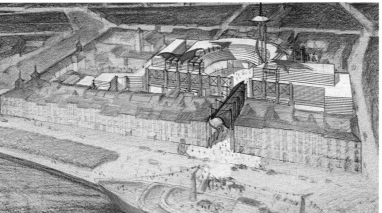

ABOVE:
The large chais of a firm in Bordeaux at the end of the 19th century.
OPPOSITE:
Prefigurative drawing of the "Cité mondiale du Vin" in the Chartrons.
BELOW:
In colour, *three drawings showing the location, the schematic structure and the scheme proposed in 1988 by*

the architect and town planner Ricardo Bofill for the restructuring of the La Bastide district opposite the Chartrons on the right bank of the river. In the middle, *diagram for the revitalization of the disused quays and warehouses in the port proposed in 1988 by the architects Reichen and Robert (see pp.206–211 for details of the project).*

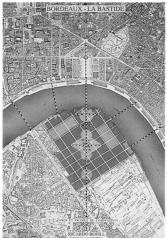

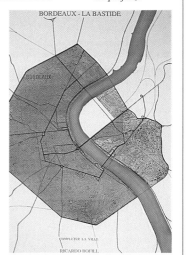

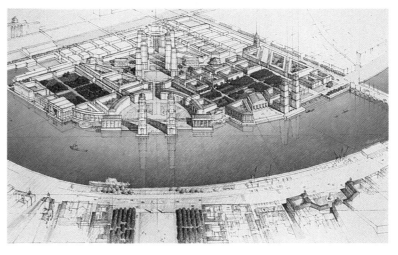

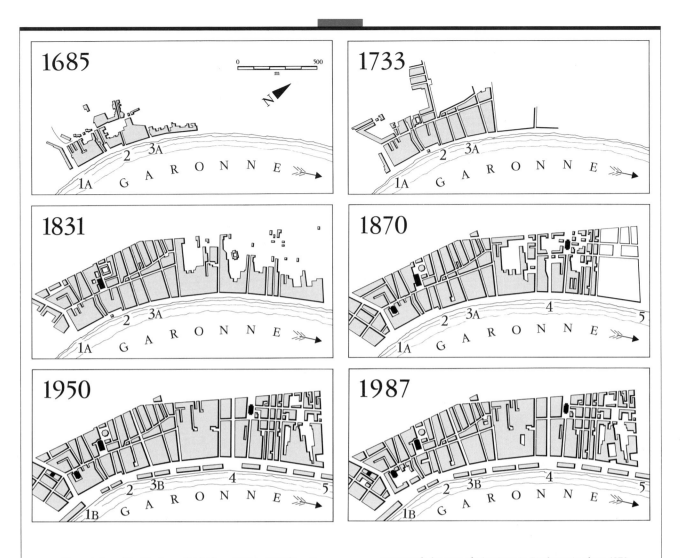

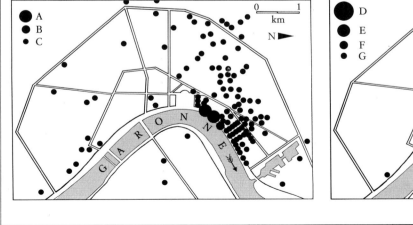

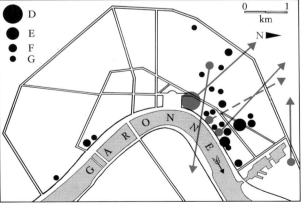

ABOVE: *The evolution of the Chartrons district from 1685 to 1987 from the plan by Masse (1685), plan by Lattre in (1733), plan by Pierrugues in (1831), archives of the département of the Gironde (1870), plan by the ministry of town planning (1950), plan by the Bordeaux town-planning agency (1987). (Cartography by Philippe Dangles, research by Françoise Clémandot).*
Key: *1A: Pavé des Chartrons; 1B: Cours Xavier Arnozan; 2: Rue Raze; 3A: Rue St-Esprit; 3B: Cours de la Martinique; 4: Cours du Médoc; 5: Rue Chantecrit.*

BELOW: Left, *location of négociants in Bordeaux in about 1970 (A: 10 négociants; B: 5 négociants; C: 1 négociant).*
BELOW: Right, *the main négociant firms in the 1970s and 1980s. D: 20–50 employees; E: 50–100 employees; F: 100–150 employees; G: more than 250 employees. In red: firms that have recently left the centre of Bordeaux and exiled themselves to the industrial suburbs. The broken lines show the relocation projects being studied for departure in the 1990s. (Cartography after Philippe Roudié).*

Château Marbuzet at St-Estèphe.

THE SPIRIT OF BORDEAUX

PORTFOLIO OF PHOTOGRAPHS BY
MICHEL GUILLARD, PARIS

Since 1978, Michel Guillard has devoted one of his talents – photography – to revealing the many aspects of the culture of the wines of Bordeaux. He has an intimate knowledge of the many landscapes, châteaux and *chais* and has become a privileged visitor of this wine-producing society – both rural and urban. The relationship he has patiently built up between himself, the men, and their vineyards can be felt in his photographs: he manages to reflect in them the magic of this corner of the wine-producing world. He presents an eloquent and inspired portrait of the spirit of the Bordeaux region. In this unique collection of photographs he has found the material for several beautiful books:

Château Lafite Rothschild at Pauillac.

Bordeaux (1981), *Médoc, presqu'île du vin* (1982), *les Charentes, pays du Cognac* (1983), *Yquem* (1985), *Couleur France* (1987) and *Château Margaux* (1988).

Since 1983 Michel Guillard has been co-editor of the famous French magazine *L'Amateur de Bordeaux*, with his wife Catherine and the journalist Jean-Paul Kauffmann. This refined publication is totally unique in its oenological and cultural approach. His desire to enlarge the scope of *L'Amateur* to feature the architecture of the wine châteaux has resulted (with the collaboration of Marc Walter) in his becoming involved in the Châteaux Bordeaux project. The Centre Georges Pompidou has also given him the diplomatic mission of enlisting sponsorship from 30 or so private individuals to help finance, with the State, this important cultural project. JEAN DETHIER

TOP: *Vineyard landscape at Baurech (Premières Côtes de Bordeaux).* BOTTOM: *The Château Canon vineyard at St-Emilion.*

The Château Lachesnaye estate at Cussac-Fort-Médoc.

Nestling in its poplar grove like a kasbah in an oasis of palm trees Château Lanessan pokes its monumental roofs and chimneys above the vegetation. It was built in the heart of the Médoc in a British-inspired style by the architect Duphot in 1875.

TOP: *Vineyard landscapes in the Sauternes region.* BOTTOM: *The surroundings of Château d'Yquem.*

The esplanade of Château Tayac overlooking the Gironde at St-Seurin-de-Bourg (Côtes de Bourg).

BORDEAUX'S PRESENT
FOR THE

AND SOME VISIONS FUTURE

THE PRESENT AND FUTURE OF WINE ARCHITECTURE

JEAN DETHIER

The most striking aspect of the Bordeaux region at the end of the 1980s is the fact that the traditional regional balance between the rural and urban aspects of the wine economy has been called into question. The acquisition of economic independence of the châteaux in recent times[1] is said to have caused a corresponding reduction in the power of the *négociants* based in Bordeaux, particularly in the Chartrons district. This famous area is increasingly resembling an immense run-down neighbourhood beside the river, while in the vineyard, new buildings and equipment are multiplying in and around the châteaux. The traditional bipolar economic structure (rural producers and urban merchants) has been replaced by a much more complex one in which the legacies of the old system coexist with the beginnings of a more efficient organization which is creating the basis for a new self-sufficiency in the châteaux. The owners of these new economic principalities tend to look after the promotion of their own wines in external markets both near and far. This situation has reinforced their awareness of their own heritage, which is increasingly being translated into investment in properties which are rarely worthy of the term architecture. But this self-awareness also tends to include a certain disaffection for their traditional economic partners, the *négociants*, and a degree of indifference with regard to the environment.

The appearance of this rural environment has badly deteriorated in the last 10, 20, or 30 years. Its wonderful landscapes have often been spoiled by numerous installations and equipment decided upon, or even devised, by the public authorities or the private sector. So many wine-producing villages and towns have been disfigured by large advertisement billboards, by electric wires and tangled telephone lines that destroy the visual and spatial coherence of the vineyard.[2] There have also unfortunately been innumerable cases of planning permission being granted for housing and various public or private buildings in sensitive vineyard sites or in their immediate vicinity.[3] However, these developments are not the inevitable result of the demands of modern life. There are many countries and regions where the conservation of the environment is a key consideration of the community. This is the case in Europe in the well-managed countryside of Britain, Ireland, Austria, Holland, Denmark and Sweden and in the United States, particularly in the Napa Valley, the most famous California vineyard.

Is it possible not to be shocked by the sight of the gigantic oil installation built at Pauillac between the river (with its autonomous port) and the vines of the châteaux that are famous around the world? This is an unfortunate eyesore in terms of the harmony and ecology of the vineyard. We should therefore be relieved that a part of the installation (built in the 1920s and 1930s) for refining oil was dismantled in 1988, to be moved outside the Bordeaux region. However, the company responsible intends to retain the gigantic metal vats for the storage of its huge regional stocks of gas and oil. Their presence at the heart of the Médoc has led some critics to call this site "Château Shell" – an irony that reveals one of the aspects of the territorial conflict between the vineyard and industrial urbanization.

Just as damaging from the point of view of the noble culture and heritage of the region was the decision taken in 1988 to demolish the beautiful neo-classical structure of the (disused) wine château of Piétru on the Ambès peninsular[4] (despite the fact that it was about to be classified as a historical monument) so as to make room for heavy industry on this former *palus* vineyard. The remains of this château could at least have been partially transferred to another site in order to create, for example, an open-air regional museum of architecture, such as exists in northern Europe (even though none has yet been devoted to the architecture of wine production). As for the fine, late 18th-century neo-classical château in the former wine-producing estate of Alty at St-Louis-de-Montferrand (in the same region of

the Bec d'Ambès), it was acquired by the same administration and knowingly abandoned and finally dismembered by vandals around 1980.

But the project that has been most discussed in the region recently concerns the establishment 15 kilometres (9 miles) to the south of Bordeaux of a "technopolis", i.e., a vast urban zone created from nothing and intended to accommodate around "service centres" the "latest technologies in various areas of research, innovation and production". This ambitious project to change the infrastructure of the region is called "Bordeaux-Technopolis" and aspires to be "a melting pot in which an essential raw material – intelligence – is concentrated." In 20 or 30 years, this scientific park should cover an area of 1,200 hectares (4.5 square miles) in the communes of Léognan, Martillac, Labrède and Saucats. It is to be situated between Château de La Brède, the historical and wine-producing residence of the political philosopher Montesquieu, and Château La Louvière, another famous wine-producing estate, belonging to André Lurton. The latter started a lively argument with the authorities in 1987 because he thinks, along with other people, that this project will take up land that is of potential interest to vine growing in this famous region of the Graves. It is to be hoped that all the intelligence involved in this giant project and in its bordering territories will be able to avoid this new example of the conflict between vineyard and urbanization.

LACK OF TOURIST FACILITIES IN THE VINEYARD

Having made the majestic trip across the Gironde in a ferry (between Blaye and Lamarque), the visitor might expect, when reaching the privileged territory of the Médoc, to find a pleasant shore, a symbolic gateway of welcome. However, all that is to be found is a dreary esplanade surrounded by huts and ruined buildings. In addition, the roads often lack any helpful signposting to indicate the way to the vineyards (in particular the Médoc vineyard from the direction of Bordeaux) and in general fail to point out interesting circuits for the wine tourist.[5] As for those who wish to sightsee by other means, e.g. bicycle,[6] river,[7] foot, horse, hot-air balloon or aeroplane,[8] they will unfortunately be disappointed in their fruitless attempt to explore the heart of the Bordeaux region.

The territory does, however, offer great potential for all types of tourism, but they have not yet been developed. Fortunately, in 1990, the T.G.V. (French very high-speed train) will reach the town of Bordeaux. This could lead to the revitalization of a dense regional railway network covering some hundred kilometres of wine-producing *terroirs* in which all the stations have prestigious names:

Margaux, Pauillac, Moulis, Barsac, Lalande-de-Pomerol, St-Emilion, Pessac, Blaye. However the outstanding tourist and economic opportunities presented by a regional wine train[9] are not being considered by the national State railway company or local authorities. Despite the fact that the railway infrastructure of the region is obviously underused, this institution has, however, begun to recognize the new opportunity represented by wine tourism.[10] To develop this type of activity requires a degree of cooperation and an infrastructure designed within the terms of a national and regional development policy and involving the participation of the many interested parties particularly those in the hotel and catering industry. It has to be admitted that the Bordeaux vineyard is fairly ill-equipped, as far as welcoming tourists is concerned. With a few exceptions (which fortunately are spread throughout the various areas and price bands), the range of services provides a remarkable contrast with the quality and international reputation of the wines. Some hoteliers in the centre of Bordeaux[11] are becoming concerned about the huge gap between the limited facilities on offer and the existing or potentially considerable demand.

Thus, wine tourism, which could provide considerable impetus towards a re-establishment of the balance between town and country in the Bordeaux region, does not yet seem to have been really taken into consideration, despite the benefits and what is at stake. On the other hand, the natural heritage of the remarkable landscapes of the Bordeaux vineyard is increasingly under threat.[12] If the serious deterioration to which it is victim is not quickly dealt with by credible and effective measures, the very potential for economic development based on viticultural tourism will be affected.

THE DECLINE OF TOWN PLANNING IN THE WINE WORLD

Changes in the urban nature of wine production may be detected within a development whose contradictions are only apparent: the clear growth in urbanization (around the built-up area of Bordeaux and other towns involved in the wine trade) and the progressive exclusion of the urban centre from the viticultural activity of the region. The town of Bordeaux had about 125,000 inhabitants in the 1920s and 1930s; today the urban district of Bordeaux comprises more than 600,000 inhabitants and covers 26 outlying communes. At the heart of this territorial expansion (which is visually often very confused), at the very centre of the metropolis of Bordeaux, a process of decline has started in the two main aspects of its economy: the ancient river port and the wine district of the Chartrons. The former is in such a state of abandonment that in 1987 the authorities dismantled almost all the huge cranes – the monumental vestiges of the past glory of this great urban port – from along the ancient urban quays. In the town centre, only the occasional presence of tourist cruise ships serves as a reminder of its former maritime role. As with so many other old ports in urban centres, the new port has been moved downstream. As a result, the dozen huge concrete warehouses built in the 1920s and 1930s (between the architectural façade of the historic centre and the river) are today only empty shells, most of which have no new role.[13] This image of economic decline at the centre of the regional capital is, unfortunately, made worse by the disused image of the Chartrons district which covers a distance of about two kilometres (one and a quarter miles) by the old port.

Numerous factors have contributed in the last 30 years to the decline in the power and importance of the activities of the wine trade, which had been centred in this district of Bordeaux since the 17th century. In particular, the effects of the diminished or transformed role of the *négociants* have combined with various factors concerning the changing urban structure. The wine that used to be transported by ship is now carried on lorries which are faced with serious parking and delivery problems in the network of narrow and overcrowded streets. In addition, since the present layout of the *maisons de négoce* is narrow and restricting,[14] the possibility of converting them *in situ* to meet the new requirements for modern equipment is considerably reduced. These factors, and others have led to an exodus of many of the large trading houses to the suburbs, where they are dispersed among the mass of general industry. This anonymity is reinforced by the options (or rather, the lack of them) these firms have with regard to the architecture of their new premises – ordinary factories with no distinctive outer sign of their viticultural role. There is a total loss of identity here, which is aggravated by the fact that these firms are no longer supported by the historical prestige of the Chartrons district. It is as if the language used for tasting the wines of Bordeaux had been suddenly replaced by a vocabulary that was limited to a few words of a language as basic as Esperanto.[15]

Fortunately, some recent projects give grounds for hope that there will be at least a partial reversal of the tendency to impoverish a district that was once so rich. In the 1970s, at the southern end of the Chartrons, towards the town centre, the Lainé warehouses, which were built at the beginning of the 19th century in an industrial neo-classical style, were converted in an exemplary way into a regional centre of art and modern culture (ignoring, however, the regional and *a fortiori* wine-producing culture). Just opposite, in the oldest block of the Chartrons along the river, the building of a large complex which will be the headquarters of the "Cité Mondiale du Vin" was started in 1987. Although its architecture is questionable, this project (which is competing with others that are equally ambitious at Paris-Bercy and Osaka) should be considered as a sign of the desire to revitalize activities linked to the wine trade in the Chartrons. But will this artificial graft be a success?

As yet, there has been no public debate concerning a vital project of urban and socio-economic planning to revitalize this entire wine district, which remains the largest in France (since the destruction of its counterpart in Paris, the Bercy district). In the absence of such a development, the decline of the Chartrons continues, encouraging the relocation of firms that are resolved to survive there or elsewhere. This is the case notably for the firm of Cruse, which was founded in 1819, and which urgently needs to find new premises in the Chartrons or else to consider – against its will – being exiled to the industrial suburbs.

Similarly, the de Luze company (founded in the Chartrons by a Swiss baron in 1820) urgently needs to adopt a new business strategy entailing important decisions about its location, premises and architecture. It can either remain in Bordeaux and establish itself there permanently (with the considerable advantage of having 30,000 square metres/36,000 square yards of land in the middle of the Chartrons), which entails becoming integrated, with the agreement of the authorities, in a comprehensive plan of long and short term redevelopment in the district; or it can leave Bordeaux for good and move into new buildings. Like Cruse, de Luze would no doubt prefer to stay in the Chartrons.

THE CONFLICT BETWEEN THE TOWN AND THE VINEYARD

Outside Bordeaux is a suburb where five wine châteaux have survived in the prestigious *terroir* of the Graves.[16] Whereas vines used to surround the town until the 19th century, the anarchic urbanization that has been invading this land over the last century or so has destroyed the image of an idyllic balance between town and countryside (which now only survives in St-Emilion). Only a few islands of vines remain in a rising tide of houses.

This is why the first château in the world to be designed for the purpose of wine production, the venerable Haut-Brion, built in 1525, now finds that the entire perimeter of its 45-hectare (110 acres) vineyard is surrounded by an unplanned environment of unattractive suburban homes and buildings. A booklet published by Château Haut-Brion itself gives us the following surprising information: "In 1934, André Gilbert (a banker and owner of the château since 1922), intended to offer Haut-Brion to

the Bordeaux town council on condition that they undertook to maintain the vineyard in perpetuity. This must have seemed far too long a time to the town authorities because the proposition was rejected".[17] It was the American banker Clarence Dillon who bought Haut-Brion in 1934 and the star-spangled banner has been flying at the entrance to the estate ever since.

But now we have a situation where the classiest of the ancient châteaux is surrounded by the most ordinary urban landscape! This curious urbanizing revenge by the middle classes on the wine-producing aristocracy could have been done in a stylish way by the use of architecture of a harmonious quality around the last vineyards in the built-up area of Bordeaux – the last vestiges of a wonderful rural landscape in an urban medium, a situation that is unique in the world.

We can therefore dream[18] of a development in the heart of the built-up area of Bordeaux which, *in extremis*, would manage to safeguard its wine-producing Central Park or Regent's Park, the upkeep of which would not cost the community anything. In the absence of such "agro-urban" creativity, we may deplore the spectacle of tens of old wine châteaux around Bordeaux that have been abandoned or are even in a state of ruin. Even the one that is managed by the State, at Blanquefort in the northern suburbs, as an agricultural college for wine production – the 18th-century Château Dillon – is badly dilapidated. How can the authorities hope to instill a respect for their own heritage in the future wine professionals who are training there?

There are only very few examples of disused wine châteaux being converted in an intelligent manner into public buildings (town halls, etc.) or private ones (hotels, etc.). The most interesting case is the conversion of Château Cordeillan-Bages, an old wine château outside Pauillac, into a luxury hotel. At Blanquefort, the commune has acquired the estate of the old Château Dulamon: the huge residence has been transformed into an educational establishment and its spectacular grounds (with their artificial grottos) have become a public park at the very gates of Bordeaux.

THE EFFECTS OF THE OENOLOGICAL REVOLUTION ON PROPERTY

Since the 1970s, the oenological revolution, which originated in Bordeaux, has, like other factors mentioned later, had a direct effect on many wine-producing estates. The increased practice of bottling "au château" and the need to treat and preserve the increased quantities of wine produced by improved techniques have made it necessary to increase the capacity, of the *cuviers*, the *chais* and the storerooms.

The new oenology thus contributed to the

THE RENAISSANCE OF THE WINE CHATEAUX BETWEEN 1970 AND 1980

In the 1970s and 1980s several wine châteaux in the Bordeaux region undertook extensive and ambitious conversion work. This redevelopment was intended to highlight their architecture and their modern wine-making installations. Châteaux Canon, Castéra, Figeac, Mission Haut-Brion, Lafite Rothschild, La Louvière, Lascombes, Lynch-Bages, Margaux, Mouton Rothschild, Phélan Ségur, Yquem and Pichon-Longueville-Comtesse de Lalande are notable examples of this new wave of wine architecture.

The latter is particularly significant as it has involved a decade of renovation work to modernize this great wine château to meet modern needs whilst still remaining faithful to the regional tradition. Pichon-Longueville is situated in Pauillac and covers an area of 72 hectares (178 acres). It was classified as a second-growth grand cru in 1855 and has been in the family of May-Eliane de Lencquesaing since 1925 (the latter took over the running of the estate with her husband in 1978). The elegant château, built with ochred stone by the architect Duphot in 1840, is surrounded by beautiful and romantic gardens which border on the

famous "Route des Châteaux". This château is one of the few in the Médoc which is permanently inhabited by its owners. From 1979–1989 the château's owners have undertaken an extensive modernization programme to celebrate the tricentenary of this renowned vineyard. The scheme devised by the Mazières architects from Bordeaux encompasses the entire property and more than 3,500 square metres (4,200 square yards). Several of the original 19th-century buildings have been renovated and some new elements have also been cleverly interwoven into the existing structure in order to extend and modernize the wine-making installations. The new, semi-underground chais constitute the focal point of the scheme. More than 2,000 barrels can be arranged in an architecturally dramatic area which is 80 metres (260 feet) long and punctuated by a spectacular row of columns. A vast terrace has been built above the chais to extend the area for receiving visitors. From here the onlooker can best appreciate the whole château complex within the setting of the Gironde landscape and one of the most prestigious vineyard sites in France.

demand for building work in numerous châteaux where no architectural initiatives had been taken for two or three generations. Hence the sometimes rather improvised nature of the extensions built. Too many châteaux suddenly surrounded themselves with new buildings which were not really in keeping with the quality environment necessary for the maintenance or regeneration of their prestigious cultural image. These expansion problems have too often been solved solely in terms of functional and technical efficiency and without assessing their architectural significance. In the château, the advice of the best oenologists was secured but when new buildings were constructed, the equivalent specialist advice was very rarely sought. These short-term plans had a devaluing effect on the overall harmony of the vineyard.

Fortunately, some owners cared about establishing a balance between their historical and architectural heritage and the modern necessities of new machinery. Many of them have, perhaps by instinct, not attempted to create a visual relation between the old and new buildings. This approach, which is curious in that it is without precedent around Bordeaux, seems to have been devised in 1972 at Château Haut-Brion by the architect R. Morin, who started the practice of installing new *chais* entirely underground. The same solution was adopted by the Mazières architects in various châteaux: the new *chais* at Margaux, Yquem and Pichon-Longueville-Comtesse de Lalande. In 1988, the new *chai* designed by the architect Ricardo Bofill for Château Lafite Rothschild was finished. His design produces a theatrical arrangement of piled-up barrels in concentric curves around the halo of a central "well of light". Above the large underground reinforced-concrete cellar more rows of the precious vineyard will soon be planted.

However, this desire to modernize the *chais* started in the 1920s and 1930s with Philippe de Rothschild's decision to redesign Château Mouton by inventing – thanks to the talents of the theatre architect Charles Siclis – a new theatrical design for the place where the wine was matured and a

prestigious setting where he could invite his guests. Half a century later, this innovative design continues to attract attention. The alterations carried out to the *chais* at Cos d'Estournel may be interpreted in the following way. A clever use of light creates the objective and affective conditions for the "scenographic presentation of wine" which simply creates an atmosphere of beauty and contemplation: a sort of wine mysticism.

A common feature of many new *chais* is that they religiously continue to use oak barrels for the *élevage* and ageing of the wine. Here the contributions of popular ancient tradition have been reconciled with the recommendations of the new science of wine: a miraculous harmony between the legacy of history and the ambitions of modernity, between cultural heritage and technological efficiency. In almost all modern *cuviers*, there has been a clear evolution through successive generations in the manufacture of the *cuves*. Originally they were all made of oak, then cement appeared, followed by metal. Since the 1970s and 1980s, they have mostly been made of stainless steel. Some châteaux equipped in this way did not want to destroy their old wooden vats and keep them simply as a reminder of their past, as at Château Lynch-Bages. These rooms are then used for receiving guests or wine tasting. Other owners have remained faithful to traditional methods by continuing to use wooden vats today; the architect Lee has managed to make very harmonious use of them in his work at Château Canon. Others again, for example at Margaux, Lafite or Montrose, try to reconcile the use of wooden vats (placed in full view) with that of stainless steel ones (positioned more discreetly). This provides the topic for a debate that

LEFT: *Label with architectural motif from the Sterling Vineyards in California.*
RIGHT: *Label used from 1966 onwards by Robert Mondavi. "Robert Mondavi is a great lord of the vineyard. His wines are the best in America. His winery is a magnificent building in the Spanish mission style and is the most elegant and most classic piece of wine architecture in California". Philippine de Rothschild, owner of Château Mouton Rothschild at Pauillac (Médoc) in "Paris Match", September 1988.*

STERLING VINEYARDS®

ESTATE BOTTLED

1983
Napa Valley
PINOT NOIR
ALCOHOL 13.5% BY VOLUME
PRODUCED AND BOTTLED BY
ROBERT MONDAVI WINERY
OAKVILLE, CALIFORNIA

is all the more interesting in that it is not limited to factors of oenological technology but takes account of elements of a sentimental, cultural or even presentational nature.

However, this debate has not yet been concluded. This is why the owner often remains limited to merely lining up these *cuves* in two (or four) parallel rows, more reminiscent of the efficiency of a commercial dairy than the prestige of a wine château. In recent modification work, there has often been a lack of the cultural reflection that is necessary to confer more urbanity and dignity on this birth place of the great wines. We might also expect the rooms designated for visitor's wine tasting to be more grandiose in order to make the ritual appear more sacred.

Some châteaux have tried to increase their cultural and artistic role by establishing private museums that are open to the public. This is true of some fairly modest châteaux (Mongenan at Portets) and some *crus bourgeois* (Maucaillou in the Médoc) as well as those that are very well-known, such as Château Mouton Rothschild, which has an admirable collection of old *objets d'art* based on the theme of wine. In addition, outside the field of viticulture, facilities for sporting activities with aristocratic connotations can also be found in the Médoc châteaux: polo at Château Giscours and a collection of horse carriages at Lanessan and Malleret.

The improvement of the cultural image of the châteaux is also the result of the fact that, over the last decade, many have had their façades cleaned by sandblasting: they have thus regained the radiant beauty of the ochre yellow stone that is typical of the region. This rejuvenating treatment has occasionally been accompanied by other restoration work, such as at Château Margaux or Château Figeac. The improvements to the exteriors of the châteaux have sometimes been extended to the interiors, with furniture being restored and decorations carried out in keeping with the style of the building. For example, in Châteaux Loudenne, Cérons or Margaux, where there are wonderful examples of Empire furniture. Some châteaux, such as Lascombes at Margaux, have recently had alterations done in order to be better equipped for receiving visitors, which reveals a new departure in public relations in the vineyard.

All this progress should not obscure the fact that there are still some outstanding châteaux (inhabited and producing wine) which are in a lamentable condition. This is unfortunately true of the magnificent Château L'Hospital (18th-century) at Portets in the Graves. Here the Swiss proprietor has allowed this architectural masterpiece to fall into a state of decay that is quite inadmissible.

Some of the old châteaux have recently acquired a new fame. At the heart of the Tursan vineyard to the south of Bordeaux, in the Landes, Michel Guérard, the famous chef, and his wife Christine, decided in 1987 to assign the architects Jean de Gastines and Patrick Dillon the task of installing new *chais* and *cuviers* at Château de Bachen.[19] The result is a particularly pleasing marriage of oenology and architecture, of efficiency and theatricality and of culture and economy.

This same concern for presenting an image of refinement has led other Bordeaux châteaux to redesign their grounds and gardens – around a large landscape garden at Mouton Rothschild, at Lagrange and at less well-known estates, whose cultural efforts are all the more remarkable. This is also the case at Château Castéra at St-Germain-d'Esteuil in the Médoc, where English landscape designers began work in 1987.

Conversely, the harmony of magnificent châteaux situated in areas of great natural beauty is being threatened. One of these (at St-Yzans-de-Médoc) has built military-looking lodgings for its staff in its immediate surroundings and massive *cuves* for storing wine beside the river which – on the site of an old and charming little port – gives the château the unfortunate appearance of a factory. Perhaps these mistakes, which are difficult and expensive to put right, are due to the fact that this château is managed from abroad by a foreign company which is not very sensitive to the spirit of the Bordeaux vineyard where one of its distant properties is located? This question is all the more serious because of the increasing number of châteaux owned by institutional investors whose head office is in Paris, London, Montreal or Tokyo. Fortunately there are also some remarkable examples of the participation of companies from outside the Bordeaux region to improve efficiency. We shall see later that this is true of Château Pichon-Longueville,[20] with the collaboration of the AXA insurance company which is based in Paris and has acquired a majority shareholding in this famous vineyard.

However, the now multinational character of investment in the vineyard is a two way process: although Château Haut-Brion has been bought by Americans, various Frenchmen including people from Bordeaux have purchased American vineyards, particularly in California's Napa Valley, which we will examine by way of a comparison between the two wine cultures. In fact, this wine-producing region is the only other where, during the 1960s, 1970s and 1980s, the concept of a type of architecture that is specific to wine has been widely put into practice. However we should also remember, although this is outside the present subject, that the conditions for regional economic development (the basis of all property investment)

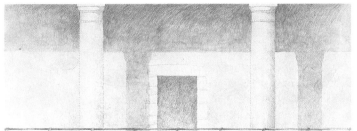

Drawings by the architects Jean de Gastines and Patrick Dillon for the redevelopment in 1989 of the chais and cuviers at Château de Bachen in the heart of the Tursan vineyard, south of Bordeaux.

FOLLOWING DOUBLE PAGE: *The new underground second-year chai designed by the architect Ricardo Bofill at Château Lafite (Pauillac) at the request of Eric de Rothschild. Completed in 1987.*

THE CREATION OF AN UNDERGROUND MECCA IN THE MEDOC

CONVERSATIONS WITH ERIC DE ROTHSCHILD, OWNER
OF CHATEAU LAFITE AND WITH
THE ARCHITECT RICARDO BOFILL, THE DESIGNER
OF HIS NEW UNDERGROUND CHAI

CONVERSATION WITH ERIC DE ROTHSCHILD

Jean Dethier: What were your reasons behind the construction of a new *chai* in 1982?

Eric de Rothschild: There were two main reasons that justified this project. On the one hand, as everyone knows, the modern techniques brought about by the application of oenology have resulted in an increase in yields and in greater consistency in harvests. On the other hand, we now store more wines at the château and we keep them for much longer than before. It therefore seemed indispensible to build a new "second-year" *chai*.

JD: As an owner how did you reach your decision?

EdR: There was a long and slow evolution in our thinking. We first thought of only carrying out limited alterations by building various extensions wherever possible. There was a real temptation to tinker in this way so as to keep the costs down. But the desire for efficiency soon gained the upper hand, resulting in the planning of a completely new project.

JD: What factors did you consider to define the requirements for the project?

EdR: I wanted to store nearly 2,000 barrels in the *chai* in the most efficient way possible, so as to make the greatest possible economies – in the available space – in terms of the time and energy involved in the various wine-making operations. This idea led me to consider a square plan but with the barrels arranged in circles. In the end, along with Ricardo Bofill, I opted for an intermediate solution: the octagon.

JD: How did the idea for an underground *chai* come about?

EdR: I was anxious for the temperature of the *chai* to be constant and self-regulated without having to resort to the artificial and unnatural techniques of air-conditioning. This was a question of ethics as well as common sense. In addition, considering the value of wine-producing land, I envisaged burying the building, covering it with two or three metres of soil and replanting vines on top.

JD: How did you set about choosing an architect?

EdR: First of all I asked local architects to do some sketches, but they lacked something. I thus realized the problem was a difficult one to solve and that only a very skillful design could address the main aspect of the project, that of the internal space. Then in 1984, I hit upon the name of my friend Ricardo Bofill.

JD: How did you collaborate with him?

EdR: We enjoyed a friendly exchange of ideas and spent many fascinating weekends at Lafite planning the successive phases of the project.

JD: Your new *chai* has provoked a lot of enthusiastic comments from visitors on account of the theatricality of the setting and the dramatic presentation of the barrels. Was this one of the effects you were looking for?

EdR: Not really, not directly. I would prefer to see it as the mystique of the place, the translation into physical form of our wine ethic. But this circular, and therefore central, arrangement has one very great advantage: it saves a great deal of manpower. Four times a year, nearly 2,000 barrels have to be moved. With 50 metres (164 feet) less movement per barrel, this amounts to a saving of nearly 300 kilometres (186 miles) of barrel-rolling every year.

JD: In your opinion is the future of fine wines a cultural one?

EdR: All refinement is cultural. The enjoyment of wine is similar to the appreciation of architecture. And the building of this *chai* with Ricardo has given me a great deal of pleasure.

JD: Which recent pieces of wine architecture do you find interesting in the Bordeaux region or abroad?

EdR: I have not yet visited Clos Pégase – so I shall reserve my opinion about it – but, apart from that, nothing really caught my eye in California. In southwest France, the current project by Michel Guérard's architects seem very interesting.[1]

CONVERSATION WITH RICARDO BOFILL

Jean Dethier: What were the various phases of study in this project?

Ricardo Bofill: The internal design of the underground building was defined at the start of the project, without any later modifications. This was possible because Eric had a specification that was very demanding and precise, which was stimulating for the creative process. I immediately attached a great deal of importance to studying the setting to ensure that it was suitable. By playing with the light, particularly the light I had filtering in from the centre of the structure, I wanted to create an atmosphere of semi-darkness.

JD: How did you decide on the exterior architectural form of this underground cellar, which was going to have an entrance in the hillside?

RB: The were two projects in this respect. I perhaps got the inspiration for the first from the powerful pieces of architecture that Vauban has built in the region, particularly at Fort Médoc. I had imagined a large supporting wall with a batter – at an angle – framed by two monumental stairways. Eric expressed the fear that this white concrete wall, which would face south, might absorb too much heat and upset the temperature balance inside the *chai*. I said to Eric: "In terms of aesthetics, I don't agree with you, but technically-speaking you are obviously right." We therefore adopted the second solution: an entrance cut into the side of the hill and bordered by two large supporting walls converging towards the entrance to the *chai*.

JD: Did you know that one of your former colleagues is co-winner of one of the architectural consultations organized for the Châteaux Bordeaux exhibition and that – along with his associate Jean de Gastines[2] – he is going to build a remarkable piece of architecture at Pichon-Longueville at Pauillac, near your own *chai*?

RB: No, I didn't know. Who is it?

JD: Patrick Dillon.[2]

RB: That's wonderful. I am very pleased for him. He worked with me for nearly ten years. He's a very talented architect . . . .

1 The new *chais* and *cuviers* at Château de Bachen were designed by Jean de Gastines and Patrick Dillon.
2 See the biographical notes on Ricardo Bofill, Jean de Gastines and Patrick Dillon at the end of the book.

are very different in the two vineyards, as financial investment in the Napa Valley has been greatly encouraged because of its tax privileges (tax shelters). In short, until 1986, it was possible to shelter considerable sums of money in the California vineyard.

THE CALIFORNIA CHALLENGE

To the north of San Francisco is the Napa Valley and in 1988, it celebrated the 150th anniversary of the first planting of vineyards by European emigrants. Germans, Italians, French and other pioneers created estates where the architecture of the buildings was inspired by the traditions of their respective countries. There are thus about 50 wine "châteaux" that give evidence of the architectural eclecticism of the 19th century. Prohibition (1919-33) caused a slowing down – and even a halt – to this development. It only resumed again in the 1970s, at about the same time as the oenological renaissance of the Bordeaux vineyard. The comparison between these two wine cultures is therefore interesting.

Numerous estates in the Napa Valley have been recently created by well-known media personalities: the widow of Walt Disney, film-makers or architects as famous as Coppola or Turnbull, families renowned for their private collections of contemporary art, such as that of Jan and Mitsuko Schrem and many others. These new arrivals have provoked a spirit of fierce competition in their efforts to create ambitious state-of-the-art wineries. Thus, by very different means, these wine producers rediscovered a spirit similar to the historical conditions that prevailed in the Bordeaux region in the 18th and 19th centuries. They too recognized the vital necessity of combining a cultural and architectural strategy with an oenological strategy to promote fine wines.

In 1966, Robert Mondavi was the first to illustrate this viticultural renewal by creating, at Oakville, an ambitious winery which seems to recreate the famous California missions built by Spanish priests in the 16th century. The reception buildings are arranged in a V-shape around a large

green, which is extended into the vineyard towards the surrounding hills. It is a place of harmonious tranquility to which Margrit Biever, Robert Mondavi's wife, has added a cultural note. She organizes art exhibitions there and a jazz festival which is now famous. It is also a place of gastronomic pilgrimage where the best French chefs are invited: Guérard, Bocuse, Chapel, Troisgros etc.

Since 1985, a joint oenological venture has been set up between California and the Bordeaux region, between the Napa and the Médoc. The Mondavi winery and Château Mouton Rothschild have jointly created an up-market wine called "Opus One". On the label are the twin silhouettes of the late Philippe de Rothschild and of Robert Mondavi; since 1966 the labels on all his bottles of wine have shown the image of his winery.[21]

Then, in 1972, Peter Newton built the Sterling Vineyards winery. Here he introduced the radically new concept of receiving visitors in the buildings where the wine is made. *Chais* and *cuviers*, work rooms and storage rooms – nearly all of them can be visited like a living museum designed specifically for entertaining considerable numbers of visitors (200,000 in 1985).

The winery is organized to absorb the flow of visitors in an independent, one-way circuit, with useful information supplied at various points. This innovatory idea is translated into the architecture of the building by the creation of two distinct levels. Only the top level, which has galleries and balconies, is accessible to the public, and thus for the first time the theatrical effect of a museum is applied to viticultural architecture. This self-guided tour consists of a route (lasting about half an hour) that alternates between intimate views of the winery and grandiose views of the untouched vineyard landscape of the Napa Valley. The position of the winery, not in the valley, but rather on a peaceful hill

OPPOSITE: *Exterior and interior view of the chais and cuviers of the winery run jointly by Messrs. Turnbull (who designed them) and Johnson at Oakville in the Napa Valley.*

BELOW: *Project for the reconstruction for Château Dauzac at Labarde (Médoc), drawn in 1985 by the French architect Olivier Fougerat-La Bertussie, at the request of the owners, Félix and Hervé Chatellier.*

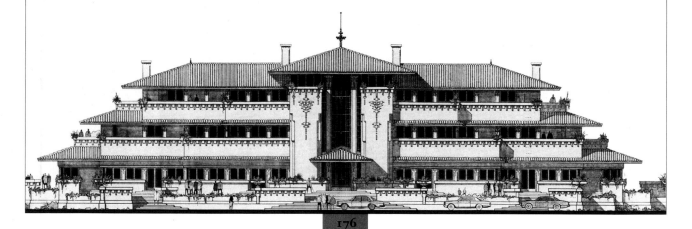

Clos Pégase, the most prestigious wine building in the United States. The owners of this Napa Valley vineyard Jan and Mitsuko Schrem organized a national architectural competition to ensure the best possible design. The winner was Michael Graves, considered to be one of the leading lights of the post-modern trend in America. The buildings and residence on the hill were finished in Calistoga in 1987. This winery is now a major tourist attraction in California.

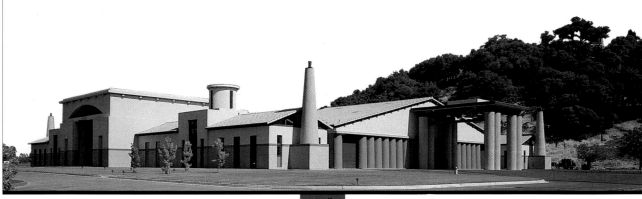

TOP: *Arranged around an inner garden are;* left, *the monumental entrance portal and* above, *the building containing the wooden vats.* BOTTOM: Below, *the façade of the building containing the stainless-steel vats with its two wings (offices and service buildings), as seen from the road.* Left, *the same façade seen at an angle with the reception wing and the offices (in the foreground). The reception rooms, which are in the background, are not visible here.*

that rises some 60 metres (197 feet) above the vineyard, has made necessary the installation of a small cable-car – costing five dollars – to provide access to this Mecca of wine production.

In this way, the new commercial and cultural concept of wine has been formulated into a coherent whole. It creates a strong brand image based on architecture and theatrical effect, in which modern methods of production and a harmonious landscape are skilfully combined.

Next door to Sterling Vineyards, also at Calistoga, is Clos Pégase, which derives its name from a work by the Bordeaux painter Odilon Redon (1840-1916) which Jan and Mitsuko Schrem keep in their collection of modern art. Concerned about art and architectural excellence, they launched a major architectural competition to produce the best scheme for Clos Pégase. Among the competitors were Ricardo Bofill (who, immediately afterwards, built the *chai* at Château Lafite-Rothschild at Pauillac) and Patrick Dillon (who, along with Jean de Gastines, went on to create the new installations for wine production at Château de Bachen in the Landes and Château Pichon-Longueville at Pauillac).

The design that was chosen and built was the one put forward by Michael Graves – one of the leading lights of post-modern architecture in the United States. His architectural scheme refers to European influences in two ways: Italy in its choice of warm chromatic harmonies from the villas of Tuscany, and France in the spirit of the design, which bears a resemblance to the Bordeaux wine château. At the top of an impressive hill is the beautiful owner's residence, with its Japanese gardens, the private museum and the guest house. At the foot of the hill, on the edge of the vineyard, the *chais* and *cuviers* are situated, along with the reception and administrative buildings. The whole complex, which is both powerful and elegant, immediately strikes the visitor as being the epitome of a beautiful winery. Thus, for an estimated cost of between 10 and 15 million dollars,[22] Clos Pégase represents an essential contribution to the renaissance of viticultural architecture.

THE NAPA PATCHWORK

Other recent California wineries, having less means at their disposal, also present interesting examples of wine architecture, making happy use of the American tradition of wooden constructions. This is true of the buildings designed by the architect Turnbull (from San Francisco) both for Cakebread Cellars and for his associate (a lawyer) and himself at the Johnson and Turnbull Winery. These functional and economic wine-producing buildings also reveal the architect's concern for creating an air of refinement. There are many other recent wine-producing

buildings in the Napa Valley that deserve commenting upon. Among the 150 or so wineries that now exist there, a clear tendency towards diversification of architectural expression is evident – some of it questionable when it veers towards kitsch, and some of it really dreadful when it is garishly eye-catching.

The Napa Valley is a sort of patchwork presenting alternating examples of the best and the worst in viticultural architecture. The worst is probably in the middle of the valley, where gigantic installations pride themselves on the enormous industrial buildings of their wine factories and where the confusion is increased by a tendency towards unplanned urbanization.[23] Fortunately, the authorities have managed to halt this process by legislation (the Agricultural Preserve Act) which, in principle, prevents the development of land that is used for vine growing. Similarly, commercial advertising is very strictly controlled and is not allowed to disfigure the vineyard.

CALIFORNIA AND THE BORDEAUX REGION

A considerable number of individual and collective initiatives combined with other factors together make up an overall viticultural strategy that brings out the best in the land and wines of the Napa Valley. Updated ideas taken from the Bordeaux region as well as new techniques have been put into practice. Wine tourism was invented in Bordeaux but it has since been considerably developed in California. The Napa offers interesting wine tours and many hotels and restaurants that are full of charm and character. The tradition invented in the Bordeaux region in the old days – but restricted to the aristocracy – of château hospitality has been modernized and made more democratic by the Americans. A disused railway has been brought back into service to create a wine train. In short, a new creativity is being applied to viticultural architecture, which is now considered to be a profitable cultural and promotional investment. This indisputable wealth of ideas and creativity should result in a healthy degree of international (or interregional) competition between vineyards.

Nevertheless, the assets of the Bordeaux vineyard are considerable. Up until now, it has always had an exceptional ability to regenerate itself so as to be better equipped to deal with the future. We only need to remember the state of destitution into which it has been plunged in the early 20th century (for two or three decades) in order to appreciate the extraordinary renaissance that has taken place since the 1960s. Thus, many Bordeaux vineyards that were lying fallow in the 1950s are now living symbols of a striking degree of viticultural and economic renewal, e.g. Château Giscours. All that remains to be done now, in the midst of the momentum that is building up in the region, is to combine this economic development with the complementary elements of a cultural strategy which is able to put right certain past mistakes, to compensate for the various shortfalls already mentioned and, above all, to update the Bordeaux wine culture.

THE FUTURE BEYOND THE PITFALLS

With regard to the future, we can make a preliminary and necessarily superficial outline for a cultural policy which could be capable of restoring wine architecture to its rightful position. I can give no formulas, just some ideas that will serve to initiate public debate. What elements of regional tradition should we try to modernize, revitalize, extend; what methods should we use to create a new interaction between viticulture and culture? This debate is necessary to clarify the ways of remaining faithful to a tradition without betraying it by sterile copies or parodies; to define the best use that can be made of existing resources that are still to be developed. It is indispensible to invent a strategy for the future in which we will continue to be conscious and worthy of the values of the past.

As a result of the research for the Châteaux Bordeaux project, which lasted two years (1986-88) and in the course of about 30 assignments in the wine-producing region of Bordeaux here – simplified and grouped into four specific courses of action – are some ideas that seem to herald a common future on the cultural and economic level.

TOWN AND COUNTRY PLANNING IN THE REGION

■ Reduce – or at least stabilize – the economic imbalance that has been created between town and country in the wine trade.
■ Develop the bipolar economy of a new rural and urban wine tourism, in particular by making the regional railway network and other undeveloped resources profitable.
■ Protect the beauty and integrity of the landscape and specific sites in the vineyard by conservation or restoration projects.
■ Create a national wine park in the Médoc and protect other areas of natural beauty in the Bordeaux region.

TOWN PLANNING

■ Regenerate town planning specifically related to the wine trade by reinforcing – or creating – urban centres to stem the recent tendency for firms to move out of the city centre to the suburbs. The proposed plans of action fall into three categories:
– Revitalize the Chartrons district in Bordeaux and convert the disused harbour warehouses there for use by the wine trade and other related businesses;
– Arrange for the setting up of a regional business park for the wine trade in the suburbs;
– Protect and enhance the architectural heritage of the wine trade in Bordeaux.
■ Reduce the conflict between the town and the vineyard by the following four projects:
– Devise a new style of urban development and settlement on the edges of the vineyards in the built-up area of Bordeaux, in particular at Pessac and Mérignac;
– Study the possible creation of a university wine château on the site of the ancient vineyard of the Luchey (property of the State) at Mérignac, in the centre of the built-up area of Bordeaux;
– Define the means of preventing the spread of urban development to the vineyards and their surroundings;
– Attempt to achieve a fruitful coexistence and a new interaction between the scientific "technopolis" project and viticulture in the Graves vineyard.

ARCHITECTURE

■ Provide a study and a detailed knowledge of the architectural heritage of wine production (and its specific characteristics).
■ Promote the creative and innovative conversion for new purposes of the many disused wine buildings of architectural interst – rural or urban, large or small.
■ Stimulate the design and construction of new, specifically viticultural architecture which can combine the spirit of the regional tradition with contemporary innovation.

COMMUNICATION AND USE OF THE MEDIA

■ Remedy the cultural amnesia or ignorance of the many riches of the cultural and architectural heritage of the wines of Bordeaux.
■ Develop considerably the artistic and media assets of the vineyard.

Although some of these main ideas have already been envisaged by various of the private and public investors in the region, what is required is an overall strategy. Of course this will not be easy to implement and there are many obstacles to be overcome. The history and development of the Châteaux Bordeaux project have given us an idea of the difficulties we are faced with. In fact, of the studies that were put forward at the outset of the project, three did not materialize.

One of the most original ideas consisted in inviting about ten European architects to design a new and emblematic wine château which could meet new requirements and ambitions. On the instigation of Michel Cantal-Dupart, this led to the idea of a university wine-château (just as the university hospital was invented in the 19th century): a place where theory and practice, oenological science and its application can complement one another in an appropriate cultural context. When it was put to our first sponsors – owners of several well-known wine châteaux – the idea was well-received and encouraged. Several of them suggested the Luchey in the commune of Mérignac as a potential site. This famous 19th-century vineyard of some 15 hectares (37 acres) – which later became a military camp (now disused) – borders directly on the vineyards of Château Haut-Brion and two other wine-producing estates that have escaped urbanization, Pape-Clément and Pique-Caillou. Situated in the middle of the built-up area of Bordeaux and between three important points – the historical centre of the town, the university and the international airport – it appeared to be the ideal spot.

But despite what was at stake, influential decision-makers in the Gironde thwarted our plans and our hopes for a university viticultural château. With it went what could have been proof of the existence of a local energy and commitment and also the cornerstone for the development of a regional wine park, requiring several hundred hectares of magnificent vines at the very centre of the city of Bordeaux.

For different reasons, the project for the study of a national wine park in the Médoc did not come about. The same was true of the project for the development and promotion of an upmarket type of wine tourism that could overcome the lack of hotel and restaurant facilities. The idea was to make use of the great potential of the region's rail network by creating a "wine train". However, the study of this luxury train, which was to have been assigned to the famous designer Philippe Starck who could have reinvented the idea of pleasurable rail travel, has unfortunately remained at the platform.

Was this a strategic setback caused by the pitfalls? Not really; we were perhaps too eager and our projects too ambitious. Owing to the size of the vineyard area, we were able with our European collaborators to turn to other subjects which have produced some interesting propositions. This line of theoretical research quickly brought about a new and decisive phase: in the spring of 1988, several of the region's leading economic figures, who were sympathetic to our initiative, offered their support. It was then necessary to outline a range of projects that would, in a practical way, address the specific problems of development so as to arrive at a series of studies for the architectural redevelopment of the premises concerned. All this was based on a diverse set of projects which corresponded to the large number of urban and rural centres involved in the wine trade of the region. Some firms – Cruze and de Luze – thus expected our collaboration to present them with a scheme that would enable them to carry out urgent conversion work in the middle of Bordeaux, thereby providing a new future for the Chartrons district.

In addition, a wine château in the Médoc – Pichon Longueville, a second-growth *grand cru classé* – helped us to understand the process of architectural consultation with the aim of providing a complete and exemplary renovation of its huge production and reception facilities which are arranged around a 19th-century residence. This series of projects (six in total) revealed a concern for quality innovative architecture within the realistic framework of the specific requirements of our business partners, all three of whom are part of large national companies.

THE REALIZATION OF AN IDEA

Thus, thanks to the faith shown by these businessmen, the Centre Georges Pompidou has managed with their cooperation to explore the area of reconciliation between the economic and cultural ambitions of the wine world in the Bordeaux region. In 1988, this collaboration produced a vision of possible courses of action for the future which matched our initial hopes: a large cultural exhibition whose preliminary historical studies and suggestions for the future could serve as a basis for viticultural architecture which is closely linked to the development of the wine trade.

It is thus encouraging to discover that the company that owns Château Pichon-Longueville officially decided in August 1988 to adopt the architectural scheme devised, on our initiative, by Patrick Dillon and Jean de Gastines. It is also good to know that the company Crus et Domaines de France plans to put into effect the planned conversion of the Cruse firm as conceived by the architects Reichen and Robert, again on our suggestion. As for the project for the redevelopment of the premises belonging to the de Luze firm, a decision will be taken in 1989.

Without being too optimistic, it seems that the conditions are now right for other investors to become involved with the Châteaux Bordeaux project in the near future. The aim is clear: to explore and experiment with a new policy of fruitful cooperation between the lively forces of the wine economy and those of cultural creativity.

1 See Nicholas Faith's article p.49.

2 See Gérard Bauer's article p.125.

3 See, for example, the article "Baurech hanté par un lotissement fantôme", *Sud-Ouest*, 23 August 1988.

4 See Robert Coustet's article p.63.

5 See Paul Levy's article in the wine column of *The Observer* colour supplement, London, 24 July 1988: "Four times we tried – and four times we failed – to find (from Bordeaux) the quickest route to the Médoc."

6 There are some cycle tracks in the region, but no circuits in the vineyard.

7 There are a few places linked by ferry up– and downstream from Bordeaux, but this represents a minute proportion of the potential resources offered by the waterways in the *département*.

8 There is always the possibility of hiring a helicopter from the Airlec company at Bordeaux airport, but the prices charged (without any competition in the region) are somewhat off-putting for tourists.

9 See Jean Dethier's article in the magazine *L'Amateur de Bordeaux*, 1987, no.17.

10 In 1988, the Chambre de Commerce et d'Industrie in Bordeaux published a confidential report on wine tourism abroad, in France and in the Bordeaux region.

11 In 1988, this is true notably of the owners of the *Hôtel du Théâtre* in Bordeaux.

12 Cf note 2.

13 See p.207 and the conversion project for these disused harbour warehouses in a coherent system of buildings of public or viticultural interest for the firms that wish to redeploy in the Chartrons district.

14 See Robert Coustet's article on the Chartrons p.139.

15 Esperanto: a language invented in 1887 by the Polish eye doctor Zamenhof based on an international vocabulary and phonetic spelling.

16 The main châteaux engaging in a significant amount of vine growing in the urban area of the communes of Pessac and Mérignac are: Château Haut-Brion (53 hectares/130 acres), La Mission Haut-Brion (29 hectares/72 acres), Pape-Clément and Pique-Caillou.

17 *Château Haut-Brion*: a small promotional book with 48 illustrated pages: English version printed in France in January 1988. Quotation taken from the back of page BE-3.

18 The town planner Gérard Bauer mentions the potential for appropriate urbanization around the vineyards of Pessac and Mérignac (cf his article p.125).

19 See this project p.172.

20 See these projects pp.184-205.

21 Laube (James): "Controversial Winery Opens at Clos Pégase in Calistoga, Napa Valley", *The Wine Spectator*, 30 June 1987, p.7.

22 *Ibid.*

23 Manson (Per-Henrik), "Suburbs Squeeze Wines", *The Wine Spectator*, 30 June 1987, p.6.

Imaginary view of Château Mouton Rothschild. The artist Francis Martinuzzi depicts various architectural, landscape and cultural elements that are characteristic of this part of the Médoc.

THE REDEVELOPMENT OF
CHATEAU PICHON-LONGUEVILLE
IN THE MEDOC

Rising up in a superb and untouched landscape of Médoc vineyards, along the famous "Route des Châteaux", is the memorable and picturesque silhouette of a wine château built in 1851 in a neo-Renaissance style by the architect Charles Burguet. This former residence of the Barons of Pichon-Longueville overlooks the river in a *terroir* of nearly 60 hectares (148 acres) to the north of the stream that marks the boundary of the Pauillac and St-Julien *appellations*. Although the fame of the wines of Pichon-Longueville, a second-growth *grand cru classé*, has long been established, the various owners of this magnificent château have hardly ever lived there in the 20th century.

Managed from afar, it has been the victim of a succession of architectural improvisations as far as the building or extension of *chais*, *cuviers* and other outbuildings are concerned. These are now in a state of architectural chaos which is damaging to the originally well-ordered château, its grounds and its vineyard. In 1987, the Société AXA-Millésimes acquired this vineyard and put Jean-Michel Cazes in charge of its management. The latter immediately realized the necessity of modernizing the wine-making equipment by installing high-performance and efficient facilities which were better adapted to the size of the vineyard. We met him in the spring of 1988 when we were looking for a "château-partner" to help set up one of the European architectural consultations for the Châteaux Bordeaux project.

This cooperation between the Centre Georges Pompidou and this wine château produced a stimulating and creative interaction. The programme for the competition was elaborated as each party put forward its ideas. Jean-Michel Cazes specified his requirements as far as the technical side was concerned: a *chai* to take 2,000 barrels (1,300 square metres/1,550 square yards), a *cuvier* for 30 vats (750 square metres/900 square yards), storerooms for bottles (1,300 square metres/1,550 square yards) and a wine-making plant (600 square metres/720 square yards).

To this scheme covering about 4,000 square metres (4,780 square yards), he wanted to add various buildings for administration and for receiving visitors. Indeed, he hopes the château will play an important part in the wine tourism that is starting up in the region. To reinforce this idea, we suggested he should also include an area with a cultural orientation: this could be a wine museum and perhaps a place to house the Châteaux Bordeaux exhibition when it finishes travelling around the world.

Three architects were then invited to design a comprehensive project around the neo-classical residence which was to be redeveloped as a reception centre for eminent guests and seminars. In August 1988, the projects were put before a panel of judges chaired by Claude Bébéar. The result of this was an official and definite decision: work on the project designed by Jean de Gastines and Patrick Dillon would start in 1989! This is a perfect example of the virtues of wholehearted cooperation between business and cultural partners who are motivated by the same desire to promote quality. Thus, one of the most ambitious building projects in the wine-producing region of Bordeaux will come into being.

JEAN DETHIER

THIS CONSULTATION WITH EUROPEAN ARCHITECTS WAS SUCCESSFULLY CARRIED OUT THANKS TO THE FINANCIAL ASSISTANCE GIVEN BY CHATEAU PICHON-LONGUEVILLE (SOCIETE AXA-MILLESIMES) IN ADDITION TO ITS PARTICIPATION IN THE SPONSORSHIP OF THE CHATEAUX BORDEAUX PROJECT.

OPPOSITE: Top, *the site of Château Pichon-Longueville at the southern end of the commune of Pauillac near the Gironde.*
Middle, *the neo-Renaissance château (1851) and 19th-century buildings surrounding it. (Paintings by Jean-Philippe Garric, SAA, Toulouse, 1988)*
Bottom left, *detail from a map dating from 1751 showing the wine-producing terroirs between Pauillac and St-Julien.* Bottom right, *the château and its annexes in 1987 (on the left: the chais and cuviers; in the middle: the 19th-century residence; on the right: offices and various buildings). In the foreground is the "Route des châteaux du Médoc".*
BELOW: *Project (not taken up) by the Hairabédian architects.*

ABOVE: *COMMEMORATIVE BRONZE PLAQUE
FOR THE INAUGURATION OF THE RESIDENCE
AT CHATEAU PICHON-LONGUEVILLE IN 1851
BUILT BY CHARLES BURGUET.*
OPPOSITE: *TWO VIEWS OF EACH OF THE
MODELS OF THE THREE TEAMS OF
ARCHITECTS INVITED TO DESIGN SCHEMES IN
1988 FOR THE ARCHITECTURAL
REDEVELOPMENT OF THE SURROUNDINGS OF
CHATEAU PICHON-LONGUEVILLE AT PAUILLAC.
FOR THE SAKE OF COMPARISON, THE MODELS
ARE SHOWN AT THE SAME ANGLE AND IN THE
SAME SCALE IN EACH COLUMN. THESE
MODELS INCLUDE THE RESIDENCE, BUILT IN A
NEO-RENAISSANCE STYLE, WHICH NEEDED TO
BE INTEGRATED INTO THE HEART OF THE
COMPOSITION.* TOP, *THE WINNING PROJECT,
WHOSE CONSTRUCTION STARTED IN 1989.
MODEL BY ETIENNE FOLLENFANT FOR THE
PROJECT BY PATRICK DILLON AND JEAN DE
GASTINES.* MIDDLE, *MODEL BY MANUEL
BROMERA FOR THE PROJECT BY VINCENTE
ALBERTO USTARROZ AND MANUEL MARIA
INIGUEZ.* BOTTOM, *MODEL BY ALAIN PRAS
FOR THE PROJECT BY FERNANDO MONTES.*

———————————

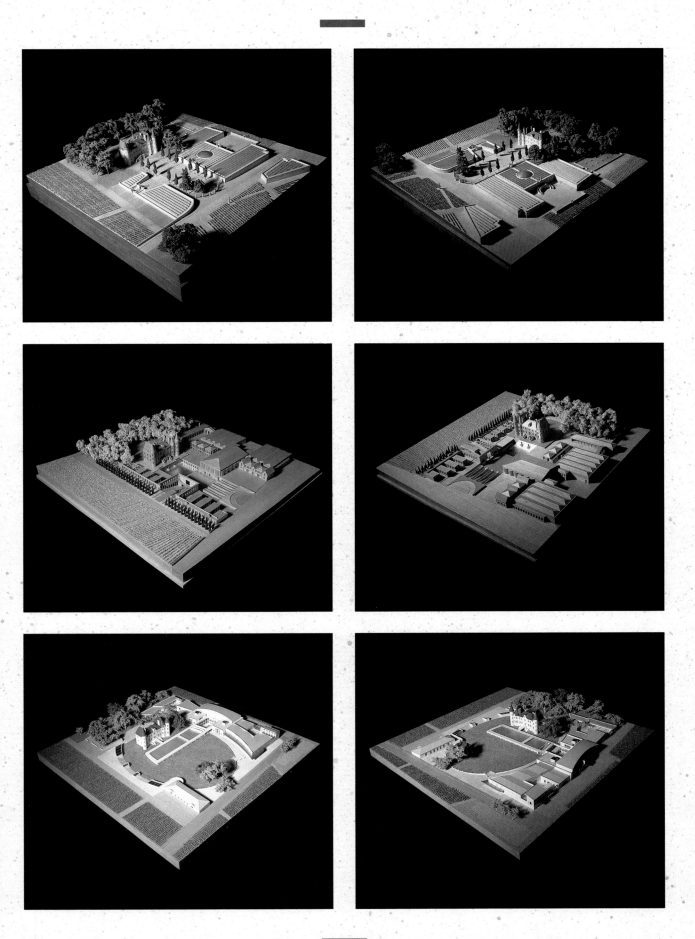

ABOVE: *The new monumental entrance portal linking the vineyard
to the esplanade of the château.*
OPPOSITE: *Model of the architectural scheme.*

PROJECT
FOR THE REDEVELOPMENT
OF CHATEAU PICHON-LONGUEVILLE
AT PAUILLAC

PRIZE-WINNING PROJECT
PATRICK DILLON AND
JEAN DE GASTINES, PARIS

WITH THE ASSISTANCE OF
CHRISTIAN BRAHAMI, VITICULTURAL ADVISER,
THE ARCHITECTS BITA HODJAT AND REZA TAHMASSEBI
AND THE COLOURIST DAN BENESCH
MODEL BY ETIENNE FOLLENFANT

THE DESIGNERS AND THEIR PROJECT

PATRICK DILLON was born in 1952 in Panama. After studying architecture at the Rice University in Houston (Texas), he worked with the architect Ricardo Bofill (for nearly ten years) on various projects in Spain, Algeria, France (Paris and Marne-la-Vallée) and the United States. In the latter, they studied a project for the wine-producing estate of Clos Pégase in the Napa Valley, California. This orientation towards viticultural architecture was taken a stage further when, in 1986, he joined forces with the French architect, Jean de Gastines, in Paris.

JEAN DE GASTINES was born in Casablanca in 1957. He studied architecture at the Ecole des Beaux-Arts in Paris. He worked with the architect Frank Gehry (California) on various projects, including a study for the New York residence of Christophe de Mesnil (daughter of the famous creator of the De Mesnil Foundation in Houston) whose Paris residence he went on to design in 1980.

In 1987, they were responsible for the renovation of a ruined winery adjacent to Château de Bachen (a neo-classical residence near Eugénie-les-Bains, 120 kilometres/75 miles south of Bordeaux, in the Landes). The owners, Michel and Christine Guérard, saw this rebuilding as a way to bring about a renaissance in this Tursan vineyard. The architects presented them with a rational and subtle design that balanced the virtues of tradition with those of modernity.

The scheme is sensitively adapted to its superb surroundings and offers a unique perspective of the landscape. The access road gradually sinks into the ground between the parallel rows of vines and comes out in a small square plaza, sunken five metres (16 feet) below ground level. It is bordered on the château side by the two-storey building containing the *chais* and *cuviers* and, opposite, by an open-air theatre to seat about 100 people. This wine château is a memorable place of quiet harmony where the new wine-making strategy of the famous chef will be able to flourish.

In 1988, they were invited by the Centre Georges Pompidou to take part in the European consultations organized as part of the Châteaux Bordeaux project and were assigned the study of two wine-producing sites in the Bordeaux region.   RUTH EATON

IN THIS PROJECT for Château Pichon-Longueville, we come across a theme already encountered in the Château de Bachen project: how to construct a large industrial building that does not rival the architecture of the nearby château but which, on the contrary, emphasizes and reaffirms its presence?

Our approach to this project involves first of all re-establishing a perfect equilibrium between the three components of the wine-producing unit represented by the vineyard, the château and the *chais*. Inspired by the architecture of the Médoc countryside, the new *chais* are the natural extension of the Bordeaux wall, which is sometimes transformed into gates, windows or sculptures. The tiled shed roofs are meant to evoke the geometry of the surrounding vines. The wall – whose height is determined by the base of the château – allows a pre-existent horizontality to be re-established. The château is thus given a central position and regains its dominance within the overall composition.

The wall opens out near the vineyard to become an amphitheatre with a monumental gate leading to the vineyard. Opposite this amphitheatre, the entrance to the *chais* consists of a door surmounted by a "window in the sky" and two obelisks, thereby reminding the visitor of various features of the Médoc landscape (towers, crucifixes, sculptures). Whereas the architecture of the *chais* is deliberately austere on the outside, inside it is allowed full expression. Here, all the ritual and the theatrical spirit of the process of vinification is articulated. The *cuvier*, in a central position, is circular in shape. On either side are the barrel cellar and the area reserved for bottling, all organized around the service courtyard where the grape harvests will be delivered. On the upper floor are the administrative offices and a short circuit for visitors, who will be able to see everything from this vantage point without obstructing the work.

For us, the new architecture of Pichon-Longueville is a fusion of diverse elements of the Médoc landscape, the château and the vineyard.

PATRICK DILLON AND JEAN DE GASTINES

ABOVE: *Bird's-eye view of the whole redevelopment. At the back, against the park, is the residence built in 1851. In the middle, the new lake and the main gate opening on to the road. To the left: the museum (in the foreground) and the tiers of the open-air theatre flanked by the reception building. To the right (from the background to the foreground): building for viticultural equipment, chais and circular cuvier (square building with service courtyard), storerooms (beside the road) and space for future expansion on the other side of this road.*
BELOW: *Plan of the new project in its terroir.*

FACADE NORD-EST
Route des Chateaux
Ech 1:200

0   5   10

FACADE NORD
Reception de la Vendange et Administration
Ech 1:200

0   5   10

COUPE-FACADE AA
Ech 1:200

0   5   10

OPPOSITE: Top, *axial view of the new chai.* Middle, *three elevations showing the relationship between the old residence and the new buildings.* Bottom, *interior view of the new circular cuvier with overhead lighting.* TOP: *Sketch for the design of the monumental portal.* MIDDLE: *Overall plan of the new buildings. At the bottom, from right to left, the museum, the open-air theatre, the reception. In the middle, the residence (1851) and the lake. At the top, from left to right, the chai, the circular cuvier and the storeroom.* BOTTOM: *Axial view of the château from the "route des châteaux du Médoc". On the left, the museum and open-air theatre. On the right, the new cuvier with its monumental entrance.*

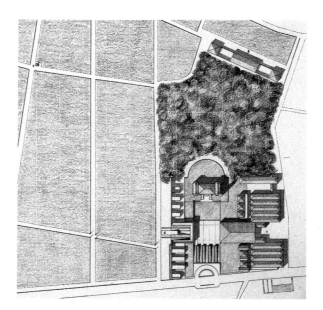

ABOVE: *Overall plan of the project.*
OPPOSITE: *Model of the new buildings surrounding the château.*

PROJECT
FOR THE REDEVELOPMENT
OF CHATEAU PICHON-LONGUEVILLE
AT PAUILLAC

VINCENTE ALBERTO USTARROZ
AND MANUEL MARIA INIGUEZ, PAMPLONA

MODEL BY MANUEL BOMERA

ALBERTO USTARROZ and MANUEL INIGUEZ were both born in Pamplona. A taste for architectural post cards, history and drawing led them to enrol, in 1965, in the Faculty of Architecture at the Catholic University of Pamplona, founded in 1955. They finished their studies in 1971 and decided to form a partnership which has continued ever since. Believing in furthering their knowledge by means of travel, for almost 20 years they have toured Europe and North Africa during the summer months purely to study architecture.

Since 1977, they have taught at the San Sebastián School of Architecture (University of the Basque country), which they helped to found, along with some friends: José Linazasoro, Miguel Garay, Ignacio Gallaraga, Unzurrunzaja and others.

They have a declared enthusiasm for ancient Greek architecture and the Roman foundations of the Middle East. If their favourite building had to be cited, we could safely say it was the Erechthéion (421-405 BC). Their favourite architect? Brunelleschi (San Lorenzo in Florence), although they also admire Karl Friedrich Schinkel and Henri Labrouste (Bibliothèque Ste-Geneviève in Paris). Favourite city? No hesitation – Rome!

These architects, with their passion for study, build few buildings and set themselves high standards. Their designs are regularly published in Spanish magazines, including *Arquitectura* and *El Croquis*, and international ones such as *Architectural Design* and *AAM*.

After a brief period marked by the influence of Aldo Rossi, they quickly established their reputation in classical and vernacular architecture. The rural centre of Cordobilla (near Pamplona), which they built in 1979, is the touchstone of their commitment to the lonely path of architecture approached from the point of historicism.

Of their recent work, we will mention the restoration of the Lesaka town hall in the Basque country and the new medical centre in the same village, which both earned them the European Prize for the Reconstruction of a Town in 1987. However, there was one big disappointment: their scheme for the new Faculty of Philosophy at San Sebastián, which they worked on continuously between 1980-83, will not be built – the rectorate considered it to be too elegant.

In 1988, they toured the United States, first at the University of Miami as visiting professors, then at Harvard, Puerto Rico and other places as lecturers.

MAURICE CULOT

IN THE SPRING OF 1988, Château Pichon-Longueville gave us the impression of an incongruous collection of buildings containing some interesting architectural elements. First of all, of course, there was the vast central building, constructed in 1851 in a neo-Renaissance style, which serves as a residence: it is spectacular, memorable and emblematic of the Médoc. In its immediate surroundings were various buildings: the neo-classical façade of an 18th-century orangery; a beautiful monumental well-coping in the form of a Doric column; a 19th-century building and, finally, the southern façade of the *chais* and *cuviers*. We therefore decided to retain these fragments to enhance the sense of history but also so that they could become the focal point of a new architectural redeployment. Our scheme has been designed along two perpendicular axes: one starts at the residence and goes towards the river (east to west); the other runs north to south and connects the *terroir* of the vineyard and the château (parallel to the road). Our composition is organized around these two lines which are intended to make the old and new buildings into a coherent unit that is both rational and theatrical.

Between the road and the main façade of the old château, we have created a two-level esplanade. On the same level as the road is a semi-circular belvedere with several fountains. From this point, you have a view of the lower level of the esplanade, towards which water is channeled down several sloping planes. Tiny canals irrigate the square below, ending in a large stretch of water at the foot of the château, which is reflected in it. To the left (south) of this space which has been designed for theatre performances – are the public reception areas and an underground museum of architecture lit by large parallel skylights. The line of the latter is broken to accommodate the large tiers of an open-air theatre, whose steps allow visitors easy access from the vineyard towards the lowered central square.

To the right (north) of this esplanade all the new functional buildings are arranged. In the centre of the structure is the rectangular *cuvier*, with the repetitive curves of the outside walls suggesting the roundness of precious vats of wine. The square buildings of the *chai* and the storerooms are placed at a tangent to the *cuvier*. This three-pole arrangement is organized around a rear service courtyard. Along the central esplanade on either side of the *cuvier*, there is on the one hand a small 19th-century building which has been completely converted into a tasting room and a shop, and on the other, a new building for receiving guests.

MANUEL INIGUEZ AND ALBERTO USTARROZ

ABOVE: *Axial view towards the château from the road;*
on the right is the new cuvier.
MIDDLE: *Side esplanade linking the vineyard with the sunken central piazza.*

BELOW: *The esplanade seen looking from the château towards*
the Gironde: on the left is the new cuvier.

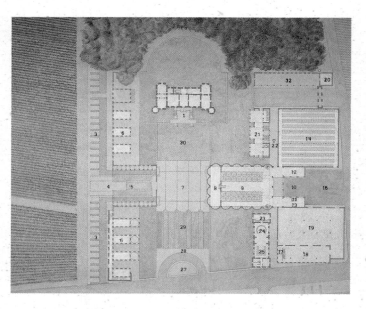

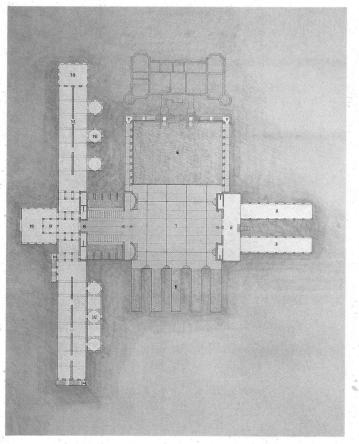

ABOVE: Top, *overall plan of the project on the upper level: 1. Château 2. Visitors' car park 3. Entrance to château 4. Reception area 5. Large cuvier 6. Delivery of grapes 7. Chai 8. Agricultural courtyard 9. Bottling 10. Storage 11. Reception room 12. Wine tasting room 13. Belvedere 14. Fountain.*
Bottom, *detailed plan of buildings on lower level: 1. Reception area 2. Reception hall 3. Chai 4. Fountains 5. Lake 6. Entrance to museum 7. Audiovisual presentation 8. Museum.*
OPPOSITE: Top, *overall view of project.*
Middle, *cross section: on the left, the museum and the tiers of the open-air theatre; on the right, the cuvier; in the background, elevation of the residence (1851).*
Bottom, *bird's-eye view of the architectural layout.*

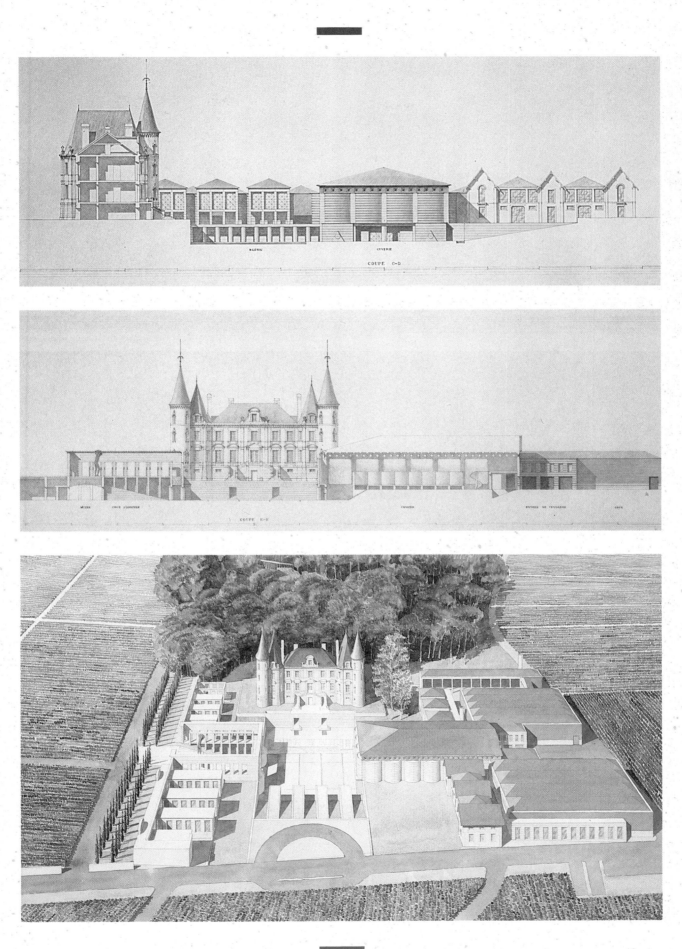

COUPE C-D

COUPE E-F

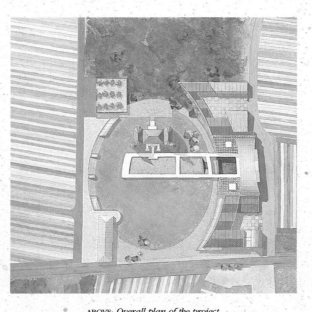

ABOVE: *Overall plan of the project.*
OPPOSITE: *Model of the architectural scheme.*

PROJECT
FOR THE REDEVELOPMENT
OF CHATEAU PICHON-LONGUEVILLE
AT PAUILLAC

FERNANDO MONTES, PARIS

IN COLLABORATION
WITH HUGUES TOUTON
MODEL BY ALAIN PRAS

THE DESIGNER AND HIS PROJECT

"L'horizon, surligné d'accents vaporeux, semble écrit en petits
caractères, d'une encre plus ou moins
pâle selon les jeux de lumière.
De ce qui est plus proche, je ne jouis plus que comme d'un
tableau." F. Ponge, *Le Paysage*

FERNANDO MONTES, born in 1941 at Quinteros (Chile), is one of those creative people who have decided to settle in Paris and who, by their innovative approach, have enriched French culture. Since the end of the 1960s, his buildings, designs and teachings have played an important role in defining modern architecture. He considers himself to be one of the spiritual heirs to Le Corbusier and Robert Mallet-Stevens, but also has a great admiration for Aldo Rossi, and his first buildings coincided with the start of the post-modernism movement in France.

The buildings he constructed in the new town of Cergy-Pontoise near Paris are like a manifesto: their semi-circular design is organized according to a plan intended to recreate urbanity in towns where social activity is too often lacking. In the project he designed for the town hall at Massy-Palaiseau in the Essonne in 1986, he was concerned with the expressive and symbolic worth of the building and attempted to structure this administrative complex like a city. On the other hand, in his project for the Opéra Populaire in the Place de la Bastille (Paris), he wanted to find new solutions for the problems raised in the 1920s and 1930s. This same approach is evident in the housing development in the Belleville district of Paris.

Montes regards architecture as a constant interchange of ideas between the old and the new – a process that, while it rejects precepts and formulas, does not regard this as the necessary condition for architectural development. For Montes, tradition has a rightful place at the centre of the reconstruction of the environment using the most sophisticated elements of the electronic age.

In short, his accumulated experience makes him one of the most pertinent representatives of a school of architectural thought that rejects dogma and ideology and is open to the influences of the changing modern world.

GERARD-GEORGES LEMAIRE

IT IS HARD to imagine a more revealing road than the *départementale 2* that goes to Pauillac in the Médoc. On one side is Château Comtesse and on the other side the château of the old Barons. The latter, Pichon-Longueville, could be considered as the perfect example of an unfinished picture in this extraordinary collection of Médoc châteaux. It is such a superlative château that even after one fleeting sight of it from the road coming from Bordeaux, it is impossible to forget. It is a château label come to life.

None of the other, much more successful châteaux along this wine road through the Médoc has the same architectural primitiveness which creates such an impression. However, the château could be transformed to create a more mysterious, more majestic or simply more up-to-date image of a modern wine-producing concern. Thus, the architectural aims of this project entail completing and revitalizing Pichon-Longueville.

What hope do we have of success? The project entails a complete programme of modernization that incorporates every aspect of the estate, agricultural, technical, commercial and cultural. Architecture is used to help reflect the marked process of evolution that is taking place on the estate, to help establish a coherence among the multitude of advances and investments. It seems certain that the mistakes of the past, which involved knocking up sheds in response to an urgent need for expansion, will not be repeated in the future. A wine château can no longer be reduced to merely a coincidence in space between the residence and the *chais* and an unimaginative merging of the domestic and the technical functions. A modern wine-producing concern is no longer entirely centred around the residential château. The latter certainly continues to be the part of the complex that has the most potential in terms of promotion and on that account plays a decisive role in the image of a wine that is to be marketed throughout the world.

However, due to the public's growing interest in the secrets of the *élevage* of the wine, the *chais* and the *cuviers* now also have an indisputable promotional role. The functional areas have become the ones that are most specific to a new type of viticultural architecture. The stereotype of the traditional château is being gradually changed into a visual concept that is more ambiguous. A comparison could be made with an abbey where the actual church is merely one of its component parts.

The second task we have set ourselves is to find a new place for the château in the overall composition. Our strategy involves choosing a basic figure: the ellipse. This adaptable shape which the cubists (Braque, Gris, Picasso), in their search for a means to express the newfound freedom of invention, used with such effect. In this context, the ellipse allows us to adjust the design whereby the existing château (which hitherto has been floating in space through lack of reference points and lack of surrounding buildings) is firmly positioned like the anchor escapement in the mechanics of a clock. The other main buildings (*chais*, *cuviers*, grounds, museum) are at the same time logically organized around this focal point.

FERNANDO MONTES

BELOW: *On the left, one of the turrets of the residence (1851); in the foreground is the new chai which is partially buried and extended by a patio. In the background is the cuvier and the other wine buildings.*

ABOVE: *Overall view of the project. In the foreground is the new concave main gate by the road; on the left, the end of the museum is extended by tiers; on the right, the group of wine buildings is dominated by the cuvier.*

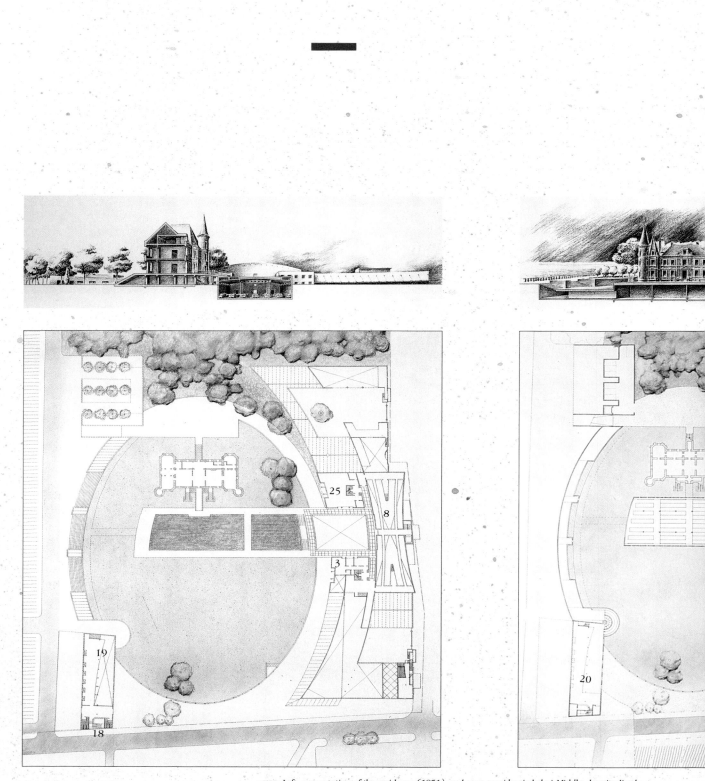

TOP: Left, *cross section of the residence (1851) and new, semi-buried chai. Middle, longitudinal section. From left to right, the underground museum topped by tiers, the semi-buried chai, the patio and the cuvier. Right, section through the wine buildings, with the cuvier in the middle.*
BOTTOM: *Overall plans of the new buildings on the three different levels: 1. Entrance gallery 2. Reception 3. Administration 4. Cloister 5. Meeting room 6. Delivery of grapes 7. Pressing*

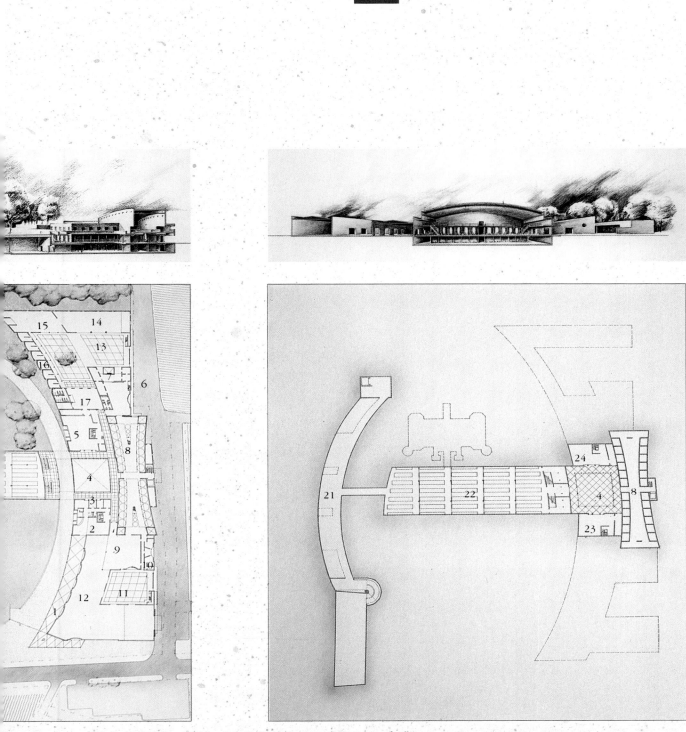

8. Cuvier 9. Bottling 10. Laboratory 11. Dispatch courtyard 12. Storage of pallets
13. Agricultural courtyard 14. Shed for machines 15. Workshop 16. Dormitories 17. Canteen
18. Entrance to museum 19. Museum (high room) 20. Museum (intermediate room)
21. Museum (large room) 22. Large chai 23. Wine tasting room 24. Reception room
25. Audiovisual presentation.

A NEW HOME FOR THE NEGOCIANT FIRM CRUSE IN THE CHARTRONS DISTRICT OF BORDEAUX

PROJECT BY BERNARD REICHEN AND PHILIPPE ROBERT, PARIS

WITH THE ASSISTANCE OF ANNE CARLES-STEFANO (TOWN-PLANNING STUDIES) AND ROMAIN REUTHIER (ARCHITECTURAL STUDIES)

Since the 17th century, the Chartrons district, in the historical centre of Bordeaux, has been the symbol of the urban aspect of the region's viticultural economy. In the 1960s, this district started to decline, mainly because of the relocation of several *négociant* houses out of the town centre to the anonymity of the industrial suburbs.

This process of dispersal has led to a serious loss of identity and prestige among companies which are nevertheless responsible for spreading the reputation of the wines of Bordeaux throughout the world. Moreover, some very old firms have expressed their desire to remain in the Chartrons so long as they can redeploy themselves in a modern, functional and permanent way. But such modernization is only feasible within the framework of an overall plan for the redevelopment of the whole area.

Two large firms – Cruse and de Luze – have entrusted us, as part of the Châteaux Bordeaux project, with the task of finding architects and town planners to solve this complex problem, so vital for them and for the city. You will find the study for the de Luze firm on page 251.

The project on the following pages for the Cruse firm has considered in detail the economic, technological and practical problems involved. The heads of these companies are anxious that their premises should be redeveloped in the best possible way so as to allow technological progress and the continued pursuit of quality. A detailed analysis of the land and property at their disposal and their immediate surroundings, has brought a unique opportunity to light: the re-use of an abandoned warehouse in the port. The delicate task of converting an old industrial building into modern premises for a large *négociant* firm was entrusted to two specialists: Philippe Robert and Bernard Reichen in Paris. The integration of the project within the district also presupposed a study of its urban context and the Centre Pompidou has also given the architects the task of outlining a plan for the redevelopment of the surrounding area.

The latter has been defined as an overall scheme of renewal for the two kilometres (one and a quarter miles) of deserted quays of the old port and of its dozen large warehouses that stretch from the Chartrons to the centre of Bordeaux. The plan envisaged for this privileged site between the river and the historic wine trade quarter would include a long promenade (flanked by a tourist tram alongside the river) which, starting from the city centre, would be the home for hotels, businesses, gardens, small markets, art galleries, cultural areas, cafés, restaurants, open-air museums etc. To the right, at the end of the Cours du Médoc (and while we wait for the possible extension of this road by a bridge to the future district of "La Bastide" on the right bank), a group of buildings designed for modern systems of communication could be erected. Beyond this pivotal point, the warehouses would be converted for the various business needs of the wine trade, in particular, to house *négociant* firms such as Cruse.

The intention is therefore not to create a "monofunctional" area, nor a continuous façade of new buildings – quite the contrary. In order to allow a clear view between the river and the interesting old façades of the Chartrons, the quay would be spaced out with esplanades and gardens. Indeed, the project proposes converting only some of the existing disused warehouses, and would not necessarily use the whole building. Some parts would thus be demolished so as to keep in general terms, autonomous square segments measuring 30 metres (33 yards) per side – an option offering flexibility and avoiding the creation of massive structures forming a screen between the river and the town. The intention of this project is to reconcile the future with the past, to ensure the survival of the wine economy by maintaining urban vitality in one of the most beautiful ports in France.

JEAN DETHIER

THE SUCCESSFUL CONSULTATION WITH ARCHITECTS FOR THE REDEVELOPMENT OF CRUSE AND DE LUZE WAS POSSIBLE THANKS TO THE SPECIFIC FINANCIAL ASSISTANCE GIVEN BY THESE TWO COMPANIES, IN ADDITION TO THEIR PARTICIPATION IN THE SPONSORSHIP OF THE CHATEAUX BORDEAUX PROJECT.

OPPOSITE: Top, *the Chartrons district with the Esplanade des Quinconces to the left. In red, the disused warehouses beside the river and, in mauve, the site of premises belonging to the firm of Cruse.*
Middle and bottom, *the urban site and the warehouses intended for conversion.*

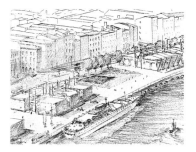

THE DESIGNERS AND THEIR PROJECT

BERNARD REICHEN AND PHILIPPE ROBERT are two young architects (born in 1943 and 1941 respectively) who, for the last 20 years, have been driven by the same passion: how to change what already exists.

At the beginning of the 1970s – a period that was not good for getting new commissions – they decided to set up their own firm. In the difficult business climate, they distinguished themselves from the rest of their profession by devoting themselves to restoration work. Their enthusiasm for this type of work, their campaigning on its behalf and their numerous projects has raised them to the rank of specialists and pioneers. By their efforts they have succeeded in elevating such architecture to a new level.

Restoration, conversion, recycling of architectural elements and any work intended to revitalize old buildings gives them pleasure. By working on already existing structures, they are rediscovering what they call the "architecture of the interior". They appropriate everything for the reworking of the architecture and the remnants of the old buildings (chimneys, boiler rooms . . .) are features of the new design. Their enthusiasm for this art have led them to organize exhibitions. Robert was an organizer of the famous "Créer dans le créé" exhibition at the Centre Georges Pompidou in Paris in 1986.

From the Usine Leblan (Lille), the Etablissements Prouvost (Tourcoing), the Halles Centrales of Lille, the Usines Japy (Belfort), and the Halle aux Grains in Blois to numerous other projects, their mastery of building within existing structures is evident. But it was their work on the Grande Halle at La Villette in Paris that gave them international renown.

Their activities are not limited to prestigious buildings protected by the Monuments Historiques. They also work on unglamorous buildings, such as the old Hôpital Marie Lannelongue, Rue de Tolbiac, Paris. Their skill allows them to place the past and the present side by side in the most effective fashion. This is apparent in the Ecole Maternelle, Rue Beauregard, Paris.   PASCALE BLIN

THE CRUSE FIRM, which established itself at 124 Quai des Chartrons in 1802, now occupies an area of more than 19,000 square metres (23,000 square yards) divided among various old buildings. The premises were obviously not designed to house the complex modern technological equipment of a large wine company. This inefficiency is incompatible with the requirements of a company in a period of expansion. The firm is headed by Marc Lenot, who sees the conversion of his premises as a strategic priority and refuses to be exiled to the suburbs outside Bordeaux. Then an alternative presented itself: why not convert one of the disused warehouses along the port? Warehouse number 16, which we found abandoned, was built around 1930 on the edge of the river. Its concrete structure covers an area of 30 metres by 120 metres (33 yards by 131 yards), with a height of 10 metres (33 feet) and its two interior levels represent a floor space of 7,000 square metres (8,000 square yards). Only the lower level of the façades, up to a height of 6 metres (20 feet), once cleaned, offer an architectural quality that is worthy of interest. We thus propose to keep only this lower part of the building and to remove its superstructure, replacing it with a steel structure on two levels and covering the 3,600 square metres (4,300 square yards) of the building with a light roof supported by cables. The idea is to suggest the image of the ships, freighters and cranes that used to characterize the port.

This arrangement allows 10,000 square metres (12,000 square yards) of floor space on three levels. The ground floor – thanks to the old walls which provide good insulation – can be used for storage space by arranging the *cuves* among the existing pillars. Whereas the upper floors (which have no constraints of this type since the new structure will be constructed without internal supports), can house the working areas for processing, bottling or packaging. There is a bridge to the intermediate level allowing access for lorries and alleviating the local traffic problem. The centre of the building contains the offices, the laboratories and the lifts and staircases. At the top is a belvedere with a view of the river.

The building presents an architectural silhouette that is urbane, contemporary, light and elegant. It is also rational, since it accommodates two complementary activities that are indissociable today: functional efficiency and public accessibility.   PHILIPPE ROBERT

TOP: *Four preliminary sketches for the conversion of the quay area and the disused warehouses in the middle of the town of Bordeaux.* Page opposite: *cruising boats moored alongside new tourist facilities.* Above, left: *the extension of the Place des Quinconces towards the river;* middle: *a warehouse divided into three small sections for museums or art galleries;* right: *proposed new square where the Cours du Médoc opens on to the river.*

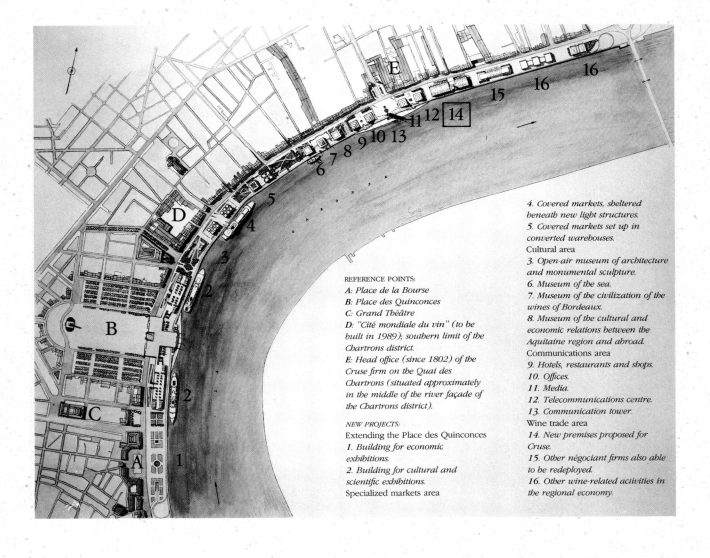

REFERENCE POINTS:

A: Place de la Bourse
B: Place des Quinconces
C: Grand Théâtre
D: "Cité mondiale du vin" (to be built in 1989); southern limit of the Chartrons district.
E: Head office (since 1802) of the Cruse firm on the Quai des Chartrons (situated approximately in the middle of the river façade of the Chartrons district).

NEW PROJECTS:
Extending the Place des Quinconces
1. Building for economic exhibitions.
2. Building for cultural and scientific exhibitions.
Specialized markets area

4. Covered markets, sheltered beneath new light structures.
5. Covered markets set up in converted warehouses.
Cultural area
3. Open-air museum of architecture and monumental sculpture.
6. Museum of the sea.
7. Museum of the civilization of the wines of Bordeaux.
8. Museum of the cultural and economic relations between the Aquitaine region and abroad.
Communications area
9. Hotels, restaurants and shops.
10. Offices.
11. Media.
12. Telecommunications centre.
13. Communication tower.
Wine trade area
14. New premises proposed for Cruse.
15. Other négociant firms also able to be redeployed.
16. Other wine-related activities in the regional economy.

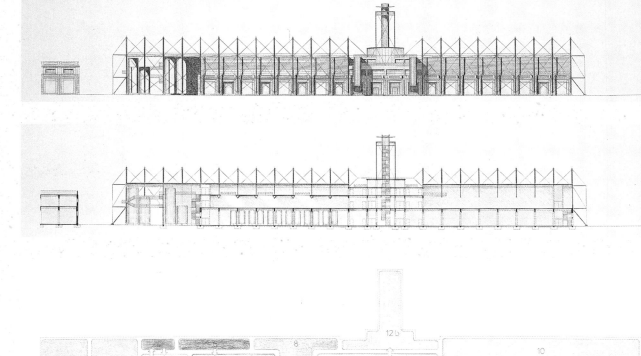

1. Exterior cuvier
2. Laboratory, tasting room and processing 3. Interior cuvier 4. Processing
5–9. Bottling line (5. Arrival of empties and bottling; 6. Arrival and storage of dry matter; 7. Packaging;

8. Additional packaging; 9. Checking, placing on pallets and dispatch) 10. Storage of finished products 11. Storage of wines 12a. Reception of visitors 12b. Wine-tasting area

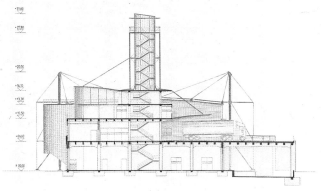

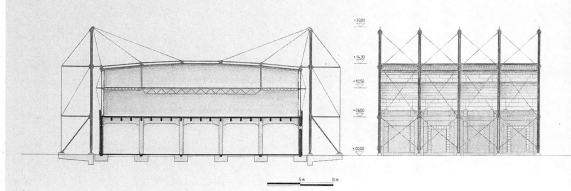

5 m   10 m

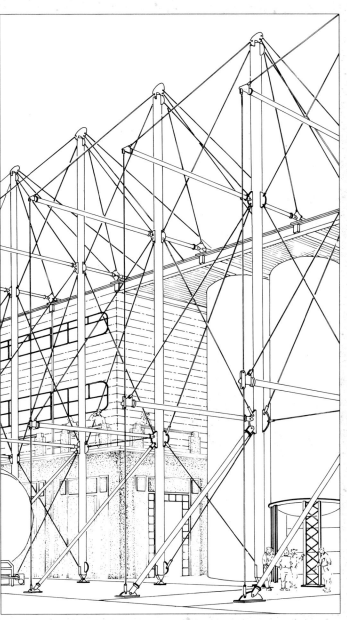

OPPOSITE: Top, *façade, facing the river, of the converted warehouse and longitudinal section of the redeveloped building.* Centre, *organizational diagram of the functions on three levels (theoretical longitudinal section) and cross section in the middle of the redeveloped building.* Bottom, *on the left, cross section revealing the concrete structure of the lower part of the old preserved warehouse. This structure is raised by two levels; the new roof is guyed. On the right, the external architecture of four modules for the new façade.*

LEFT: Top, *view in perspective of the southern end of the converted warehouse with its guyed roof and its large exterior wine vats.* Bottom, *shaded site plan of the converted warehouse in its urban context.*

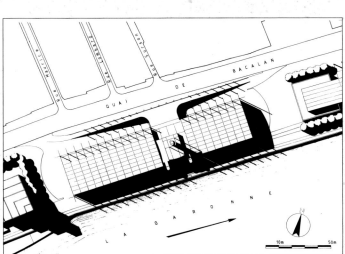

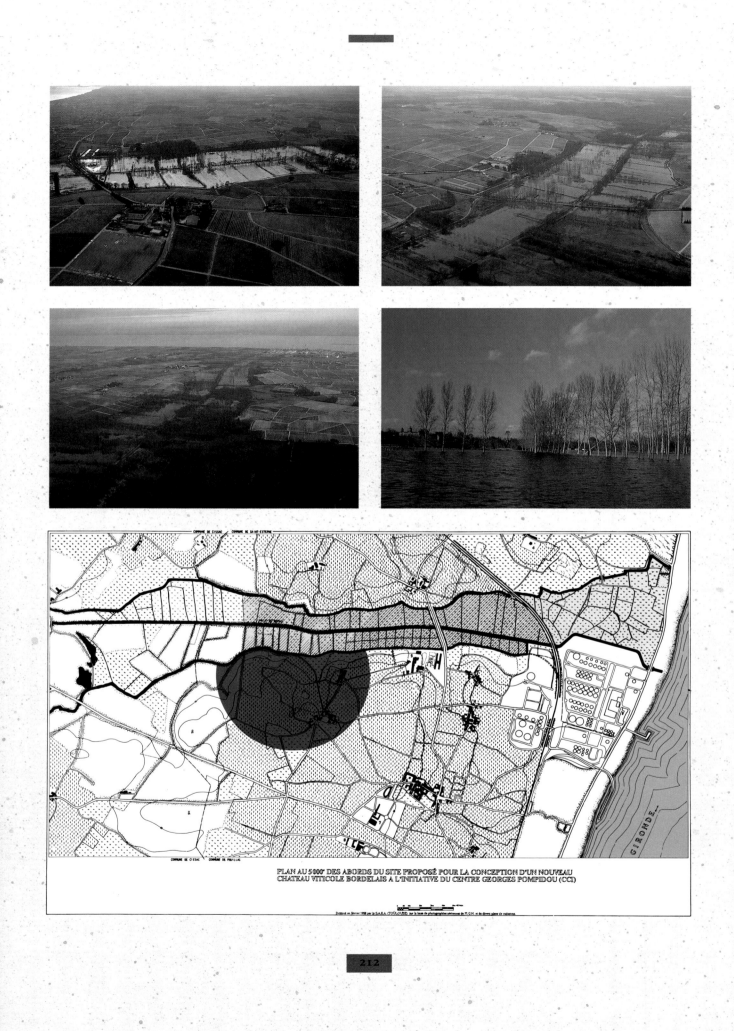

PLAN AU 5000° DES ABORDS DU SITE PROPOSÉ POUR LA CONCEPTION D'UN NOUVEAU
CHATEAU VITICOLE BORDELAIS A L'INITIATIVE DU CENTRE GEORGES POMPIDOU (CCI)

SIX IMAGINARY CHATEAUX IN THE MEDOC

At the heart of the Médoc, in the commune of Pauillac, the 60-hectare (148 acres) vineyard of Château Duhart-Milon is to be found. This vast and beautiful estate is closely bordered by prestigious neighbours: the châteaux of Lafite-Rothschild, Mouton Rothschild and Cos d'Estournel. But this fourth-growth *cru classé* is unique in the Bordeaux region. There is no château residence and the *chais* and the *cuviers* are located five kilometres (three miles) away in the centre of the town of Pauillac. This property attracted our attention when, at the beginning of 1988, we were searching for wine-growing sites which required a new architectural development as part of the Châteaux Bordeaux project.

With the agreement of the owner – who coined the expression of the "intellectual loan" of his land – the Centre Georges Pompidou invited six European architects to submit their designs for a wine château. Of course, this would be an imaginary château, but it would be anchored in the real or possible world – a modern vision of a historical concept. It was thus necessary to take account of the château tradition and of the various recent or future socio-economic developments – including the emergence of a new wine tourism in the region, facilitated by the proximity of the Médoc railway, along which a "wine train" could run.

The theoretical site proposed for examination by the architects extends beyond the *terroir* of the above-mentioned vineyard and includes the attractive valley of the Jalle du Breuil, which is liable to flooding and which opens into the Gironde nearby. Apart from the classic components of a wine château of the region (residence, *chais*, *cuvier*, cellars, storerooms, various utility rooms etc.), the architects were also asked to design various complementary centres of activity, notably facilities for visitors and a cultural museum, a part of which could serve as "a wine embassy" for the wines from neighbouring *appellations*.

Unlike the projects studied for the Chartrons urban district or for the redevelopment of Château Pichon-Longueville (where all the precise data needed to be realistically taken into account), the architects in this instance enjoyed great freedom of interpretation, both on the architectural level and as regards the wine-making process envisaged. It was also agreed that each team of architects and their collaborators were to decide for themselves which of the different options were to be incorporated in their scheme.

Some projects may seem less realistic than others. But surely the purpose of planning for the future is to free ourselves from tried and tested models, while still having respect for them. It was in this spirit that this particular site and project were proposed to the architects for their thoughts.

JEAN DETHIER

THIS PROCESS OF CONSULTATION WITH SIX EUROPEAN ARCHITECTURAL FIRMS WAS POSSIBLE THANKS TO THE FINANCIAL ASSISTANCE GIVEN BY THE BANQUE FRANÇAISE DU COMMERCE EXTERIEURE (BFCE), IN ADDITION TO ITS PARTICIPATION IN THE SPONSORSHIP OF THE CHATEAUX BORDEAUX PROJECT.

OPPOSITE: Top, *aerial photographs of the valley during its seasonal flooding (January 1988)*. Bottom, *plan of the site, with the Jalle du Breuil, in pale blue, flowing into the Gironde. In red, a schematic representation of the part of the Duhart-Milon vineyard proposed for the site of the imaginary château with various annexes.*

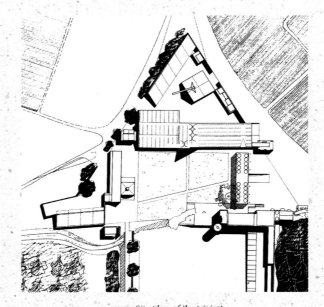

ABOVE: *Site plan of the project.*
OPPOSITE: *Imaginary label for the new château.*

CHATEAU DIXON-PIMLOTT

JEREMY AND FENELLA DIXON WITH MARK PIMLOTT, LONDON

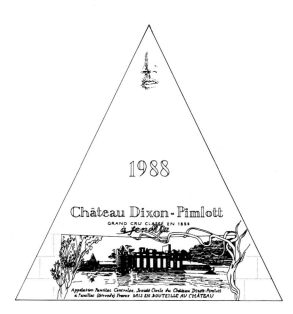

WITH THE ASSISTANCE OF THE PAINTER CARL LUBIN
MODEL BY RICHARD ARMIGER

THERE COULD NOT BE a more English firm of architects than Jeremy Dixon and his partners. The origins of the firm go back to the early 1970s when a group of young students graduated from the Architectural Association in London with the intention of working together.

Jeremy Dixon with his wife Fenella (born in 1939 and 1938 respectively) established a practice in London that came to prominence with successful designs for housing in London. These designs for St Mark's Road, Lanark Road and Ashmill Street (instead of slavishly following the destructive urban thinking of the modern movement) adopt principles of design that relate the houses to the tradition of the London street. They have been described as post-modern because they have assumed into their designs elements that are familiar.

The talent of Jeremy Dixon and his partners lies in assimilating ideas and feelings about places and then once these sensations have been absorbed producing a synthesis that is not derivative but still familiar. A great deal of detailed research goes into every project however small. Every commission is a learning process. On winning the competition for the extension to the Royal Opera House, in London's Covent Garden, Dixon (with BDP) began detailed research which covered the entire opera world. It is this concern for the client and the wish to fulfill his requirements, almost by osmosis, that makes Dixon an exceptional architect. At a time when many architects are making grand gestures to achieve a high public profile, the quiet and recessive nature of the Dixon approach is as unusual as it is welcome.

For the Châteaux Bordeaux project a team of three – Jeremy Dixon, Fenella Dixon and Mark Pimlott – was formed to produce the competition design. Each member of the team made a particular contribution but it was Mark Pimlott who finally drew the scheme. He has worked with the Dixons on a number of projects since 1984. He is Canadian by birth, and, like them, a graduate of the Architectural Association in London. His work includes urban schemes in Montreal (1982) and Barcelona (1985), and, with Peter St John, a prizewinning project for the Indira Gandhi National Centre for Arts, New Delhi (1986).   COLIN AMERY

THE QUALITY OF THE typical Bordeaux château is unselfconscious and self-evident. It could be said that there is a sense of English restraint in the manner of the château, which avoids grandeur and does not reveal everything at first encounter; the content has to be discovered. The visitor's memory holds onto special sensations: the odour of the *chais* at work; the feel of walking on stone and earth floors; the absence of daylight; the preoccupation with ageing in natural processes. It is said that the character of the wine dictates the character of the château. Therefore,

we asked the estate's owner for a description of the wine from Duhart-Milon. The words he used were "drinkable, affordable, approachable". In working on the project we have tried to retain something of these impressions.

The château buildings are sited on a triangle of land that unites on its three sides the vineyard, the village of Milon, and the valley. The front façade of the château looks across the valley onto a garden that is arranged around the theme of water. The public approach to the buildings is from a new road that runs along the southern edge of the valley. The main gateway leads to a raised causeway across the water meadow, and a small bridge crosses the canal that bisects the valley longitudinally. The main aspect is a rectangle of water flanked by existing woodlands, a boxed-in lake, revealing the château at the far end. The approach continues along one side of the lake and the château ensemble becomes visible as an informal composition of buildings giving equal prominence to the *chais* and the château itself.

The visitor arrives in a courtyard of buildings open on one side to the lake and with the vineyard visible through the walls of a transparent *cuvier*. The gardens of the château continue down to the other edge of the lake bordered by a wall that is part of the museum. The approach sequence is thereby extended right around the lake ending up in an informal path in the woods and the folly by the canal.

The arrangement for the functional buildings is very straightforward with the various stages of the winemaking process arranged in sequence around the courtyard. The grapes arrive after harvesting at a special terrace that lies between the *cuvier* and the château. The *cuvier* and its modern equipment naturally give rise to a steel and glass building. Whereas the maturing and storage areas are more traditional in their aspect. A visit around the estate would follow the same sequence: château, *cuvier*, *chais*, *cave* and tasting room. This tour starts in the daylight and gradually gets darker, ending with a descent into an underground *cave* in almost total darkness, only lit by grotto-like *lunettes* looking back over the surface of the lake. To arrive at the tasting room above is to come back into the daylight. This room is at the top of the château's tower which represents the focal point of the composition of the buildings. From the tower it is possible for the first time to see the vineyard and the valley and to understand the layout of the château buildings within the landscape.

The architectural manner of the project allows the various buildings to have an individual expression: overall consistency is not sought, but rather a gentle intermingling of styles and building technology that represents the contemporary state of architectural affairs as we see it.

JEREMY & FENELLA DIXON AND MARK PIMLOTT

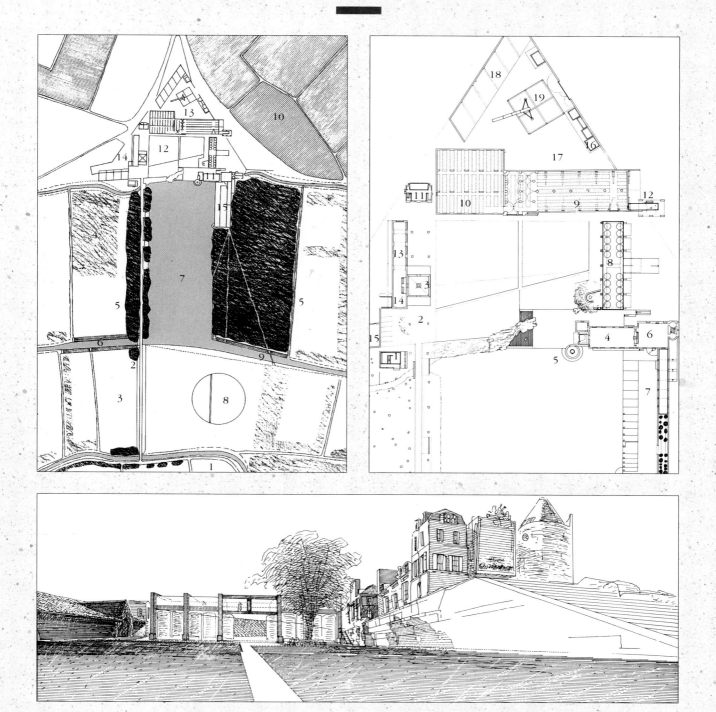

TOP LEFT: *plan of the whole project in its setting in the vineyard. 1. New road 2. Château driveway 3. Jalle du Breuil 4. Existing trees 5. New plantings 6. Canal 7. Lake 8. Sheep hill 9. Bridge between Pauillac and St-Estèphe 10. Vineyard 11. Château 12. Château courtyard 13. Agricultural courtyard 14. Wine-making building 15. Museum and garden.*

TOP RIGHT: *site plan of the various buildings. 1. Manager's house 2. Entrance courtyard 3. Cooperage 4. Château 5. Wine-tasting room 6. Owner's residence 7. Museum 8. Cuvier 9. First-year chai 10. Second-year chai 11. Cellarmaster's house 12. Régisseur's house 13. Bottling 14. Packing 15. Storage of pallets 16. Offices 17. Agricultural courtyard 18. Sheds 19. Fertiliser store 20. Lake.*
MIDDLE: *View facing the cuvier.*
BOTTOM: *Interior view of cuvier.*

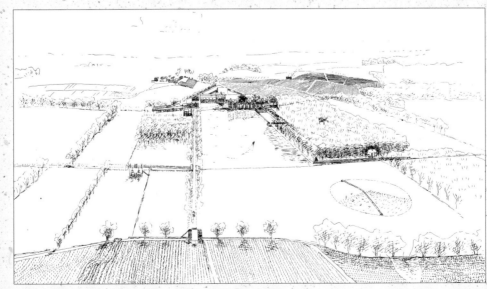

ABOVE: *General view of the château from the new lake.*
(Oil on canvas by Carl Laubin, 1988).

LEFT: *View down onto the whole of the developed site.*

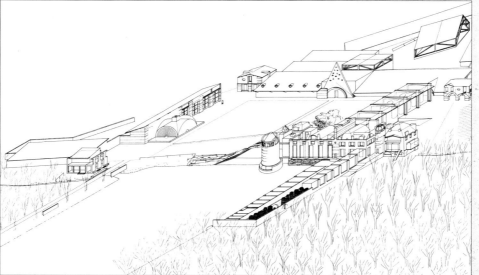

RIGHT: *Bird's-eye view of all the château buildings.*

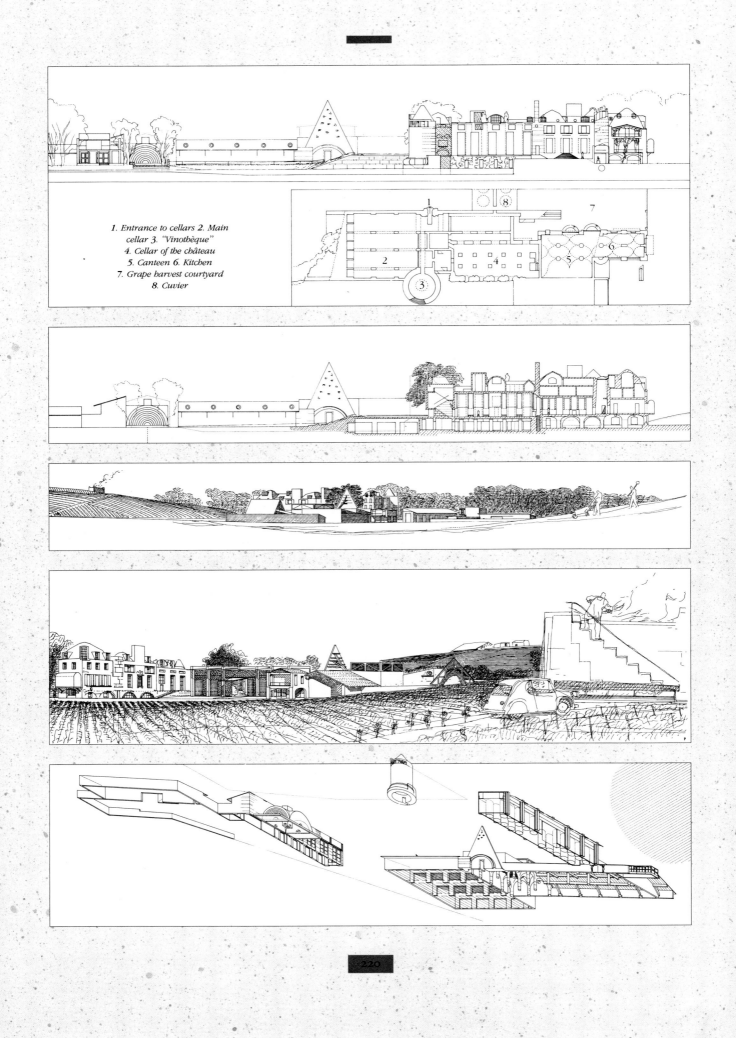

1. Entrance to cellars 2. Main
cellar 3. "Vinothèque"
4. Cellar of the château
5. Canteen 6. Kitchen
7. Grape harvest courtyard
8. Cuvier

OPPOSITE: *Various aspects of the project: elevations, plan, perspective and axonometric projection.*

ABOVE: *The chai and cuvier of the château.*

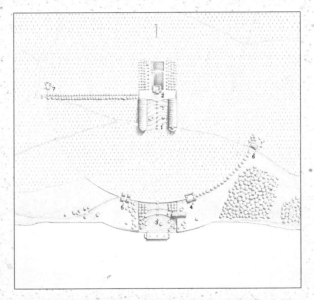

ABOVE: *Site plan of the various château buildings beside the lake. 1. Wine-making installations 2. Owner's residence 3. Club and its tennis court 4. Museum 5. "Wine embassies" 6. Cellarmaster's residence 7. Warden's house.*
OPPOSITE: *Plan and perspective of the château with its linear chais and cuviers.*

CHATEAU LIPSKY

FLORENCE LIPSKY AND PASCAL ROLLET, GRENOBLE
AND VINCENT DEFOS DU RAU, BORDEAUX

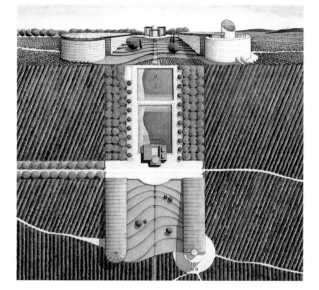

WITH THE ASSISTANCE OF THE SCULPTOR JEAN-FRANÇOIS GAVOTY
AND THE ADDITIONAL SUPPORT
OF CHATEAU BRANE-CANTENAC, MARGAUX
AND THE GROUPE CRATERRE, GRENOBLE

THE DESIGNERS AND THEIR PROJECT

FLORENCE, PASCAL and VINCENT are three unusual young architects. Pascal Rollet (born in 1960 in Grenoble) and Vincent Defos du Rau (born in 1958 in Dax) met at Mayotte (Comores) when they were still students but with several projects to their credit. These projects were built with earth, and marked a new architectural departure. In this way, they developed the methods of the Groupe Craterre in Grenoble, which consist of respect for the naturalness of the material coupled with technological inventiveness. In 1985, Pascal won first prize in a competition intended to promote wooden architecture, and with the firm Jourda & Perraudin, worked on perfecting the technical details of the building for the Ecole d'Architecture in Lyon.

In 1986, Florence won the Louis Katz special prize in the international Van Allen competition for the best graphic work and in 1987, she designed the book *Le Corbusier et la Méditerranée*. Their latest piece of work, "Une maison pour demain", a prototype for the house of the future for the Habiter 88 exhibition in Paris (La Villette), shows all the virtues of their professionalism. The project combines earth, for the most intimate spaces, with canvas for the contact between the house and the surrounding sky – technological ingenuity combined with simplicity of spatial structure. Three promising young architects indeed . . . BRUNO QUEYSANNE

IN THE 18TH CENTURY, the wine-producing estates that had access to the Gironde created small ports from where they sold their wine. In 1988, the creation of a new wine château places us in a similar situation: to initiate renewed cultural exchange and contact with the outside world. Thus our project encompasses the waterside area which would play an important role in the reception of visitors.

The visitor is taken by boat to this reception area, which is inspired by the very British notion of the club – the most elegant way of creating a comfortable setting in which people from all parts of the world can devote themselves to their common passion. This "club house" is a ship which is moored alongside the quay. It has three masts made of glass and aluminium and its great unfurled sails shelter the upper deck and the passengers' cabins. These are in fact private apartments which overlook the vineyard and the châteaux.

From the club to the cellarmaster's residence – the whole architecture gravitates around the wine château. To reach the latter, the visitor goes by foot along a straight path made of green marble which crosses the vineyard and which is marked out with blue lights at night. The visit starts with the *cuvier*, an enormous stainless steel tanker inside which the fermentation vats are arranged in an arc, like a cathedral organ. Light from an overhead window dramatizes this cylindrical space. This spectacle is orchestrated by the cellarmaster who is positioned in the middle of the vinification tower with push-button controls.

Whereas the *cuvier* is testimony of modern man's capacity to transform his environment, the *chais* (and the other buildings involved in wine production) maintain their strong links with the *terroir*. They are built from plain earth, from the same earth that has made the region prosperous. Compressed into light casings using the *pisé* method, the earth is built into thick, solid walls. The structure built in this way is a great asset in maintaining a stable temperature, allowing the wine to age in oak barrels at a temperature of between 13 and 16 °C (55 and 61°F). Our *chais* will provide the best guarantee of coolness and humidity without any artificial ventilation or air conditioning.

The quality of the building can be appreciated when moving among the barrels that have been arranged in strict lines in the shadowy light under the vaults of these large naves. After visiting the bottling plant, the hypostyle area of the packing cases, the cooperage and the cellar, the tour finishes at the top of the *cuvier*: a circular ramp leads to the wine-tasting room. Suspended between the ground and the sky, it offers a magnificent panoramic view of the *terroir*.

With its façade of green copper studded with brass, the owner's château residence looks out on a sea of green marble and vineyards opening onto the club. The marble path climbs the turfed terraced steps up to the rotunda of the entrance, where three circular areas are symbolically arranged on top of one another, from bottom to top: the owner's personal cellar, the reception room and the office-library. In the actual residence, only the large dining-room will be visible to the public, since the family apartments are kept hidden behind a wall of privacy. Meals are served at a long table in front of an immense window which allows the vineyards to form a theatrical backdrop. Indeed this is the scene for a one-act play: "in praise of the art of living".

FLORENCE LIPSKY, VINCENT DEFOS DU RAU,
AND PASCAL ROLLET

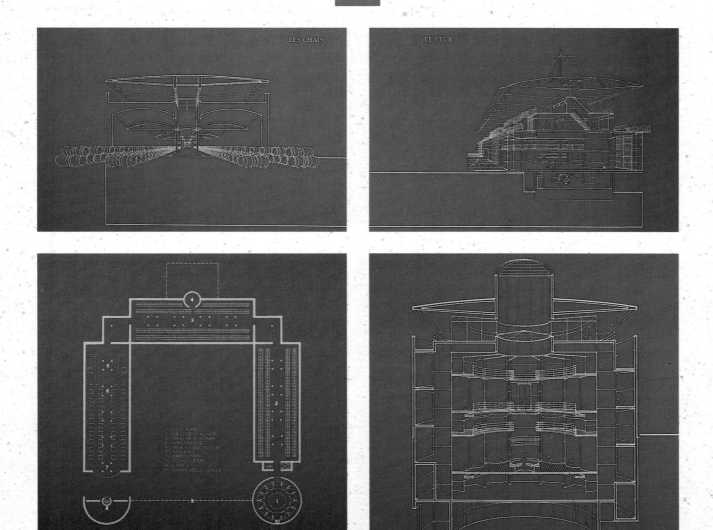

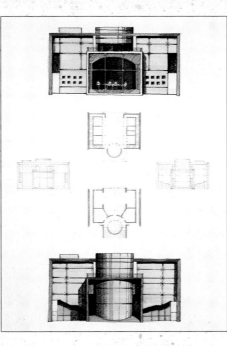

TOP: Left, *interior perspective of the chais.*
Right, *section in perspective of the club.*
MIDDLE: Left, *plan of the two parallel
buildings containing the wine-producing*
machinery. Right, *section of the cuvier and
its helical ramp.*
BOTTOM: *Façades, plans and sections of the
château.*

ABOVE: *Part of the château built on the water.*
OPPOSITE: *General plan of the architectural scheme.*

CHATEAU MONTES

FERNANDO MONTES, PARIS

WITH THE ASSISTANCE
OF HUGUES TOUTON
MODEL BY ALAIN PRAS

THE PROJECT

*"Et à ce propos, je dirai quelque chose de ce genre d'industrie (de transformation) qui
consiste à placer la matière au bon endroit, au bon contact . . . et à attendre."*
Francis Ponge, Pièces, *Le Vin*

THE MEDOC

The first thing to note is that, in the Médoc, the whole takes precedence over the parts. The difference between the areas can be so abstract that they are not obvious and the division of the land can become purely conceptual. To complicate the boundaries still further, fences are rare here.

The Graves is not the same as the Médoc, and not just because of the different system of *appellations d'origines contrôlées* or because of the absence of a historical classification of the wine. The unique character of the wine-growing region that exists in the Médoc is missing in the Graves. The Landes and the Médoc have many things in common. Naturally, they have the same background of ocean, land and river. But they also have a shared concern for maintaining the ecological balance to conserve the environment in this utopia.

This art of agriculture (*Sanctas Rusticitas*) perhaps dates back to the Venezia of the 16th century with the strict distinction between dry and wet, or permeable and absorbent soil. In fact the Médoc with its pinewoods in an area of marshland and producing great wine every year is a good example of the putting into practice of experimental techniques and of the *"usanza nuova"* of French agriculture.

THE PROJECT

We are faced with a problem today – the problem of modernizing, destroying or redefining the concept of the wine château. Is the château a farm? Or is it a villa?

It has the composite and open structure of the modern farm as envisaged by Le Corbusier in *Les trois établissements humains*. But like the Palladian villa of Venezia, the Bordeaux château is primarily an emblem and then a place of habitation. An emblem of what? In former times, although wine was greatly enjoyed, it continued to be regarded as any other agricultural product. It was only in this century that the wine, which was returned to the châteaux from the Chartrons after the setting up of an international sales network, took off and became what it is today: a luxury product with such added value that the place of production has been bestowed with a magical air.

Like the *haute couture* houses or the top-class perfumers, the châteaux are looking for a clear and objective explanation of their success. Very few of them manage to extend their market to reach new consumers without devaluing their image. Successful examples are Cartier and Mouton. An unsuccessful example is Cardin. The Palladian villa is meant to be both an urbane presence in the country and a sublimation of the ordinary qualities of the countryside. A monumental and splendid object, it gleams in the middle of a field of maize. It can control vast stretches of land with its numerous connected activities and developments.

The Bordeaux château has the same duality: urbane and rural. It is urbane because of the proximity of Bordeaux, the origin of its occupants and the links that unite it with the rest of the world via the wine trade. It is rural because it is a centre of agricultural production and without this role, there is no future; hardly any châteaux have survived without their vines. However, these châteaux are now also linked with leisure activities. As the estates evolved, the *vita rustica* has given way to the emergence of a new factor: wine tourism.

The link between the road and the château, the exterior and interior, the integration of the various buildings that make up the estate, the architectural link between the various activities concerning the production and sale of wine. What can compare with this bringing together of diverse elements? The intermediate space surrounding the château is not a village square. It lacks the necessary diversity and reference points to become one. Nor can it be compared with a cloister of an abbey – the empty space being marked off by a string of specialized buildings – because it is much too extrovert in character. However, from the village square, it has inherited its open structure and the scale required for the machinery and for access to the road; from the cloister, it has learnt how to unify its composite elements. The château is an area of contradiction, yet it is unambiguous, it is both a place of rustic simplicity and an adornment.

FERNANDO MONTES

NB. See the biographical note on Fernando Montes on page 202.

BELOW: *General view of the château with the residence above the water in the foreground, reached by an entrance ramp; on the right, the museum and the chai.*

ABOVE: *View down on the courtyard of the château and, in the background, the residence opening out onto the valley.*

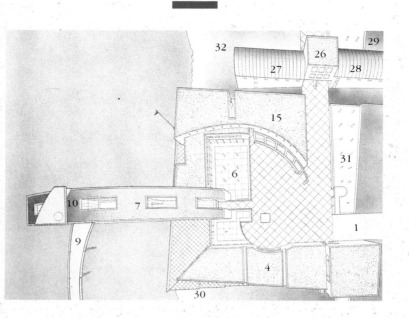

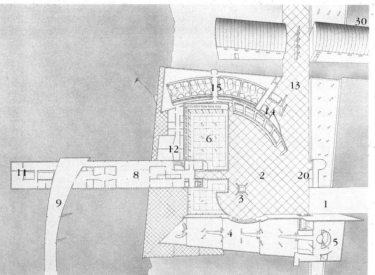

General plans of the buildings on three levels: 1. Visitors' entrance 2. Château courtyard 3. Skylight of the wine-tasting area 4. Museum 5. Museum restaurant 6. Cloister 7. Château 8. Château restaurant 9. Access ramp to the château 10. Belvedere 11. Owner's residence 12. Administration 13. Delivery of grapes 14. Presses

15. Cuviers 16. First-year chai 17. Second-year chai 18. Bottling 19. Storage of pallets 20. Dispatch 21. Cellars 22. Wine-tasting area 23. Auditorium 24. "Wine embassies" 25. Cooperage 26. Cellarmaster's house 27. Lodgings for grape harvesters 28. Sheds 29. Agricultural courtyard 30. Grounds 31. Orchard 32. Pasture.

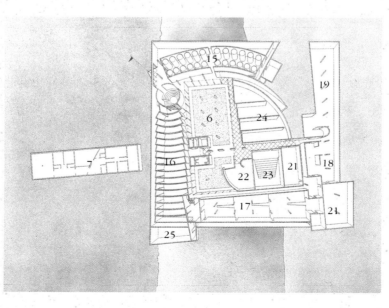

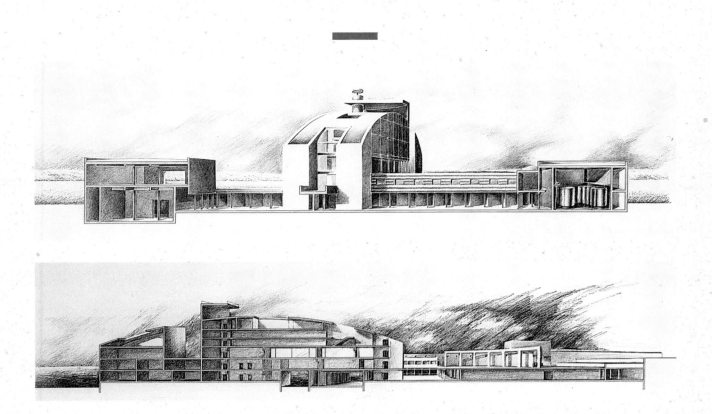

TOP: *Two sections through the buildings.*
BOTTOM: *View of the chais in perspective.*

ABOVE: *Preliminary sketches for the project.*
OPPOSITE: *First study model for the buildings.*

CHATEAU NIVELLE

BERTRAND NIVELLE, BORDEAUX

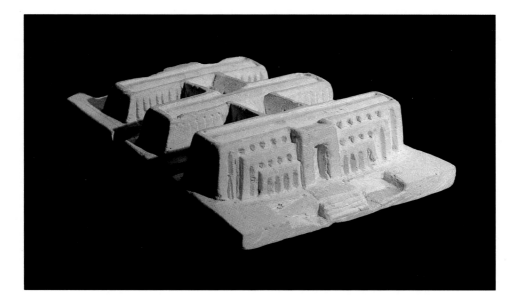

WITH THE ASSISTANCE OF
HENRI BRESLER, CONSULTANT,
MICHEL ROLLAND, OENOLOGIST,
AND BENOIT EYQUEM, COLLABORATOR

BERTRAND NIVELLE was born in 1955. He obtained his architects' diploma in 1983 after studying at the Ecole d'Architecture in Bordeaux where he now practices.

In 1985, a grant from the ministry for foreign affairs, "Villa Médicis hors les murs", enabled him to work with the Italian architect and painter, Massimo Scolari on the Noah's Ark project for the 17th Triennale of Milan (1986). This work continued his exploration of the possibilities offered to him by techniques as diverse as video film and design. With five other architects and the firm BBS-Production, he co-produced *Les Traces* (1984), a video film about the Spanish and French work of Ricardo Bofill. The film was awarded a prize at the 2nd International Festival of Architectural Film (FIFARC) in Bordeaux. He was also invited to exhibit in the design section of the 3rd FIFARC, for which he created the "*Lit-Bateau*" – floating architecture with poetic images linked to sailing and sleep. The piece, which was selected for the Salon des Artistes Décorateurs (SAD), was shown in Paris in the same year.

Bertrand Nivelle has taken part in various restoration projects in the protected area of Bordeaux and participated in numerous competitions. In 1981, he won the competition for the restoration of the balustrade and the lighting of the Pont de Pierre in Bordeaux (with Giacinto-Loisier). Then in 1986 he won the competition for the restructuring of the Atrium-Casino in Dax (Landes), a 1930s building by André Granet which, because of present-day cultural requirements, has had to be redesigned.

As well as having several articles published, "Architecture et dessin" in *Techniques et Architecture* (1986), "Letto-Batello, una tipologia intermedia" in *Domus* (1987), Bertrand Nivelle in parallel with his architectural activities is also an active painter. In the drawings and comments he makes in his notebooks – preliminary sketches which form a basis for his thoughts – he tries to grasp the moment when a roof becomes a pediment, when the town becomes a flotilla, the bed a boat, the coating a skin. This repertory of structures and ideas anticipates his future work and provides a source of reference for him to dip into.

ROSELINE GIUSTI

HAVING VISITED the 20 largest properties in the Médoc, I imagined a château whose architecture and character could rival the carefully created wine concealed in the cellars. Following the logic of the Médoc, it would be positioned on a site where vines do not grow, in the characteristic setting of a *jalle*. This slight depression between two gravel hills would provide shelter in its dense vegetation, but I wondered how to approach this ideal site.

Then I remembered the comment of a vigneron and poet: "wine is the juice of the sun and the earth and its basic state is dry, not wet; therefore, the mythical substance that is its most opposite is water". The château would be built so as to protect it from the flooded land and it follows that my first sketches gave it the form of a boat. Thus, protected from the frost and the light, its hull would provide a space where the wine would be allowed to settle. Above, the deck of this platform, 120 by 90 metres (130 by 100 yards), would serve as the foundation for the château, which would be open to the public, to the vines and to various entertainments. It would be divided into three independent units: the hotel-museum, the *cuvier* and the reception areas being the key places of interest to visit in the building.

In the first unit, the hotel-museum, the visitor, having seen to the formalities of his stay, would find information about the vine and the origins of the château. In the centre of the building, he would enter the second unit, the *cuvier*, where he would find hidden in one of the vats the passage leading down to the *chais*. There, in a vast ambulatory, he would learn about the work involved in the maturing of the wine. The visitor would then find himself in the stairway-corridor, winding around the wine-tasting rooms of the third unit. In the reception room, the guests would be able to meet the people responsible for ensuring the quality of the vintages and perhaps even form lasting friendships.

BERTRAND NIVELLE

NOTE ON THE VINIFICATION PROPOSED FOR THE CHATEAU

This 50-hectare (124 acres) property is subdivided into 35 parcels of land and produces an average of 2,500 hl per year. The hand-harvested grapes are placed in carts with a capacity of 25-30 hl. A conveyor belt leads to the machine which crushes and destalks the grapes before they are sorted. The crushed grapes are put in vats of different capacities. The vats are made of stainless steel and are divided into two: the upper part, self-emptying for alcoholic fermentation and the lower part to catch the flow from the first. The automatic regulation of the temperatures of the vats to control the rate of fermentation is carried out from the laboratory by an internal flag system.

After the juice has run out and after the grapes have been pressed, the *vin de goutte* and the *vin de presse* undergo malolactic fermentation separately before descending, by the force of gravity, to the underground *chais*. The new barrels are filled by a distribution ramp and then moved by a pre-programmed crane to their places on a positioning block. Underneath, the stainless-steel washing area is concealed from view: only the barrels are displayed in the *chais*. The first- and second-year decanting operations are carried out by the so-called "barrel-to-barrel" method with pressurized air replacing the traditional bellows.

At the end of the first year, the cranes move the 1,500 barrels to the second-year *chai*, further along the row. Taking all the barrels together, gives a perspective that is 110 m (120 yds) long. Fining is carried out in the barrel after which the wines are put in a 1,000 hl, glass-fibre and reinforced-concrete vat. By means of a pump, this vat fills exactly three vats for drawing off wine. The bottling plant is automatically supplied with empty bottles, corks, labels, capsules, cases. It creates two products: wine for bulk sale in pallet boxes and the traditional wooden cases of wine. Most of the stock remains in the storeroom and will be recorded on a computer for future consignments. The remainder will be placed in the cellar which connects the *chais* to the tasting rooms.

BERTRAND NIVELLE AND MICHEL ROLLAND

Preliminary sketches for an architectural proposal and, at the bottom, for the interior layout of the chais and cuviers.

TOP: *Sections and façades of the buildings.*
BOTTOM: *Detailed plans of the interior organization on three levels.*
LEVEL − 1
A. Visitors' reception B. First- and second-year chais
C. Bottling D. Automatic stock E. Delivery and dispatch
F. Technical buildings, equipment shed and cooperage
G. Wine-tasting room H. Ageing cellar.

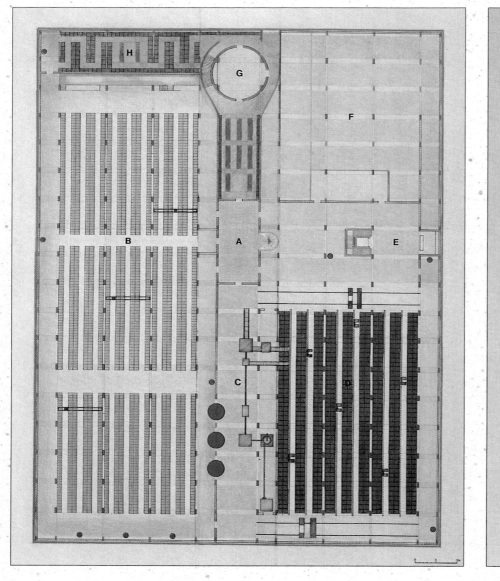

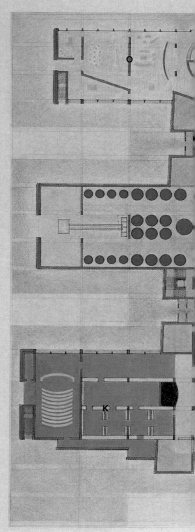

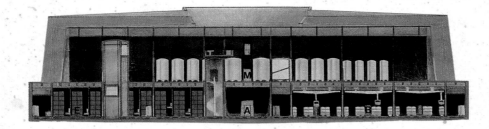

LEVEL 0
I. Main entrance hall J. Châteaux Bordeaux museum K. Wine museum L. Gallery for temporary exhibitions M. Cuvier N. Wine-tasting room O. Sitting rooms, library, music room P. Grape-harvesters' room.
LEVEL + 1
Q. Guest rooms R. Offices and administration S. Bridge T. Private sitting rooms U. Reception rooms.

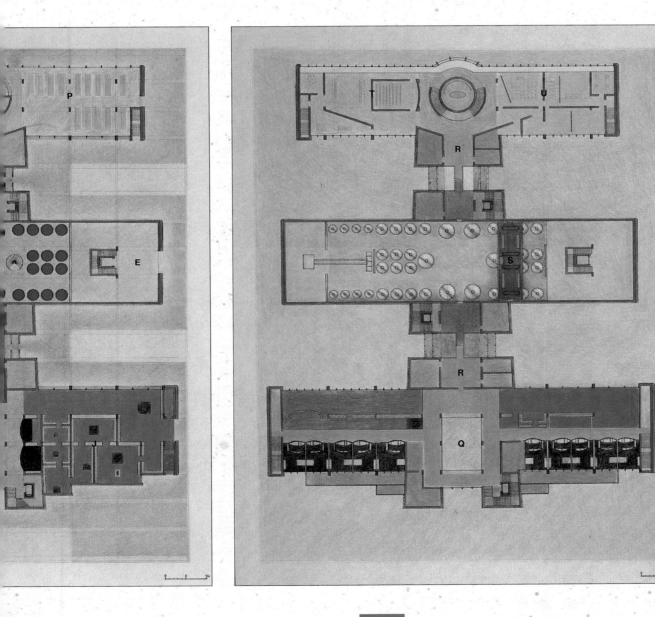

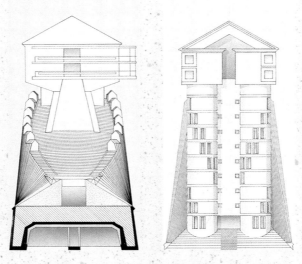

ABOVE: *Sections and elevations of the main building of the château.*
OPPOSITE: *View in perspective of the château placed on
its substructure of chais and cuviers.*

CHATEAU REICHLIN

BRUNO REICHLIN, GENEVA

WITH THE ASSISTANCE OF THE ARCHITECTS
THOMAS HASLER, GABRIELE AND ADOLF STILLER
AND THE ARCHITECTURAL STUDENTS
PHILIPPE MEYLAN AND MICHAEL VOCHTING
MODEL BY ADOLF STILLER

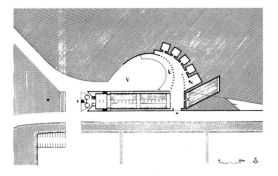

THE DESIGNER AND HIS PROJECT

BRUNO REICHLIN was born in 1941 in Lucerne. He spent his youth in Switzerland in the Ticino. He shares a studio in Lugano with his associate, Fabio Reinhart, with whom he has designed most of his projects.

Bruno Reichlin belongs to a kind of formalist school of architecture. This does not meant to say that he treats architectural forms in an arbitrary manner, wanting to free them of any expression of constructive or functional constraints. He is a formalist to the extent that he is interested in the processes of creation, generation and transformation of architectural structures beyond purely positivist reasons of usage or solidity.

Bruno Reichlin is concerned with carrying out a formal analysis of the "languages" of architecture and takes an interest in the work of linguists and semiologists. The fact that he now teaches at the Ecole d'Architecture in Geneva, is both a coincidence and a return to basics. These architectural interests will perhaps explain why his first work to be built, the Casa Tonini at Toricella (Ticino, 1972-74) is the direct result of his interpretation of the Palladian theme of the villa with a symmetrical plan. By the pertinence and the precision of his analyses, Bruno Reichlin has also transformed the way we look at the works of the most renowned architect of the century, Le Corbusier, whom he has celebrated at the Centre Pompidou.

His analysis is based on methodical and tireless questioning. He questions the identity of things but his eyes do not wander into the abstract; they remain firmly fixed on the material nature of the architecture.

JACQUES LUCAN

THE WINE-PRODUCING LANDSCAPE of the Bordeaux region is a monument of agrarian culture and, as such, deserves to be preserved. It is a territory that has been cultivated and built upon with ingenuity and concern for maintaining the equilibrium and harmony.

The beauty of this setting stems less from the quality of particular architectural monuments than from the geography of the land: the beauty of the rows of poplars along the canals – those levelling waterways that make the minimal, but geologically essential, changes in the level of the land in the Médoc all the more noticeable. A discreet,

melancholy and fragile beauty which is revealed when the cold rain of winter transforms the low terraces into a marshland that stretches as far as the eye can see and when the Gironde becomes a pool of turbid water. But it is the many Bordeaux châteaux that characterize the landscape that is already familiar to the traveller because it repeats the same gentle images and legends of all that belongs to the past, to nostalgic but distant contemplation.

This architectural project rests on these statements. The new wine château cannot merely continue the history of its predecessors, copying their typology and even their architecture. The new château openly proclaims its differences from its ancestors. Standing aloof it is a comment on the past and forms a postscript for what has gone before. This distancing is in any case implicit in the design programme: the building of a wine museum presupposes an introspective dimension, whereas the area for wine tasting and the related tourist amenities introduce a recreational and didactic dimension which relegates the primary function of the wine château to second place. It would thus be simplistic to claim that this new château is simply a distillation of the historical notion of the Bordeaux château.

The introspective dimension justifies the architectural bias. The *cuvier*, *chais*, château cellar, wine-tasting area which have become public as much as production places, then the residence of the owner and his staff, and finally the museum and the guest house – although arranged around a circuit for visitors that follows the logic of production, they will nevertheless be presented in an artificial way instead of being separated into distinct areas. All the fundamental elements will be arranged together inside an immense building. The wine-tasting area opens onto a perspective of the vats, the château cellar and the first-year *chais* forming a "shrine" beneath the wine tasters' feet.

Temple, giant vat, warehouse, machine, petrified saurian or coleopteron – the new château evokes all these images at once without any of them being completely assumed. It has the semblance of a traditional wine château, like the decorative Cos d'Estournel which is its counterpart on the opposite slope of the Jalle de Breuil.

BRUNO REICHLIN

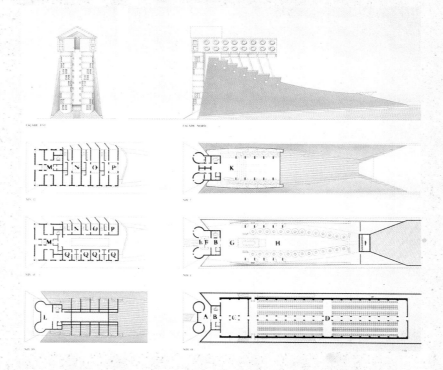

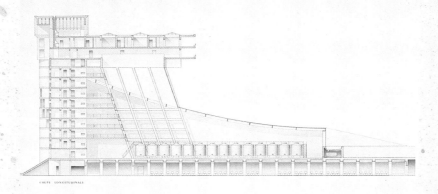

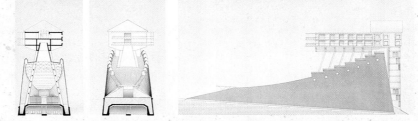

OPPOSITE: *Site plan of the château beside the lake.*
ABOVE: *Elevations, sections and plans of the château at different levels:*
A. Delivery B. Centre for distribution C. Cellar of the château D. First-year chai E. Entrance for
the public F. Reception of visitors G. Wine-tasting area H. Cuvier I. Delivery of grapes
J. Accommodation for guests K. Museum L. Technical buildings M. Owner's residence
N. Régisseur's quarters O. Cellarmaster's quarters P. Manager's quarters Q. Guest rooms
R. Second-year chai S. Bottling T. Storage of crates and pallets U. Agricultural
and viticultural equipment V. Courtyard W. Lake.

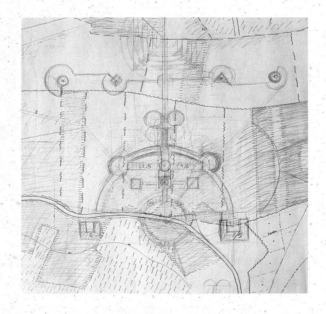

ABOVE: *Preliminary sketch for the general construction of the*
château on its site. The water of the river is shown at the top of the drawing.
OPPOSITE: *Sketch of site plan of the château*

CHATEAU VANDENHOVE

CHARLES VANDENHOVE, LIEGE

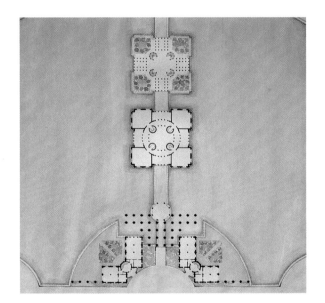

WITH THE ASSISTANCE OF
JACQUES SEQUARIS AND ANGELO DORE,
MARIE-LOUISE DELAIRESSE, ALAIN DIRIX,
STEPHANE MEYRANT, PRUDENT DE WISPELAERE,
ALAIN SABBE AND AFAGH MOHAMMADI
MODEL BY FRANZ BAUMANS

CHARLES VENDENHOVE was born in 1927 in the village of Teuven (Belgium) at the centre of a triangle formed by the three European towns of Liège, Maastricht and Aix-la-Chapelle. He grew up in the rural surroundings of his father's large farm, built in the typical style of the Meuse region. He studied architecture from 1945-51, first at Liège, then at the Ecole Nationale de la Cambre in Brussels. It was there that the avant-garde teachings of two great Belgian pioneers, Victor Bourgeois and Henry van de Velde, left a lasting impression on him.

After finishing his studies, he went into partnership with the Belgian architect, Lucien Kroll. Whilst travelling around Europe, they met Le Corbusier and Gropius, and also Gi Ponti and Max Bill. Their first creation, a house in Waterloo (town south of Brussels) in 1954, showed their attention to the use of new systems of construction. In 1957, Vandenhove married Jeanne Belvaux, who became his main collaborator. He set up his own architectural practice in Liège. Based on his very extensive research into prefabricated building materials, he designed his first buildings, notably the Institut National de l'Industrie Charbonnière (1960).

The 1950s saw the start of his long and fruitful collaboration with the University of Liège, for whom he built a students' residence (1962). His development as an architect was also broadened by his design for a new campus for the university. For this scheme, he built the Magasin à Livres (1961), the imposing Institut d'Education Physique (1963) and the Centre Hospitalier Universitaire (1962). This important project reveals all the aspects of his talent: his mastery in planning, his search for clear and monumental structures, his refined manner of construction, his attention to details and his taste for the grandiose.

Alongside his larger works, Vandenhove continues to work on more personal projects. The evolution of his style may be detected in the architecture of his own house (1962) and the Maison Schoffeniels in Olne (1967). The Maison Delforges in Namur (1983) reveals a new classicism. But the most striking examples of this architectural development are his subtle alterations to the old Hotel Torrentius in Liège and the redevelopment of the Hors-Château district (1979) in the same town. In this urban block he successfully achieved a remarkable blend between the old (17th-century) and new houses. In 1985, he celebrated his outstanding career with a big exhibition of his work at the Institut Français d'Architecture in Paris. Partly as a result, he acquired an international reputation which gave him the opportunity of major projects in France and Holland in particular.

GEERT BEKAERT

IN THE HEART OF THE MEDOC, in a valley that opens onto the Gironde, a multitude of canals branch out to form a network of waterways covering a width of nearly 400 metres (440 yards). The two slopes of this *jalle* are lined with the neat rows of the vineyard that marks its horizon. It is an inspired place of strange beauty which is well worth preserving. Building a château on this site thus implies a harmonious conjunction between nature and the achievements of man.

This new château must exalt the magic of the place and appeal to all the spectator's senses. Into it must be sublimated the geometry of the network of canals which connect the slopes of the valley by creating a shimmering waterside setting from which the architectural forms of the château and its outbuildings will emerge. The northern side of this stretch of water is served by an extension of the regional "wine train"; the southern side by an approach road for cars. A dike is raised up to the water level to connect the two sides. Having passed through the entrance portico, the visitor immediately sees the villas which are intended to house the guests.

Further on, he will see – on either side of an axial course – the line of the *chais* and *cuviers*. They mark the limit of the square stretch of water with the château in the middle. Beside the château are the various focal points of its structure: the wine-tasting area with its conical roof, the museum devoted to the wine architecture of the Bordeaux region, the open-air theatre and the four buildings for the "wine embassies".

By ascending to the upper terrace of the château, privileged visitors will be able to enjoy an overall view of the vineyard and to enter the base of the cobweb-like hollow sphere, which is both monumental and sculptural and which symbolizes the communion between Reason and Passion at the heart of this new estate.

CHARLES VANDENHOVE

Study for bird's-eye view of the château (in the middle)
and of the chais and cuviers (in the background).

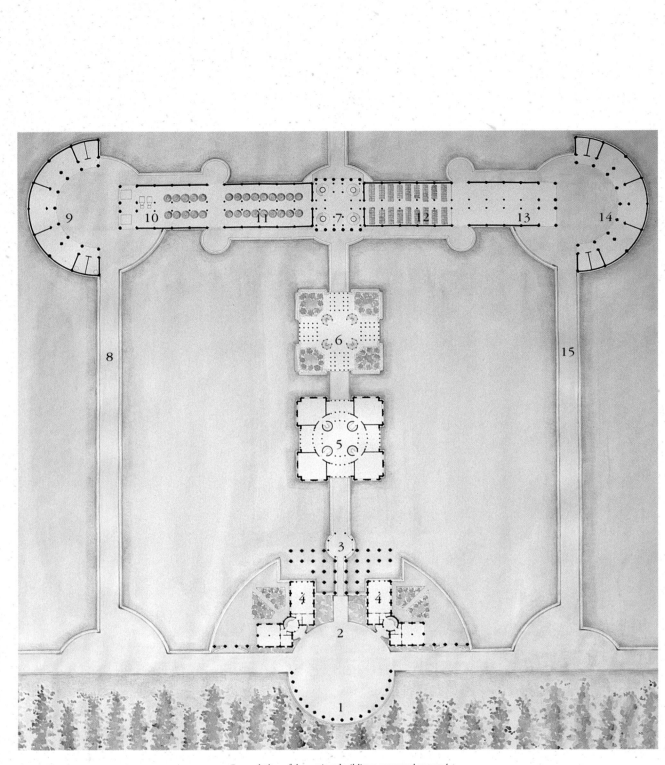

*General plan of the various buildings arranged around
the château: 1. Car park 2. Visitor's entrance 3. Portal
4. Residences 5. Château 6. Long-term cellar, museum
7. Wine-tasting area 8. Delivery of grapes 9. Workshop
and garages 10. Presses 11. Cuviers 12. Chais
13. Bottling 14. Storage of pallets 15. Dispatch.*

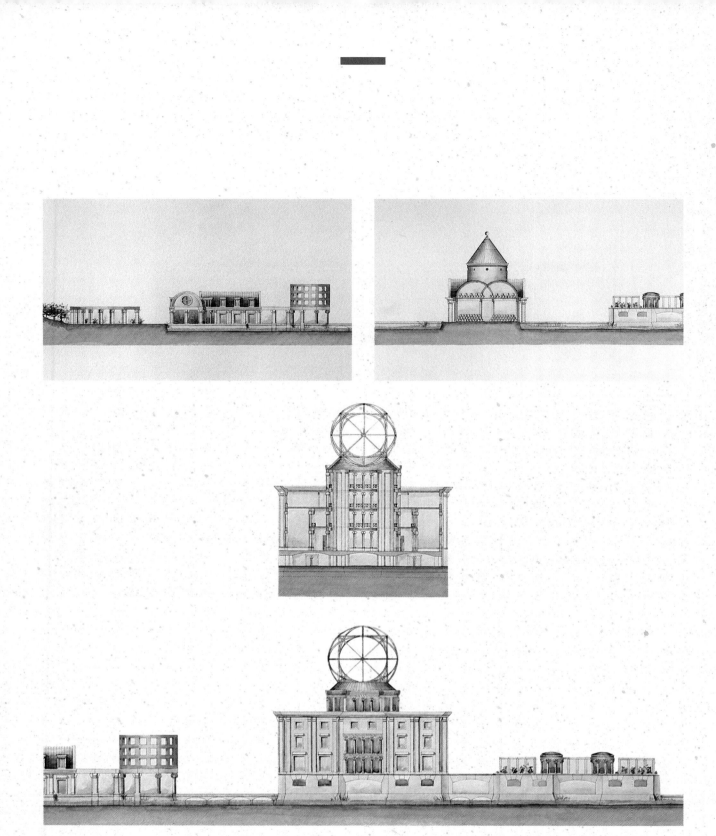

*Façades, sections and elevations of the wine-producing
buildings arranged around the château.*

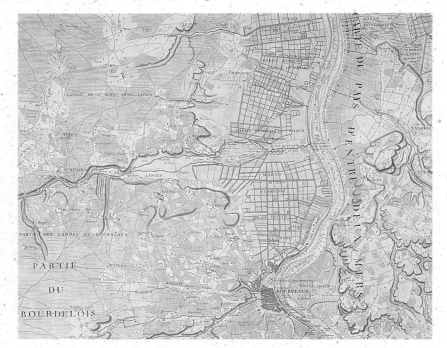

A REGIONAL BUSINESS PARK
FOR THE WINE TRADE AND A SCHEME FOR
THE FIRM OF BARTON & GUESTIER AT
BLANQUEFORT (MEDOC)

The commune of Blanquefort is situated in the northwest suburbs of Bordeaux, about six kilometres (4 miles) from the centre of the regional capital. Its geographical position makes it an important point of transition between the largest city in southwest France and the famous vineyards of the Médoc which start here.

The territory of this commune and its geographical surroundings is well serviced by road, rail and river links to the Médoc. In the 1960s and 1970s, when various large *négociant* firms decided to relocate to the suburbs, so as to have more space than was available in the Chartrons district, they established themselves at Blanquefort: C.V.B.G and Barton & Guestier, for example. In both cases, the move was unfortunately accompanied by the construction of immense new storage buildings with little architectural merit – the same danger that now threatens a very large part of the wine-producing economy of the region. The consequence was a loss of cultural identity, and thus of prestige also.

Being sensitive to this situation, the head of the Barton & Guestier company agreed to a research project. This assigned architects with a theoretical study to outline, retrospectively, what could have been a more sympathetic and effective means of developing the 40,000 square metres (50,000 square yards) of land on this remarkable site which is bordered by the Jalle de Blanquefort and marked by Château de Magnol.

In the scheme by Patrick Dillon and Jean de Gastines, this 18th-century château becomes the central point of a circular composition on which the modern installations are grafted and divided into four groups which are distinct but complementary, so as to avoid the heavy mass of a monolithic building. Rejecting the image of a wine factory, the project re-invents the idea of a wine-producing village grouped around its old château.

In addition, while surveying the surroundings of this site and those of the nearby Ford factory from a helicopter at a time of heavy rain and flooding, we were struck with the idea for a regional business park linked to the wine trade. This could serve as a new base for Bordeaux's wine merchants where the firms that could no longer survive in the Chartrons district of Bordeaux could gather together. It could be a district that could reconcile the advantages of economic activity with the virtues of innovative town and country planning, forming a collection of insular plots separated by waterways, canals and *jalles*.

JEAN DETHIER

This preliminary study was made possible thanks to the support of the Barton & Guestier company.

OPPOSITE: Top, *the new Barton & Guestier building constructed in the 1960s at Blanquefort (Médoc).* Middle, *the same building seen in its site with the 18th century Château Magnol in the foreground (left). Closer view of the same château with its vineyard in the background (right).* Opposite, *this old map of Bordeaux and its northern peripheral territories clearly shows the specific nature of the site. It is situated in the middle of the old marshes (see the network of drainage channels) near the point of convergence of the Gironde and the river (the Jalle du Breuil de Blanquefort, flowing from west to east).*

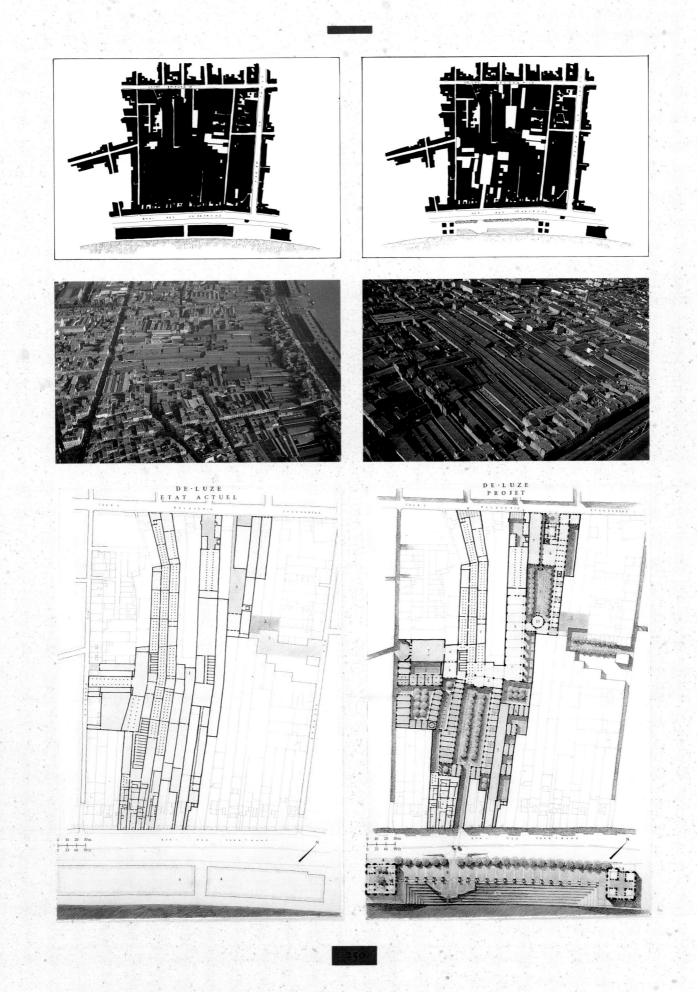

DE·LUZE
ETAT ACTUEL

DE·LUZE
PROJET

THE REDEVELOPMENT OF THE NEGOCIANT FIRM DE LUZE IN THE HISTORIC CHARTRONS DISTRICT OF BORDEAUX

PROJECT BY JEAN DE GASTINES AND PATRICK DILLON, PARIS

The *négociant* firm de Luze was founded in 1820 by a Swiss baron and set up its premises on the Chartrons quayside in Bordeaux at the peak of the wine merchants' power in the city. During the 1960s the Chartrons declined as a result of a general European trend away from urban centres. Thus, the majority of *maisons de négoce* disappeared or moved to the outskirts of Bordeaux. The traditional *négociant* premises in the historic Chartrons quarter were characterized by their unique architecture which had developed because of the confines of space in the city centre. The narrow merchants' houses extended along the quayside and were backed by a ribbon of *chais*, about 400 metres long and 10 metres wide (780 yards by 11 yards). During the 1970s and 1980s this isolated district declined and apart from the façades of the buildings situated along the quay, it is now very dilapidated and run-down. Today de Luze is one of the few remaining great *maisons de négoce* still based in the Chartrons. The owners of the company are well aware of the value of their prestigious three hectare (seven acres) site in this central quarter which has come to represent the whole history of the development of the Bordeaux wine trade. They were therefore reluctant to make the move to the suburbs in order to modernize their premises. Thus the de Luze firm was amenable to the proposal made by Jean Dethier and the Centre Georges Pompidou in 1988 to study a project for the redevelopment of its original site.

The problem was to ensure that de Luze could continue to trade in the Chartrons by modernizing its premises but at the same time retaining its architectural identity and its cultural links with the historic town of Bordeaux. The revitalization of this urban area entails that it maintains its links with both the city centre and the wine trade. We propose, therefore, to improve the access between the Chartrons and the centre of Bordeaux by building a street parallel to the river and leading directly into the heart of the new premises. We will also ensure that there is a clear view of the river by the demolition of unused warehouses which will be replaced by a river esplanade. Equally this urban area should be allowed to revitalize itself by attracting new activities and businesses with half the de Luze site to be allocated for new facilities. Parks, housing, hotels, and public amenities will therefore be constructed within the existing architectural and urban structure.

We aim to preserve the historical identity of the Chartrons. De Luze will retain its ancient quayside offices dating from the beginning of the 19th century, but the new buildings will open onto new public areas and gardens to occupy 1.5 hectares (4 acres). We are proposing a progressive architectural treatment rather than a complete solution.

Thus, de Luze would create the appropriate setting for its revitalization which would be linked to the urban and economic renaissance of the historic Chartrons quarter in the centre of Bordeaux.

JEAN DE GASTINES AND PATRICK DILLON

OPPOSITE:
Top, *two plans of the urban district of the Chartrons where the de Luze premises are situated (black represents buildings and white the areas not yet built on). To the left, the site in 1988. To the right, the envisaged scheme with new public areas (gardens and footpaths linking the district with the city centre).*
Middle, *two aerial photographs of the site in 1988. See also the two photographs on page 151.*
Bottom, *left: plan of the site in 1988. Right: detailed plan of the proposed future development. 1: Existing buildings (26,000 square metres) 2: New building for regional archives 3: Gardens and public areas 4: Hotel (6,500 square metres on three levels) 7: Land not owned by de Luze 8: New esplanade 9: Terraces 10: Public buildings A: De Luze offices (5,400 quare metres) B: reception C: Warehouse entrances F: Storage (5000 square metres) G: Bottling (1,000 square metres) H: Dispatch (shipping) (4,000 square metres) I: Warehouse exit.*

APPENDICES

BIOGRAPHICAL DICTIONARY

THE ARCHITECTS, BUILDERS AND LANDSCAPE DESIGNERS INVOLVED IN THE DESIGN OF THE CHATEAUX,
GARDENS AND WINE BUILDINGS IN THE BORDEAUX REGION, BETWEEN 1511 AND 1988.
JEAN-CLAUDE LASSERRE, PHILIPPE MAFFRE*

*The notes on landscape gardeners were written by Jean-Pierre Bériac. Those on the architects Bofill, Dillon and de Gastines were prepared by Ruth Eaton.
*The numbers at the end of the notes refer to the pages in the book where the architect or landscape gardener is mentioned. (Roman for the text, italic for the illustrations and bold for the architectural and town planning projects).

ALAUX, GUSTAVE (1816–82). Architect. Member of a long line of painters and architects. Attracted by the archaeological trend personified by Viollet-le-Duc (q.v.), he constructed or restored numerous churches in the neo-gothic style. Châteaux include Vilaure at Camarsac.

BARILLET-DESCHAMPS, PIERRE (1824–1873). Gardener. His career began in Bordeaux, where Napoleon III discovered him in 1852. Famous as gardener-in-chief of the city of Paris, where he designed the parks of Monceau, Buttes-Chaumont and Vincennes. Creator of the grounds of Château Batailley in Pauillac. (See p.116).

BILLAUDEL, JEAN-BAPTISTE, BASILIDE (1793–1851). Former student of the Ecole Polytèchnique and civil engineer, assigned to Bordeaux in 1818, where he spent his entire career. Mayor of the town and deputy to the Constituent Assembly in 1848. In collaboration with Claude Deschamps, his father-in-law (q.v.), he built Château Le Moine in Cenon in about 1825. During the construction of the bridge at Libourne, he planned a collection of merchants' dwellings with cellars beside the river.

BLAQUIERES, ALPHONSE (born 1829). Grandson of Etienne Laclotte (q.v.) and last member of that active dynasty of architects. Trained in Bordeaux, then Paris. Breaking with the classical and neo-classical tradition which dominated the work of this family, he developed a rather neo-gothic style, of which, in terms of quality and homogeneity, the most beautiful example is Château de Ricaud at Loupiac. He also built the wine châteaux of Pitray at Gardegan and St-Ahon at Blanquefort in the Médoc. (See p.84, 90, 149).

BOFILL, RICARDO (born 1939). Spanish (Catalan) architect and town planner. Considered to be one of the international leaders of post-modernism and the new neo-classical trend. He founded a multidisciplinary group in Barcelona, the Taller de Arquitectura. After numerous works in Spain, Bofill moved to Paris. In the new towns around the capital, he built numerous residential buildings inspired by a desire to reconcile the modernized virtues of neo-classical urban architecture with those of sophisticated industrial prefabrication, also managing to update the notion of architectonic adornment. In Paris, near the Gare Montparnasse, and in Montpellier (Quartier Antigone, 1979–89), he translated these principles to the heart of the city, trying to recreate a lost urbanity. In Bordeaux in 1987, he was invited to propose a very ambitious plan of urban reconstruction for the right bank of the river, opposite the old neo-classical 18th-century town. If it is carried through, this grand design could create a new focal point for the town centred around its majestic waterway and would be the major building project for the end of the century. In California in 1985, Bofill and his collaborator Patrick Dillon (q.v.) took part in the competition to design a wine château in the Napa Valley (Jan Schrem's Clos Pégase), but the judges chose Michael Graves' design (another leading light of post-modernism), which was built in 1987. In France, in the Médoc, Eric de Rothschild entrusted him with the creation of a new and spectacular circular and underground chai which was inaugurated at Château Lafite Rothschild in 1987. (See p.92, 122, 152, 170, 173, 174–175, 176, 180–181, 234).

BONFIN, RICHARD-FRANÇOIS (1730–1814). A building contractor and architect from Versailles who came to Bordeaux with Jacques-Ange Gabriel to take part in the construction of the Place Royale. He produced designs for a vast Médoc wine château at Arsac for the Comte de Ségur. In 1780, he reconstructed Château de Beauséjour in the middle of the Graves vineyard, at Mérignac.

BONNORE, JEAN-EDOUARD (born 1820). . Architect. A native of Lesparre, he settled there in 1852. In particular, two high-quality buildings in the commune of Valeyrac should be mentioned: Troussas, built in 1870 for M. Brannens, and Sipian, with its Renaissance-inspired decoration. (See p.76).

BRUN, PIERRE-CHARLES (1852–1902). Architect. Studied under Poitevin (q.v.) in Bordeaux and Uchard in Paris. He settled in Bordeaux and became the architect for the Monuments Historiques et Bâtiments Civils of the Gironde. Among his great works, including the restoration of Château Raba (1873), we should mention: the construction of Château Labeyrie at Cudos, that of Citran at Avensan between 1861 and 1864, with its chais, that of Millet at Portets for the Ravez; some chais in the Cours du Médoc and the warehouse of the Bordeaux Chambre de Commerce.

BUHLER, DENIS (1811–90) and **EUGENE** (1822–1907). Landscape designers. Successors to designers such as Thouin and Varé. The two brothers were responsible for a considerable amount of work, with many parks in southwest France due to them. Owners of Château Ripeau at St-Emilion.

Eugène designed the Parc Bordelais and the grounds surrounding Château Giscours in the Gironde. (See p.113, 116).

BURGUET, CHARLES (1821–79). From a family of Bordeaux contractors. Studied in Paris. Champion of a very broad-based eclecticism. His two main works in the Médoc, Château Pichon-Longueville at Pauillac and Château Palmer at Cantenac, constitute architectural prototypes, which contributed to the creation of the image of the Bordeaux château in the 19th century. Despite this backward-looking inspiration, Burguet is also famous for having introduced metallic architecture to Bordeaux. (See p.76, 90, 146, 185, 186).

CATROS, YVES-TOUSSAINT (born 1757 in St-Brieuc, died 1836 in Le Bouscat). Nurseryman. From a family of nurserymen, he was trained at the royal nurseries at Roule and Vincennes. Director of the royal nursery in Bordeaux in 1785, he opened his own firm in 1791, also in Bordeaux. His brother-in-law, Jean Gérand entered into partnership with him a few years later (the Catros-Gérand company still exists today). In 1795, he created an important experimental arboretum at Le Taillan in the Médoc and devoted his L'Oiseau estate at Le Bouscat to a vine nursery. He designed the grounds of Château Margaux (1810–16). (See p.116).

CHEMINADE, JEAN Active between 1530 and 1560, a master-mason, from a family of masons, who included among his clientele several parliamentarians whose names belong to the wine world, the most famous being Richard de Pichon and Jean de Pontac. For the latter, he built the main body and corner turrets that form the old part of Château Haut-Brion. (See p.66).

COMBES, GUY known as LOUIS (1757–1818). Studied under Richard-François Bonfin (q.v.) then, in Paris, under Mique and Peyre-le-Jeune. Rome prize in 1781. Back in Bordeaux in 1784, he became the leader of the Bordeaux neo-classical school, and if only because of his appointment was made architect of the *département* in the first months of the Revolution, a post he held until his death. In 1786, he designed projects for the redevelopment of the estate and reconstruction of Château d'Olivier at Léognan. In the same year, he built Château Morin at Bassens in the Ambès peninsular for the alderman Acquart which was then an important wine-producing area. His most famous creation is Château Margaux which was commissioned by the Marquis de La Colonilla in 1810. (*See p.*70, *78*, 80, 84, 88, 90, *110*).

CORCELLES, ARNAUD (1765–1843). He built Château Labégorce at Margaux and Château de Valrose at Latresne. Whereas the working buildings of the former were modified or enlarged by Burguet (q.v.), those at Valrose are still intact. At Macau in the Médoc, he built the storeroom of Château de Cantemerle. (*See p.*90).

COUSTURIER, GUILLAUME Mastermason from Tabanac in the Entre-Deux-Mers, active between 1511 and 1536. He built the old part of Château de Pic at Le Tourne for the priest of the large parish of St-Pierre in Bordeaux. At Floirac, he built Château de Feuillas which was replaced in the 18th century by a residence known by the name of Sybirol.

DECAZES, ELIE Duke (born at St-Martin-de-Laye on 28 September 1780, died in Paris on 28 October 1860). A lawyer and descended from a family of lawyers from Libourne. Began his career as a magistrate, before becoming a State dignitary. Creator of the stud farm in Libourne, honorary president of agricultural and horticultural societies, he initiated the experimental field for the synonymy of the vine in the Luxembourg nurseries. Brother-in-law to Mirbel and a friend of Thouin, he designed the park of his estate of La Grave at Bonzac where he carried out agronomic experiments.

DESCHAMPS, CLAUDE (1765-1843). Civil engineer. Famous for his Pont de Pierre and Entrepôt Lainé. Along with his son-in-law Billaudel, he built his own wine château and country house called Le Moine, situated at Cenon. (*See p.140*).

DESPINE (18th century). Architect known from an inscription that unequivocally credits him with the construction of Château du Piat at Tauriac on the right bank of the Gironde. This château, which dates

from 1781, may be considered to be a prototype of the low country house called a "chartreuse" in the Bordeaux region.

DILLON, PATRICK Architect born in Panama in 1952. His father was a builder. Studied architecture at the Rice University at Houston (Texas, USA). Set out on a cultural tour of the world, which was cut short by his meeting of Ricardo Bofill (q.v.) in Barcelona in 1978. For nine years, he was one of his collaborators, taking part in projects of the Taller de Arquitectura in Spain, Algeria and then France (Paris and Marne-la-Vallée); and in the United States, where he studied, with Bofill and his associates, the competition project organized in 1985 for the architectural design of a new winery in the Napa Valley of California: the Clos Pégase created by Jan Schrem. This new orientation towards viticultural architecture was furthered in 1986 when he left Bofill and went into partnership with the French architect Jean de Gastines in Paris. (*Further information on this team will be found in the note on Jean de Gastines and on p.190, at the top of the introduction to their joint project*). (*See p.74*, 170, 171, *172*, 173, 180, 182, 185, *187*, **188–193**, **248–251**).

DROUYN, LEON (born 1839). Architect. Carried out numerous restoration works and built Château Mondinet at Jugazan.

DUFART, JEAN-BAPTISTE (1752–1818). In 1772, he worked as a draughtsman in the offices of Victor Louis (q.v.) at the start of work on the Grand Théâtre in Bordeaux. His main work, in which he adapted his austere neo-classical style to an extremely complex scheme, was the Théâtre Français in Bordeaux. He built two wine châteaux, Beauséjour at Gironde-sur-Dropt and le Burck or Navarre at Ambès in 1786. (*See p.63, 88*).

DUPHOT, THEODORE, Michel, Jules, Henri (1810–78) and DUPHOT, ABEL, VALENTIN (1839–89). Architects. The former was a pupil at the Ecole d'Architecture in Lyon and settled in Bordeaux in 1835. He supervised the erection of Château de Cestas according to Baltard's design; he built the complex of agricultural buildings called the "Ferme Suzanne" at Château Giscours; after working on Château Pichon-Longueville-Comtesse de Lalande, he managed, after several rejected designs, to build Château Latour (1862–64) – giving it its present appearance – under the supervision of the Marquis de Beaumont-Villemanzy, and to enlarge the *chais*. Both architects must also be credited with Château Lanessan at Cussac and Château de Grenade at St-Selve and de Virelade at Virelade for the Carayon-Latour family. (*See p.74, 76*).

DUPRAT, FERDINAND (born in Bordeaux in 1887, and died at Le Bouscat in 1976). Landscape gardener. Trained at Kew Gardens in England. He specialized in the reconstruction of historic gardens and was considered to be the successor to Achille Duchêne. As well as in France, he worked in the United States, in South America, Morocco, Cuba and Turkey. In the Gironde, he was responsible for the gardens of Château Beychevelle, Gruaud-Larose, the Maison Labottière, the little garden of Château Haut-Brion, Camparian at Cenon, the restructuring of the grounds of Château Margaux (reorganized once again by Lou de Viane in the early 1980s) and the regular gardens of Château de Vayres. He provided projects for Château de Malle and for Château Coutet (both in the Sauternes area). (*See p.116, 119, 120*).

DURAND, GABRIEL (1750–1814). Architect and contractor of Normandy origin, called upon by Victor Louis (q.v.) to supervise the construction of the Grand Théâtre in Bordeaux. He settled permanently in that town after 1786 and founded a dynasty of architects. He produced schemes for M. Gaubert in Portets for the reconstruction of a wine château, which he was only to enlarge and restore. He built the small Château de Thiboeuf at Léognan.

DURAND, GABRIEL-JOSEPH (1792–1858). Architect, son of Gabriel Durand (q.v.). Town hydraulic engineer, member of the first Commission des Monuments Historiques, archaeologist and enlightened collector. His numerous official activities did not prevent him from working for private clients, but most of his orders came from public bodies. He took part in the restoration of many wine châteaux but his most successful creations in this area are Château de La Sauque at Labrède in the Graves and, in the Médoc, Château du Comte d'Aux at St-Julien, known today by the name of Talbot. These two buildings, which were erected between 1820 and 1830, are perfect illustrations of the moderation of his neo-classical style which do not go as far as the usual excesses of this period of "mannerism". (*See p.66, 70, 78, 88, 90, 115*).

DUTHOIT, EDMOND (1837–89). Architect. Born in Amiens into a family of sculptors. Trained on the job, he became one of the closest collaborators of Viollet-le-Duc (q.v.). In 1873, he opened an architectural practice in Amiens. He worked on and took a very active part in the conversion work on Château de Roquetaillade at Mazères. His knowledge of the Orient (he took part in the archaeological mission to Syria and in Melchior de Vogüe's mission to Cypress in 1862–64 as a draughtsman) was most strikingly demonstrated in Château d'Abadia (at Hendaye) and at Roquetaillade, espe-

cially in the decoration of the château's chapel. (*See p.84*).

ESCARPIT, JEAN-ALPHONSE (born in Bordeaux on 16 July 1829). Landscape designer. Son of a Bordeaux nurseryman associated with Louis-Bernard Fischer (q.v.). He created the grounds of Château du Tertre at Fronsac and of Roquetaillade.

EXPERT, ROGER HENRI (1882–1955). Architect. Studied at the Ecole Municipale des Beaux-Arts in Bordeaux, then in Paris at the Ecole Nationale des Beaux-Arts. Restored and converted Château de Calvimont at Cérons, where he died.

FERRANT or FERRAND (19th century). Architect (?). Restored the old Château du Parc (or d'Espagne) at Mérignac, which has now been demolished.

FISCHER, LOUIS-BERNARD (born in Château du Thil at Léognan on 3 April 1810, died in Bordeaux on 19 August 1873). Landscape gardener. Spent his entire career in the Bordeaux region. Creator of the public park in Bordeaux, for which he was in competition with Barillet-Deschamps (q.v.), but also of the grounds of Laburthe at Floirac, Le Thil at Léognan, Sybirol at Cenon, Les Lauriers at Lormont and Filhot at Sauternes. (*See p.116*).

GARROS, MICHEL-LOUIS (1833–1911). Architect. Pupil of the Ecole des Beaux-Arts in Paris. Settled in Bordeaux in 1860. He made his mark as an extremely active architect and built and restored numerous chapels, dwelling houses and wine châteaux. Among the latter, we note: Grattequina at Blanquefort for Frédéric Giese, a merchant in Bordeaux (1872); the luxurious château of Clément-Pichon (ex. Parempuyre) for the Duran-Dassiers (1881), a perfect example of eclecticism, combining reminders of the early Renaissance and classical residences of the 17th and 18th centuries, with beautifully preserved interior decoration; Rayne-Vigneau at Bommes; Malescot-St-Exupéry at Margaux, reconstructed for the new owner M. Fourcade (1885), using the decorative repertory of the 18th century; Lachesnaye at Cussac etc. His son Alexandre (1867–1953), also a graduate of the Ecole des Beaux-Arts in Paris, helped him in his work and succeeded him, in association with Louis Garros (1895–1956) and Marcel Garros (1898–1956). (*See p.84*, 90, 94).

GASTAMBIDE, JACQUES (1758–1839). Pupil at the Académie des Arts in Bordeaux. Most of his career as an architect was spent in Mauritius, where he emigrated in 1790. Beforehand, he had numerous successful projects including the grounds of Château de Monbadon, the enlargement of Château de Blaignac and the reconstruction of Château du Parc at Mérignac, and he had also built Château de La Canadone at St-Léon in the Entre-Deux-Mers. In view of the latter and some of his drawings, he could be attributed with the design of Château de Blésignac situated in the neighbouring commune to St-Léon.

GASTINES, JEAN DE French architect, born in Casablanca (Morocco) in 1957, whose father (Gilles) was an international property developer. Studied architecture at the Ecole des Beaux-Arts in Paris. Collaborated with the architect Franck Gehry (California) on various projects, including the study for a New York residence for Chrisophe de Mesnil (the daughter of the famous creator of the De Mesnil Foundation built in Houston by Renzo Piano) for whom he would personally design the layout of her Paris apartment in 1980. Entered into partnership with the Panamanian architect, Patrick Dillon (*q.v.*) in 1986 and created a firm in Paris, which quickly took on the role of starting a renaissance in wine architecture. Together they designed (from 1987 onwards) and built (1988–89) a new system of *chais* and *cuviers* around Château de Bachen (a neoclassical residence near Eugénie-les-Bains, 120 km south of Bordeaux in the *département* of the Landes). The owners – the famous chef Michel Guérard and his wife Christine – aim to revive this Tursan vineyard. In 1988, the two architects were invited by the Centre Pompidou (CCI) to participate in the European consultations organized as part of the Châteaux Bordeaux project. They were thus entrusted with the study of two viticultural sites in the Bordeaux region. Firstly, they studied the development (involving urban and landscape elements) of a possible "regional business park for the wine trade" at Blanquefort (Médoc) in the vicinity of the firm Barton & Guestier. Secondly, they designed (on a much more realistic and functional level, in the short term) one of the four projects for the redevelopment of the buildings surrounding Château Pichon-Longueville (a residence built in the neo-Renaissance style in 1852) at Pauillac. In August 1988, the judges unanimously accepted the project by Dillon and de Gastines. This ambitious architectural and cultural scheme could be the most important built in the Bordeaux vineyard in the 20th century. (*See p.74*, 171, *172*, 173, 176, 183, 185, *187*, **188–193**, **248–251**).

GIROUARD, JEAN (active in the second half of the 17th century). Built Château de Meyney between 1660 and 1662 along with another Bordeaux mason, Jean Tisson.

HAUSSEZ, CHARLES LEMERCIER BARON D' (1778–1854). Prefect, agronomist, mechanic, minister (exiled and pardoned) landscape designer. This polymath created the beautiful grounds of Château de Cantemerle in the Médoc.

IVOY, ARMAND-JOSEPH (born in Lille on 28 November 1778, died in Le Pian-Médoc on 19 April 1869). Owner of the estate of Geneste, in Le Pian-Médoc, where he created an important arboretum. Agronomist, member of the Société Linnéenne, creator of the grounds of Château Malleret (Le Pian-Médoc).

LABAT, RAYMOND (17th century). Master-mason from the Bordeaux region. Designer of the first Château de Parempuyre (Clément-Pichon) built after 1657, now replaced by a late 19th-century building. (*See Garros*).

LACLOTTE, JEAN (1701–61). Son of a stone-cutter and nephew of an architect. Played an important role as architect of the cathedral chapter of St-André in Bordeaux. In this capacity, he constructed a wine château on the Ambès peninsular on behalf of two canons. Unfortunately, this residence and its large accompanying *chai* and *cuvier*, are now destroyed. He built a residence with *chais* in the Rue Borie of the Chartrons in Bordeaux for a Danish *négociant*, the consul Hansen de Liliendhal.

LACLOTTE, ETIENNE (1728–1812). Son of Jean Laclotte. From 1761–72, he worked with his younger brothers Jean and Michel under the name of the Société Jean Laclotte Frères, after which he worked in partnership with his brother Jean alone for the rest of his career. Dominant figures in the building world from 1770 until the Revolution, the three brothers several times dictated the fate of the guild of architects in Bordeaux. Their family relations (they were allied to all the important contractors in the town), their official positions (they were the architects of the St-Seurin and St-André chapters), their financial skill and the strength of their firm's organization, meant that they were a powerful force in Bordeaux at that time. In addition to undertaking architectural plans and projects, they also supplied everything from land to window frames to other customers. The three (and later, two) brothers built a great number of *négociants* residences in Bordeaux, a large proportion of them in the Chartrons and in particular the famous group of residences with squinch balconies in the Pavé des Chartrons. Three wine châteaux sum up their very classical manner: Chênevert and Pique-Caillou at Mérignac and Virginia at Caudéran. Pique-Caillou, which still has a remarkable wine-producing estate in the suburbs of Bordeaux today, was Etienne Laclotte's private country house. (*See p.90*).

LACLOTTE, MICHEL (1760–1834). Son of Etienne. Architect, probably trained by his father and uncles, then by Mique in Paris in 1784. His main claim to fame is the residence he built bearing his name at St-Louis-de-Montferrand for the minister Peyronnet.

LACLOTTE, HYACINTHE (born *c.* 1765). Son of Jean one of Etienne's younger brothers. Architect, trained in Bordeaux. In 1800, he competed for the project to develop the Place des Quinconces in collaboration with Raymond Rieutord. Emigrated to the United States, where he took part in the construction of the New Orleans theatre in 1805. Later became an engineer in the United States army. He returned to Bordeaux and, again with Rieutord, restored Château d'Issan at Cantenac in 1824 and, in the same year, seems to have built Château Branaire-Ducru for Louis Duluc at St-Julien.

LAFARGUE, JULES (1825–81) and **LAFARGUE, PAUL** (1842–76). Architects of Château Bourran at Mérignac, Château Bel-Air at Ste-Foy-la-Grande, Château Pape-Clément at Pessac and Château Dulamon at Blanquefort. (*See p.84*).

LAUNAY, JACQUES (17th century). King's engineer. Redeveloped the façade overlooking the Dordogne of Château de Vayres and put in the large set of steps that provides direct access from the château to the grounds. (*See p.114*).

LE BRETON (L.L.) (born *c.* 1820). Landscape designer and nurseryman based in Paris and Orléans. In the Gironde, he designed the grounds of Châteaux Pellegrin, Bourran. Foncastel, Chênevert (Mérignac). Couhins (Villenave-d'Ornon). Dulamon (Blanquefort). Only Bourran and Dulamon (Majolan grottoes) still partially exist.

LEE, RIGBY (born 1924) and **LEE, NATHANIEL** (born 1948). Architects of British origin. Numerous contributions to various wine châteaux in the Gironde, particularly in 1987 in the building of new *chais* and *cuviers* (in wood) at Château Canon at St-Emilion. (*See p.92*, *170*).

LHOTE or **LOTHE, FRANCOIS** (1740–1808). Pupil of Gabriel at the Académie Royale d'Architecture. Settled in Bordeaux in 1776. Collaborated with Richard-François Bonfin (*q.v.*). One of his most beautiful buildings is without doubt Château de La Louvière at Léognan which he built for the powerful *négociant*, Jean-Baptiste Mareilhac in 1791. The old wine château of Castel d'Andorte may also be attributed to him. (*See p.90*).

LOUIS, LOUIS-NICOLAS (VICTOR) (1731–1800). Pupil of Le Camus and Loriot at the Académie Royale. Rome prize in 1755. At the request of the Duc de Richelieu in Bordeaux, he built his most famous work, the Grand Théâtre. At the same time, he also built several private buildings, including Château du Bouilh at St-André-de-Cubzac, which was never completed because its owner, the Marquis de La Tour du Pin stopped the work when he was appointed minister of war so as not to be suspected of using public funds to erect this luxurious residence. (*See p.13*, 66, 68, 69, 78, 90, 140, 149).

MAITRE, LOUIS-ALFRED (born in 1842). Architect. Studied under Constant Dupeux. Designed many buildings in the Médoc: Château Bages at Pauillac in 1875; Château Mouton Rothschild in 1833. The agricultural buildings of Château Montrose at St-Estèphe and of Château Léoville at St-Julien should also be noted. (*See p.84*).

MAZIERES Architects' workshop in Bordeaux, consisting of **MARCEL** (born in 1920), **PHILIPPE** (born in 1948), **BERNARD** (born in 1949) and **JEAN-MARIE** (born in 1955). Many important commissions since 1975, ranging from the restoration of properties to the fitting out of residences: Châteaux Castéra, Cantenac-Brown and Phélan-Ségur (restructuring of the property); Château Latour (exterior work and construction of wine-making and storage buildings); Château Trois-Moulins at St-Emilion (renovation); Château Lagrange (restoration of estate and residence); Château Lascombes at Margaux (construction of *cuvier* and reception area); Château Cadet-Bon at St-Emilion (fermenting room and production buildings); Château Ducru-Beaucaillou and Château Grand-Puy-Lacoste (making improvements to the properties); Giscours and La Houringue (restoration and fitting out of the estates); Branaire-Ducru (extension of the buildings); Château Marquis-de-Terme (work on *cuvier*, *chais* and residence). Finally, the beautiful underground *chais* at Château d'Yquem and at Pichon-Longueville-Comtesse de Lalande and Margaux. (*See p.92*, *134*, 169, 170).

MIAILHE, VICTOR-PIERRE (1802–71). Architect. Pupil of Poitevin (*q.v.*). Built wine châteaux for M. Deffes at Bouliac and Messrs. P. Dubois and Wetzel at Carbon-Blanc.

MINVIELLE, MARTIAL-ERNEST (1835–1914). Architect. Succeeded his father Barthélémy (1797–1882). Worked with his son Georges (1859–1936) who succeeded him after his death. His many buildings include: Château de La Tour de By (1873–75); Domaine du Fayau at Cadillac, as well as the Lataste *chais*, Château Cantenac-Brown (1866–98), Château Kirwan, Château Montbrun and the *chais* at Angludet at Cantenac; Château Lestage at Listrac;

Château Montbrun and Château Labégorce (1867–93) at Margaux and in addition outbuildings for Château Léoville-Poyferré at St-Julien-Beychevelle. (*See p.*84, 90).

MOLLIE, JEAN (*c.* 1720–92). Architect, son and brother of architects. In 1786, he built Château Nairac at Barsac, exemplary in its quality and the classical balance between the residence and the surrounding agricultural buildings. (*See p.*66, 90).

MONDET, JEAN-JULES (born in 1834). Architect. Pupil of Labbé and Danjoy. Restored numerous churches in the *département* of the Gironde, such as the Abbaye du Rivet at Aurois (transformed into a residence). Built a château for Messrs. Degre and Tamizé in Castets and Château Turpeau in the Isle-St-Georges in 1875.

MONGINOUX, ACHILLE (born in 1862). Engineer. After leaving the Ecole Nationale des Ponts et Chaussées, he started working with Alphonse Blaquière's (*q.v.*). Main known works: old *chais* of the Calvet firm in the Cours du Médoc, Bordeaux; Château Marbuzet at St-Estèphe, with colossal columned porch and Corinthian capitals – a late addition to the neo-

classical buildings in the Bordeaux region, similar particularly to those of Dufart (*q.v.*).

PERRIE, AUGUSTE (died 1886). Architect. Worked on Château de Mauvezin (1840), then at Roquetaillade (between 1849 and 1851) before the great restoration by Eugène Viollet-le-Duc and Edmond Duthoit (*q.v.*). Designed, with his brother, Château La Boulbène at Quinsac and probably the neighbouring Château Bellevue.

POITEVIN, PIERRE-ALEXANDRE (1782–1859). Trained in Paris, under Fontaine, Percier and Regnault. Architect of the Lot-et-Garonne *département*, he is mainly known for his public works which, like those of Gabriel Durand (*q.v.*), are marked by a very tempered neo-classicism. He built some residences for private individuals, and the vast Château Filhot at Sauternes for the Comte de Lur-Saluces. He completed one of the wings for a neo-gothic chapel for the minister Peyronnet's Château de Montferrand. (*See p.*70, 78, 90).

RICARD, ALPHONSE (19th century). Architect. Designed the Collège St-Genès and the enormous building

for Descas Père & Fils, on the Quai de Paludate in Bordeaux, on the site of the former Hôpital de la Manufacture – a gigantic trade building with offices, wine-tasting room and three-storeyed *chais* with metal girders, the latter now demolished. Only the main building remains and it has been converted into ordinary offices. (*See p.*149).

ROCHE, ALEXIS-HONORE (born *c.* 1760). Contractor who came from Orléans to work on the Hôtel Gobineau in 1785 at the request of Victor Louis. This residence, which is now the offices of the CIVB (Conseil Interprofessionel du Vin de Bordeaux), was to be the first part of the Place Ludovise, envisaged by Victor Louis and is practically the only evidence of the plan. Roché's masterpiece, the Maison Carrée of Arlac, cannot really be considered to be a wine château, since the vineyard that accompanies it is so small. However, just before the Revolution, Roché built a large wine château for M. Du Temple, director of the Bordeaux mint, in the parish of Salleboeuf in the Entre-Deux-Mers. This was Château de Vaquey, where the residence and the wings of the outbuildings formed a U-shaped court with side galleries. It illustrates perfectly the desire for rational archi-

tecture adapted to the demands of agricultural production which the rigours of neo-classicism met so well. (*See p.*90).

VIOLLET-LE-DUC, EUGENE (1814-79). Architect. Studied briefly with the architect J.M. Hervé, then with Achille Leclère. Vast and wide-ranging work, in which he showed his many talents as an archaeologist, writer, restorer, builder, theoretician and also a painter and a decorator. Author of the *Dictionnaire raisonné d'Architecture* and the *Dictionnaire raisonné du Mobilier français.* At the request of the Mauvezin family, he undertook large-scale restoration of the medieval Château of Roquetaillade in the Bazas region, under his direction and that of his "faithful lieutenant", Edmond Duthoit (*q.v.*). As with Château de Pierrefonds of the same period, the painted or sculpted decoration and the original layout both designed in a style harmonizing with the restored medieval architecture, made it a complete work of art. The same partnership worked in the region on Château d'Abadia at Hendaye (1865–66) with the architect, Magne. A project in 1871 for M. Lavigne, perhaps at Ste Eulalie d'Ambarés, has not yet been identified. (*See p.*84).

GLOSSARY

Allumette hollandaise (Dutch match): See *mèche*.

Ampelography: Scientific study, identification and classification of vines.

Appellation d'origine contrôlée (AOC): Collection of criteria guaranteeing the quality of a wine: precise geographical origin (region, commune, parcel of land); mixture of varieties of vine, technique of pruning the vine; maximum yield per hectare, minimum percentage of alcohol in must. Each *appellation* in France is subject to a law made by the Ministry of Agriculture.

Assemblage (blending): Mixing different wines from the same *cru*. The aim is to harmonize the production.

Barrique bordelaise: An oak barrel specifically used in the Bordeaux region with a capacity of 225 litres (49 gallons).

Borde: This term refers to an isolated house in the country in southwest France. It also used to refer to a small farm held on a *métayage* (sharecropping) agreement.

Botrytis: See *pourriture grise*.

Bordeaux mixture: Mixture of copper sulphate and lime perfected by the inhabitants of the Bordeaux region to combat mildew.

Bourdieu: A word of medieval origin that has long been used in France in notarial deeds to describe a rural estate: land and buildings, or possibly, buildings only.

Carrasson: A wooden stake used as a support for a vine stock.

Carruade: A plateau in a vineyard. In fact, a locality in the commune of Pauillac ("Les Carruades de Lafite").

Cave (cellar): The temperature must be kept cool and constant.

Caveau: Part of the *cave* or the *cellier* intended to keep bottles of wine in. Its temperature must be kept constant and it should be sheltered from humidity and light.

Cellier (wine storeroom): Synonymous with *chai*; place where the barrels of wine are kept.

Cépage: Variety of cultivated vine, e.g. Cabernet, Sémillon, Merlot, etc.

Chai: (wine storeroom): Generally built above ground level; wine is stored here in barrels. However, some are underground. In Bordeaux, the *chais* also include the administrative premises.

Chartreuse: In the Bordeaux region, a small château, low and elongated in shape.

Chartrons: Central district of Bordeaux where activities connected with the wine trade have developed over the centuries and where the wine companies are traditionally based.

Château: In the Bordeaux region, this term refers to the property and the vineyard attached to it. By identification, the "château" has become synonymous with the *cru*.

Clairet or **claret**: In the Bordeaux region, red and white vines were originally mixed together in the vineyards and their grapes were vinified together. This produced a pale red wine which the British particularly enjoyed. Hence the name "claret" which is still used in Britain to describe the red wines of Bordeaux.

Classification of 1855: On 18 April 1855, at the request of the Bordeaux chamber of commerce, the wine brokers' union of Bordeaux drew up a list of 58 *crus* of "red wines from the Gironde", focusing on the Médoc and Haut-Brion. They added 22 *crus* of sweet white wines from the Sauternes region. This list has served as a reference point for all later classifications.

Clos: A term describing a wine-producing property that is (or used to be) surrounded by walls (mostly used in Burgundy).

Collage (fining): Operation intended to clarify the wine before it is bottled. Fining is still carried out by mixing beaten egg whites into the wine in the barrels with the help of a whisk (*fouet*), hence the term "*fouettage*".

Côtes: In the Bordeaux region, this means a vineyard on the edge of a plateau or slope; this position makes it well-suited to quality vine growing (orientation, drainage, slope etc.). Examples: Côtes de Blaye, Côtes de Bourg, Premières Côtes de Bordeaux, etc.

Coulure: A pollination failure of the young vine. It manifests itself either by the withering of some of the flowers or grapes or by their unequal growth.

Courtier (broker): The intermediary between the grower and the buyer of wines. It was traditionally his job to canvass the vineyards and to offer samples to the buyer.

Croupe de graves (gravel hill): The rounded summit of a hill composed entirely of gravel. Also called "*croupe graveleuse*".

Cru (growth): In the Bordeaux region, this term is used in its individual sense to describe the production of one estate and, by extension, the *terroir* where the vines are grown. In other regions of France, it has a collective meaning referring to all the wine-producing concerns located in one *terroir*.

Culture en joualles: Alternating crops based on vines in parallel rows.

Cuvaison: Operation of fermenting the grape harvest in vats. The length of the *cuvaison* depends on the quality of the grapes, its degree of maturity and the sort of wine the cellarmaster wants to obtain.

Cuve (vat): A large container, usually made of wood, stone, concrete or stainless steel, in which the wine is fermented.

Cuvée: Contents of a vat. This word commonly means the wine coming from one vat or all the wine made at a certain point under the same conditions.

Cuvier (fermenting room): Building where the vats are located.

Deposit: In red wines, this is a sediment containing tannin and pigment which should be left undisturbed in the bottle. Decanting may be advisable for fine old wines which show a sediment. In white wine, the deposit is tasteless.

Domaine (estate, property): A wine-producing property including the château, the working buildings and the vines.

Elevage (nurturing the wine): Succession of operations allowing the wine to be brought to maturity, from vinification to bottling.

Encarrasser: To arrange the barrels (*barriques*) in several layers on top of each other (at least two, usually three, at the most five).

Fond de cuve (bottom of the vat): Sediment after wine has been allowed to settle and has then been decanted.

Fumure (manuring): Spreading manure or fertilizer on or in the soil to fertilize it to improve yield.

Fût: Wooden cask etc. in which the wine is aged. See also *barrique bordelaise*.

Garenne: A private wood with straight paths surrounding or in the grounds of a château.

Graves: Soil containing a high proportion of gravel, shingle or pebbles. By extension, this term is used to refer to those districts in the Bordeaux region which have this type of gravel soil.

Jalle: A local term for the small tributaries of the Garonne and the Gironde rivers or the drainage channels in the former marshland.

Journal: Under the *ancien régime*, this referred to an area of land which, depending on the Bordeaux region, varied between a quarter and a third of a hectare.

Maître de chai (cellarmaster): The person in charge of vinification, nurturing and looking after the ageing of the wines in an estate.

Mayne: This is a basic hamlet of a few houses in southwest France.

Mèche (wick): *Mèchage* consists in cleaning a barrel by burning a sulphured wick in it. In the 18th century, this was called the "*allumette hollandaise*" or "*allumette de chai*"

Mildew: A vine disease caused by a fungus. It appeared in Europe in the years 1880-82. The people of the Bordeaux region discovered an effective way of combating it with their Bordeaux mixture.

Millésime (vintage): Year of the harvest from which a wine originates. This date is mentioned on almost all the labels of fine wine.

Must: Grape juice which has not yet fermented or which is in the process of fermentation.

Négociant (merchant): Professional who buys the wine from the producer and sells it to the distributor. A *négociant-éleveur* makes his own wine and sells it under his own brand name.

Noblesse du bouchon: Name applied to the leading wine merchant houses in the Chartrons district of Bordeaux.

Oïdium: Fungus similar to mildew that attacks the vine. This disease, which first appeared in Europe in the middle of the 19th century, can be treated with sulphur.

Palisser: To train the vine so as to support it and keep it growing in the desired direction.

Palus: Low, damp land on the banks of the Dordogne, the Garonne and the Gironde in the Bordeaux region.

Phylloxera: A small aphis of American origin which appeared in Europe at the end of the 19th century and threatened the destruction of all French vineyards.

Plantier: A regional term meaning a parcel of land that is planted exclusively with vines, unlike the *joualles*.

Pourriture grise (grey rot): Spoilage of grapes attacked by a fungus (*botrytis*) before they mature. This same fungus can have beneficial effects, see *pourriture noble*.

Pourriture noble (noble rot): Shrivels the grapes and causes a concentration of sugars which can produce top quality sweet white wines such as Sauternes.

Premier vin: Result of selecting from among the vats produced by a harvest. The criteria of selection are based on the structure of the vineyard on the one hand and on analytic and rigorous tasting on the other. Whereas the *premiers vins* carry the name of the château, the lesser wines (*seconds vins*) carry another name.

Récoltant: A wine producer who is legally obliged to declare his harvest.

Rège: A row of vines in the Bordeaux region.

Régisseur (steward): The person responsible for the administration and organization of a vineyard.

Terroir: Land considered from the point of view of wine production.

Vignoble (vineyard): All the vines cultivated in a *cru*, an *appellation* or a region.

BIBLIOGRAPHY

THE REGION AND TOWN OF BORDEAUX

HIGOUNET (Charles ed), *Histoire de Bordeaux*. Bordeaux: Fédération Historique du Sud-Ouest, 1962-1972, 7 volumes.

MALEZVIN (T.), *Histoire du commerce de Bordeaux depuis les origines jusqu'à nos jours*. Bordeaux, 1892.

GENERAL WINE INFORMATION

ANGLADE (Pierre) and PUISAIS (Jacques), *Vins et vignobles de France*. Paris: Larousse, 1987, 640p.

DION (Roger), *Histoire de la vigne et du vin en France des origines au X1X siècle*. 1959, 768p. (New ed., Paris: Flammarion, 1977).

ENJALBERT (Henri and Bernard), *Histoire de la vigne et du vin*. Paris: Editions Bordas & Bardi, 1987, 223p.

Geographe historique des vignobles. Papers from the symposium organized in Bordeaux in 1977. Paris: Editions du CNRS, 1978, 2 volumes (215 and 199p)

JOHNSON (Hugh), *The World Atlas of Wine*. London: Mitchell Beazley, 1985, 3rd ed., 320p.

JOHNSON (Hugh) and DUIJKER (Hubrecht), *The Wine Atlas of France*. London: Mitchell Beazley, 1988, 2nd ed., 280p.

Hugh Johnson's Wine Companion. London: Mitchell Beazley, 1987, 2nd ed, 544p.

LACHIVER (Marcel), *Vins, vignes et vignerons; histoire du vignoble français*. Paris: Fayard, 1988, 714p.

LICHINE (Alexis), *Encyclopedia of Wines & Spirits*. London: Cassell, 1985, 733p.

PEYNAUD (Emile), *Le Gout du vin*. Paris, 1980, 240p.

ROYER (Claude), *Les Vignerons: usages et mentalites des pays de vignobles* (ethnological study in France). Paris: Editions Berger-Levrault, 1980, 260p.

SELLIER (Jean ed), *L'Atlas des vins de France*. Paris: Editions Oliver Orban, 1987, 206p.

THE WINES OF BORDEAUX

ANDRIEU (Pierre), *Petite histoire de Bordeaux et de son vignoble*. Montpellier: La Journée viticole, 1955, 169p.

BANQUE DE FRANCE, *Le Vin de Bordeaux*. 1978, 126p.

CHASTENET (Jacques), *L'Epopée des vins de Bordeaux*. Paris: 1980, 222p.

COCKS (Charles) and FERET (Edouard), *Bordeaux et ses vins*. 1868, 2nd ed. (13th ed. Bordeaux: Editions Féret, 1987, 472p.)

DUIJKER (Hubrecht), *The Good Wines of Bordeaux*. London: Mitchell Beazley, 1983, 200p.

DUIJKER (Hubrecht), *The Great Wines of Bordeaux*. London: Mitchell Beazley, 1983, 200p.

ENJALBERT (Henri), *Les Grands vins de Saint-Emilion, Pomerol et Fronsac*. Paris: Editions Bardi, 1983, 634p.

MERGOIL (Guy), "La Structure du vignoble girondin", *Revue géographique des Pyrenees et du Sud-Ouest*, 1961, volume 32, p.119-140.

David Peppercorn's Pocket Guide to the Wines of Bordeaux. London: Mitchell Beazley, 1988, 144p.

PEPPERCORN (David), *Bordeaux*. London: Faber and Faber, 1982, 428p.

PENNING-ROWSELL (Edmund), *The Wines of Bordeaux*. Penguin Books Ltd, 1976, 573p.

PIJASSOU (René), *Un grand vignoble de qualité: le Médoc*. Paris: Tallandier, 1980, 2 volumes, 1500p.

ROUDIE (Philippe), *Le Vignoble bordelais*. Toulouse, Privat: 1973, 193p.

ROUDIE (Philippe), *Vignobles et vignerons du Bordelais 1850-1950*. Paris: Editions du CNRS, 1988, 456p.

SEELY (James), *Great Bordeaux Wines*. London: Secker & Warburg, 1986, 362p.

THE ARCHITECTURE OF THE REGION AND TOWN OF BORDEAUX

AVISSEAU (Jean-Paul ed), *Bordeaux et l'Aquitaine: urbanisme et architecture de 1920 à 1940*. Paris: Editions Regirex, Techniques et Architecture, 1988, 298p.

BERIAC (Jean-Pierre) and MAFFRE (Philippe), *Le Bordelais néoclassique*. Bordeaux: Editions IACA, 1983, 150p.

CANTO (Monique), *Villégiatures*. Paris: Editions Colona, 1982 (photography of numerous Bordeaux wine chateaux by Anne Garde), 104p.

CARDOZE (Edmond), *les Cartes postales des châteaux de la Gironde*. Perigueux: Editions Pierre Faulac, 1985, 255p (almost 500 illustrations).

TAILLARD (Christian), *Bordeaux classique*. Toulouse: Editions Eché, 1987, 256p.

CULTURAL ASPECTS OF THE CIVILIZATION OF THE WINES OF BORDEAUX

ANONYME, *Le Médoc à travers le livre*. Bordeaux: Société des bibliophiles de Guyenne, 1978, 98p.

ROTHSCHILD (Philippe de), *Vivre la vigne; du ghetto de Francfort à Mouton Rothschild 1774-1981*. Paris: Presses de la Cité, 1981, 228p.

SUTTON (Denys), "The Marvellous Museum at Chateau Mouton", *Apollo*. New York, 1963, no. 19, p.172-192.

VEILLETET (Pierre ed), *De l'Esprit des vins: Bordeaux*. Paris: Editions Adam Biro, 1988, 224p. Photography by Anne Garde.

Vignobles et vins d'Aquitaine: histoire, art et economie. Papers from the 20th congress of regional studies held in Bordeaux in 1967. Bordeaux: Fédération historique du Sud-Ouest, 1970, 446p.

THE WINE TRADE AND THE CHARTRONS DISTRICT

CHAUVREAU (Paule), "La Formation topographique du quartier des Chartrons", *Revue historique de Bordeaux*, 1929.

COUTUREAU (Eric), *Le Developpement urbain du faubourg des Chartrons à la fin du XV111 siècle*. Historical thesis (III). University of Bordeaux, 1979.

COUTUREAU (Eric), "Le Pavé des Chartrons: oeuvre d'Etienne Laclotte", *Revue historique de Bordeaux*, 1981, p.93-207.

DETHIER (Jean), "La Conquête du droit de cité des Chartrons", *L'Amateur de Bordeaux*. Paris: 1986, no. 10, p.38-43.

MONOGRAPHS ON THE BORDEAUX WINE CHATEAUX

DETHIER (Jean), "La Magie du Bouilh ou la théâtralité viticole selon Victor Louis", *L'Amateur de Bòrdeaux*. Paris: 1986, no 13, p.42-47.

DETHIER (Jean), "Chateau Margaux", *L'Amateur de Bordeaux*. Paris: 1985, no 9, p.30-36.

DETHIER (Jean), "Chateau Saint-Georges", *L'Amateur de Bordeaux*. Paris: 1986, no. 12, p.34-37.

FAITH (Nicholas), *Château Margaux*. London: Christie's Wine Publications, 1980.

FAITH (Nicholas), *Victorian Vineyard: Chateau Loudenne and the Gilbeys*. London: Constable, 1983, 160p.

FAITH (Nicholas ed), *Château Margaux*. London: Mitchell Beazley, 1989. Photography by M. Guillard. Postface by Jean Dethier.

HIGOUNET (Charles ed), *La Seigneurie et le vignoble de Chateau Latour; histoire d'un grand cru du Medoc (X1V-XX siècle)*. Bordeaux: Fédération historique du Sud-Oeust, 1974, 2 volumes. This work includes an important text by René Pijassou.

OLNEY (Richard), *Yquem*. Paris: Flammarion, 1985. Photography by M. Guillard.

PIJASSOU (René), "Un Chateau du Médoc: Palmer", *Revue historique de Bordeaux*, 1964, no. 2, p.183-203.

RAY (Cyril), *Mouton Rothschild: the Wine, the Family, the Museum*. London: Christie's Wine Publications, 1975.

RAY (Cyril), *The Story of Chateau Lafite Rothschild*. London: Christie's Wine Publications, 1985, 140p.

EXHIBITION CATALOGUES

Les Architectes de Bordeaux et le néoclassicisme. Exhibition catalogue. Bordeaux: Municipal archives, 1970.

Bordeaux: 2000 ans d'histoire. Exhibition catalogue. Bordeaux: Musée d'Aquitaine, 1971.

In vino veritas. Exhibition catalogue directed by Lucien Logette. Paris: National archives, 1953.

Mouton Rothschild: Paintings for the Labels: 1945-1981. Boston: New York Graphic Society, 1983.

La Vigne et le vin. Exhibition catalogue. Dijon: Musée Archéologique, 1976.

La Vigne et le vin. Exhibition catalogue. Paris: Cité des Sciences et de l'Industrie; Editions de la Manufacture, Lyon, 1988.

La Vigne et le vin dans l'art. Exhibition catalogue. Paris: Musée des Arts Décoratifs, 1936.

Le Vin de France dans l'histoire. Exhibition catalogue. Paris: Archives de France, 1953.

PRACTICAL GUIDES AND CATALOGUES

BARBEY (Adelaide ed), *Aquitaine*. Paris: Editions Hachette Guide bleu, 1987.

BETGE-BREZETZ (A.), *Guide des archives de la Gironde*. Bordeaux: Departmental archives, 1973.

Guide Hachette des Vins de France. Paris: Editions Hachette, 1989.

LICHINE (Alexis), *Sur les Routes des vins de France; guide*. Paris: Editions Robert Laffont, 1987.

RENOUIL (Yves ed), *Dictionnaire du vin*. Bordeaux: Editions Féret, 1962.

INDEX OF THE CHATEAUX AND NEGOCIANTS WHOSE NAMES APPEAR IN THE TEXT OR ILLUSTRATIONS

PICTURE CREDITS

SPECIALLY COMMISSIONED PHOTOGRAPHS AND DRAWINGS

DUBAU, M., Bordeaux: p.32, 33, 40, 41 (except for middle plate), 51, 52, 61 (bottom), 62, 66, 67, 68 (top), 69 (top), 76, 78, 84, 90 (top), 115 (top, bottom), 116 (top), 119 (top), 120, 121, 127 (top left), 138, 141 (bottom), 142-143 (bottom), 144, 147 (top), 150 (top), 169 (top right), 232-237, 248 (bottom).

GUILLARD, M., Paris: p.12, 18 38, 46, 48, 49, 53, 57, 58, 59, 60, 61 (middle), 64, 65. 68-69 (bottom), 72, 73, 77, 79, 80, 81, 85, 86-87, 88, 89, 90 (bottom), 91, 92 (top, middle), 93, 94, 95, 97, 112, 116 (bottom), 177, 122, 123, 124 (bottom), 127 (top right, middle, bottom), 128, 129, 130, 131, 132-133, 134, 135, 136 (except vignette), 149 (top), 151, 154-161, 169 (colour left: top, bottom; middle right), 206 (middle left and right), 248 (top, middle), 253, 255.

PERCIVAL, F., Paris: p.75, 83, 96, 118, 124

(top), 148, 174-175, 206 (bottom).

PLANCHET, J.-C.(CCI), Paris: p.28, 29, 30-31, 54, 63, 68-69 (middle), 98-111, 114, 115 (middle), 141 (top), 145, 169 (bottom), 172, 176, 188, 190, 191, 192, 193, 200, 203, 204-205, 208-211, 212 (bottom), 222-225, 226-231, 238-241, 250-251.

SAA, Toulouse: p.47, 54, 55, 70, 71 (bottom), 82, 98-111, 119 (bottom), 124, 147 (bottom).

OTHER PICTURE SOURCES

AGENCE SCOPE, Paris: p.43 (top).
BAITZ, O., USA: p.178, 179.
BIBLIOTHEQUE NATIONALE, Paris: p.126, 142-143 (top).
BOFILL, R.: P.152 (middle left, middle right, bottom).
CIVB, Bordeaux: p.56.
DANGLES, Ph.: p.153.
DIXON, J., London: P.214-221.
EATON, R., London: p.136 (bottom), 212 (bottom).
GASTINES, J. DE, Paris: p.74.
HAUT-BRION (Château), Bordeaux: p.169 (right bottom).
HERVE C., Libourne: p.39.
IGN, Paris: p.206 (top).
INIGUEZ & USTARROZ, Pamplona: p.194, 197, 198-199.
JOHNSON, B., London: p.44-45, 164, 169 (colour left: middle).
JOHNSON REVERDY, USA: p.177.
LEMAIRE, J., Brussels: p.169 (bottom right).

LEOVILLE-BARTON (Château), St-Julien: p.42 (top).
LUZE DE, Bordeaux: p.71 (top), 139.
MARTINUZZI, F., Paris: p.183.
MOREAU, L, Grenoble: p.36, 140, 146, 150 (bottom), 152 (top).
MUSEE DES ARTS DECORATIFS, Bordeaux: p.41 (middle).
NIVELLE, B., Bordeaux: p.113.
PETUAUD-LETANG, Bordeaux: p.152 (International Wine City).
REMY, D., Studio Médoc, Pauillac: p.25, 34, 35, 187, 195, 201.
ROBERT, Ph., Paris: p.152 (middle).
SEGUIN-MOREAU, Cognac: p.90 (middle), 149 (bottom).
VANDENHOVE (Château), Liège: p.242-247.
VIGOUREUX, S., Paris : p.92 (2nd, 4th and 5th pictures from top to bottom).
WOLFSON., R., Florence: p.37.